FEAR LESS

FEAR LESS

THE AMAZING UNDERDOG STORY OF LEICESTER CITY, THE GREATEST MIRACLE IN SPORTS HISTORY

JONATHAN NORTHCROFT

NATION BOOKS
New York

Published in the United States by Nation Books,
an imprint of Perseus Books, LLC, a subsidiary of Hachette Book Group, Inc.,
116 East 16th Street, 8th Floor,
New York, NY 10003

Nation Books is a co-publishing venture of the Nation Institute and Perseus Books.

Books published by Nation Books are available at special discounts for bulk purchases in the United States by corporations, institutions, and other organizations.
For more information, please contact the
Special Markets Department at Perseus Books,
2300 Chestnut Street, Suite 200, Philadelphia, PA 19103,
or call (800) 810-4145, ext. 5000,
or e-mail special.markets@perseusbooks.com.

A CIP catalog record for this book is available from the Library of Congress.

LCCN: 2016952001
ISBN 978-1-56858-982-4 (paperback)
ISBN 978-1-56858-983-1 (e-book)

First published in the United Kingdom in 2016 by Headline Publishing Group.
UK ISBN 9781472241627

First Edition

10 9 8 7 6 5 4 3 2 1

For Jan: my first miraculous fox.

CONTENTS

ACKNOWLEDGEMENTS

Five minutes after Robert Huth's header put Leicester 3–0 up at Manchester City came a text: 'Hi mate, we should have a chat about a potential Leicester book.' In the Etihad press box, caught in the moment, I fired back: 'Good idea.'

Of course it is madness committing to a book when you've a young family, a sixty-hours-a-week newspaper job, are in the middle of uprooting to a new city, and have the end of the season and a European Championship coming up – but David Luxton caught a split second when all that seemed to matter was the sheer wonder of a fearless football team. It is the fault of David and his message that this book exists – and I owe him sincere thanks, because writing it was so much fun.

Equally 'culpable' is Jonathan Taylor of Headline Publishing, who believed in *Fearless* from day one and provided such calm and wise direction. Alessandra Bastagli offered equally shrewd and important advice. Thanks to Richard Roper, Millie Seaward, Joe Yule, Rebecca Winfield, Alessandra Bastagli and Clive Priddle too.

The core of this book, indeed of Leicester's miracle, is a unique group of players. I was deeply fortunate that Kasper Schmeichel, Marc Albrighton, Robert Huth, Wes Morgan and Andy King sat down with me. Five bright, grounded and unusual footballers, whose deep love of their dressing room, their families and their craft was striking and which I hope *Fearless* conveys. Thank you to them.

Anthony Herilhy is owed much gratitude for helping at a time when the whole world wanted its piece of Leicester. Thanks also to Jonny Lally and John Hutchinson: your book and reflections on Leicester's history were appreciated, John.

The aim was to not just portray who and what Leicester, in 2015–16, were, but offer context. Leon Britton, who has 'future coach' stamped all over him, was fascinating to listen to on the subject of playing against Leicester – thanks for your time, Leon. Pat Nevin said something so sharp in passing that it just had to be stolen and used: Cheers, Pat. Peter Schmeichel offered many interesting thoughts about Leicester over the years. Thanks also to David Morgan for his insights. I owe the deepest thanks to certain friends in the game who always come through for me and did so again here. Eddy Jennings, Chris D, Chris B, Matt, David, Owen, James Skelland: as usual I owe you.

Thanks to Simon Chadwick, who opened up a whole new line of thinking with his perspective on the Srivaddhanaprabhas, and John Williams, who helped my understanding of Leicester socially and culturally. Gavan Wilmot was important here, too. Conversations with Pete Simmons and Tony Faulkner stimulated ideas about the culture of this unique football club – and of sporting organisations generally.

Maybe it's the Sunday journalist in me but I loved going into the back stories. Allen Bethel is, as noted in chapter eight, inimitable. I could have listened to Allen talk about Stocksbridge, his life, and Jamie Vardy, all afternoon . . . and pretty much did. Thanks for so much of your time, Allen.

Boubakar Coulibaly was the most generous and genial host. I'm still blown away by the scale and standards of AAS Sarcelles – the banlieue boys who give Paris Saint Germain a run for their money. Thanks, Boubakar – and full marks for knowing Aberdeen's 1983 Cup Winners Cup line up. At JS Surenses, Pierre Ville spoke so proudly and insightfully about N'Golo Kanté: *merci* from me and Jan.

Without Tor-Kristian Karlsen's recollections and sharp insights the 'Claudio' chapter would have been distinctly 'Ligue 2', thanks TKK. And thanks Steve Madeley for describing the mayhem at 'Vardy Gras'.

Help from friends and colleagues was invaluable and typically generous. Chris Brereton, Rob Draper, Joe Bernstein, Rory Smith, Kristoff Terreur, Lee Marlow: you did important things for me and I hope to return the favours.

The Leicester story sparked so much brilliant journalism and pieces by Rob, Joe, Rory, Lee, Jason Burt, Henry Winter, Martin Samuel, Oliver Holt, Oliver Kay, Nick Harris, Rob Tanner, John Percy, Stuart James, Laurie Whitwell, Alan Smith, James Sharpe, Graeme Bryce, Barney Ronay, James Horncastle, Sam Wallace, Grant Wahl, James Astill and Gabriele Marcotti – and many others – were devoured (and probably cannibalised) in the writing of this.

Thanks for talking or telephone numbers or bits of encouragement or help and hospitality: Rob Maul, Guillem Balague, Graham Hunter, Rafael Honigstein, Neil Ashton, Ian Herbert, Phil Dickinson, Rob Hunt, Rebecca Fyfe, Francois De Pape, Jon Wilsher, Linda O'Brien, Edoardo Magro, Joe Prince-Wright, David Dick, Francis Leech, Shaul Adar, Shintaro Kano, Ole Magnus Storberget, Douglas Alexander, Jim Donnelly, Chandu Dave, Andy Miller, Suhail, Beilin, Saeed and Alli.

At the *Sunday Times*, David Walsh, Lucy Dupuis, Nick Greenslade and especially Alex Butler always have my back. They did so again here. I can't really thank them enough.

And I certainly can't thank Jan Northcroft enough: partner, translator, interviewer, collaborator, CEO and supermum: nae bad, Jan, nae bad. Without Dad, Mum and Mat, none of this would be possible – and without Jan, Ishbel and Cora, none of it would matter.

TABLES

Leicester City Squad, 2015–2016

Number	Name	Position	Nation Playing For	Year Joined
11	Marc Albrighton	Midfielder	England	2014
13	Daniel Amartey	Defender	Ghana	2016
29	Yohan Benalounane	Defender	Tunisia	2015
2	Ritchie De Laet	Defender	Belgium	2012
36	Joe Dodoo	Midfielder	England	2013
4	Danny Drinkwater	Midfielder	England	2012
28	Christian Fuchs	Defender	Austria	2015
22	Demaray Gray	Midfielder	England	2016
6	Robert Huth	Defender	Germany	2015
33	Gökhan Inler	Midfielder	Switzerland	2015
8	Matty James	Midfielder	England	2012
14	N'Golo Kanté	Midfielder	France	2015
10	Andy King	Midfielder	Wales	2006
19	Andrej Kramarić	Forward	Croatia	2015
25	Riyad Mahrez	Midfielder	Algeria	2014
5	Wes Morgan	Defender	Jamaica	2015
20	Shinji Okazaki	Forward	Japan	2015
15	Jeff Schlupp	Midfielder	Ghana	2010
1	Kasper Schmeichel	Goalkeeper	Denmark	2011
17	Danny Simpson	Defender	England	2014
23	Leonardo Ulloa	Forward	Argentina	2014
9	Jamie Vardy	Forward	England	2012
27	Marcin Wasilewski	Defender	Poland	2013

Leicester City, 2015–2016, Premier League Games

2015

Date	Home Team	Score	Away Team	City
8 August	Leicester City	4–2	Sunderland	Leicester
15 August	West Ham United	1–2	Leicester City	London
22 August	Leicester City	1–1	Tottenham Hotspur	Leicester
29 August	Bournemouth	1–1	Leicester City	Bournemouth
13 September	Leicester City	3–2	Aston Villa	Leicester
19 September	Stoke City	2–2	Leicester City	Stoke-on-Trent
26 September	Leicester City	2–5	Arsenal	Leicester
3 October	Norwich City	1–2	Leicester City	Norwich
17 October	Southampton	2–2	Leicester City	Southampton
24 October	Leicester City	1–0	Crystal Palace	Leicester
31 October	West Bromwich Albion	2–3	Leicester City	West Bromwich
7 November	Leicester City	2–1	Watford	Leicester
21 November	Newcastle United	0–3	Leicester City	Newcastle
28 November	Leicester City	1–1	Manchester United	Leicester
5 December	Swansea City	0–3	Leicester City	Swansea
14 December	Leicester City	2–1	Chelsea	Leicester
19 December	Everton	2–3	Leicester City	Liverpool
26 December	Liverpool	1–0	Leicester City	Liverpool
29 December	Leicester City	0–0	Manchester City	Leicester

Leicester City, 2015–2016, Premier League Games *(continued)*

2016

Date	Home Team	Score	Away Team	City
2 January	Leicester City	0–0	Bournemouth	Leicester
13 January	Tottenham Hotspur	0–1	Leicester City	London
16 January	Aston Villa	1–1	Leicester City	Birmingham
23 January	Leicester City	3–0	Stoke City	Leicester
2 February	Leicester City	2–0	Liverpool	Leicester
6 February	Manchester City	1–3	Leicester City	Manchester
14 February	Arsenal	2–1	Leicester City	Holloway, London
27 February	Leicester City	1–0	Norwich City	Leicester
1 March	Leicester City	2–2	West Bromwich Albion	Leicester
5 March	Watford	0–1	Leicester City	Watford
14 March	Leicester City	1–0	Newcastle United	Leicester
19 March	Crystal Palace	0–1	Leicester City	London
3 April	Leicester City	1–0	Southampton	Leicester
10 April	Sunderland	0–2	Leicester City	Sunderland
17 April	Leicester City	2–2	West Ham United	Leicester
24 April	Leicester City	4–0	Swansea City	Leicester
1 May	Manchester United	1–1	Leicester City	Manchester
7 May	Leicester City	3–1	Everton	Leicester
15 May	Chelsea	1–1	Leicester City	London

1

THE GROUP

'Why couldn't you beat a richer club? I've never seen a bag of money score a goal'

– Johan Cruyff

A bag of money has never scored a goal but plenty have provided assists. And there were Leicester, little Leicester, back in their box.

The banknotes of all the big clubs in the world seemed to weigh down the lid.

Neglected players with a nearly manager from a nonentity city: top of the Premier League? Their run had been nice, fun, but this was February and football awaited the moment it would end. Now it seemed the moment was here.

It was February 14; a grey, chilly, North London afternoon. A Valentine's Day robbed of romance, when reality bit hard on an underdog team. Arsenal 2 Leicester 1 at Emirates Stadium. Twelve of the 38 games left. Leicester, after leading had lost to a last second goal and were now top of the Premier League by a sliver.

Arsenal were just two points behind and so were surging Tottenham, who beat Manchester City in the day's later kick off. The bookmakers quickly moved Leicester out to third favourites once Arsenal's winning goal hit the net.

The scorer had been Danny Welbeck: young England striker, impeccable pedigree, a marquee £16m transfer. Arsenal's first goal came from Theo Walcott – another England thoroughbred, on a princely £140,000 per week.

And Welbeck and Walcott were merely Arsenal's substitutes. The assist for Welbeck was from a German World Cup winner, the £42m German Mesut Özil while Alexis Sanchez, iconic £32m Sanchez, played a part in Danny Simpson's pivotal sending off.

How did Leicester's strength in depth compare? With Simpson dismissed Claudio Ranieri summoned from his bench a cut-price kid (£3m Demarai Gray), an out-of-practice Polish veteran (Marcin Wasilewski) and club-developed stalwart Andy King.

These substitutes, combined, earned less than Walcott. Ranieri's entire starting XI cost around half Özil's transfer fee.

So, this seemed an appropriate way for the haves to put have-nots back in their place – and an appropriate setting. Here, at Emirates Stadium, the most lucrative sports venue on the planet, football's greatest cash machine. Where the £4m per game generated gives Arsenal greater match day revenue than Real Madrid, Barcelona, Mancester United – any team.

Where the *cheapest* season ticket costs over £1,000. Where there is steamed salmon and ice cream in the press room and in the executive boxes; if you want an informal alternative to the five-course fine dining option you can order the 'fun' menu of gourmet burgers with lobster tails.

'Will that be the goal that Arsenal look back on in May as the one that propelled them to title glory?' asked the Sky Sports commentary. Welbeck scored with the final touch of stoppage time, in his first game back after serious injury: 'The ending was like a great movie,' gushed Thierry Henry in Sky's studio. It seemed Arsenal were in the fairytale, not Leicester.

● ● ●

The Emirates' home dressing room is designed to the cerebral specifications of Arsène Wenger; a shrine to Zen and good taste. U-shaped, to eliminate pillars and posts, it has an acoustic ceiling and mood lighting. Players get not one but two lockers. The neat, small, charcoal mosaic tiles in the showers and plunge pool are the stuff of a fine boutique hotel.

The away dressing room is not bad either. Plainer but still spacious, it certainly passes the Dave Rennie test. Rennie, Leicester's physio of sixteen years, tweets wryly about substandard facilities given to visiting teams at certain football grounds. Queens Park Rangers: 'toilets right next door to the massage beds'. That kind of stuff.

No complaints about this clean, wide, pine-panelled room, though.

Waiting was Simpson, who said sorry for his red card as teammates trooped in. 'Don't worry about it, Simmer,' the replies came back.

Leicester's players sat down. Some were sanguine. 'Listen, we have lost 2–1 at Arsenal with ten men. We have been dominant. We have been brilliant. Forget it. Keep going,' Kasper Schmeichel kept saying. But others had sinking feelings. 'It literally felt like we had been relegated,' recalls Robert Huth.

There was anger about referee Martin Atkinson's punishment of Simpson – two bookings for two moderate fouls. And apologies to partners and children were starting to form in players' heads.

Entering three games billed as the sequence that would test their challenge – Liverpool at home, then Manchester City and Arsenal away – Ranieri promised everyone a week off for winning all three. Liverpool and City were dispensed with in astonishing ways, but this defeat meant going home and telling loved ones, 'Sorry – no holiday.'

Then something happened.

Then came the selfies.

The Arsenal Selfies.

Pictures were coming through on social media of a touch of triumphalism going down in that nice, Zen, home dressing room.

Arsenal players danced round Welbeck, chanting his name, and then a large bunch of them posed for a photograph. In the shot were Aaron Ramsey, Özil, Walcott, a clenched-fists Héctor Bellerín, a Victory-signing Sánchez, Olivier Giroud, Nacho Monreal, Alex Oxlade-Chamberlain, Calum Chambers and Mathieu Flamini. A group celebration pose in front of their pristine pine lockers.

Ramsey tweeted it. Oxlade-Chamberlain tweeted it. Sànchez tweeted it. So did Özil, who added an emoji of a flexed bicep and '#bigpoints'.

Chambers, Petr Čech, Laurent Koscielny, Walcott and Bellerín posted adding different celebratory tweets and Arsenal's own official feed joined the exuberance. 'DAT GUY IS BACK!' it blared, referring to Welbeck. Twitter memes from fans abounded: Welbeck as the Pope, Welbeck as a king.

And Leicester's lads saw it. Without need for ambient lighting, their mood changed. They unified again. Defiance sluiced out any despair. In the days and weeks ahead The Arsenal Selfies would become a hot subject on the private social media groups Leicester players shared.

'For me the key point in the season was when we lost to Arsenal and it was last minute. Everyone was celebrating,' says Huth. 'We were sitting in the changing room. They were doing selfies. Even though we were still top.

'We have a group on the phones. A few of the lads stuck a few [of Arsenal's] pictures up and it got the blood boiling. Certainly, it gave us an extra yard in the next few games.'

We have been dominant. We have been brilliant. Players recalibrated. Maybe Kasper was not so far away. 'We had ten men for the best part of the second half and for them to only score in the last minute and then celebrate how they did . . . it proved how good we are,' says Wes Morgan. 'I think that gave us a real boost. "Right, come on, boys, we are not going to let that happen again."'

Andy King reflects, 'A lot of people looked at that game: "This is it, the bubble has burst." We didn't look at it like that. It had taken them 95 minutes to score two past ten men.'

Kasper: 'Social media is dangerous. I'm not saying more. Very dangerous.'

• • •

Lost Amazon tribes probably know by now that Leicester were 5,000-1 to win the Premier League. If you played 5,000 seasons of the Premier League then just once would a team like Leicester win, the bookmakers said. Set your clock for the year 7016 – when the next comparable triumph is due to happen.

Another way of putting it: Liverpool had played around 5,000 matches in their history but never before come back from a 3–0 deficit at half-time until they did so to win the 2005 Champions League in Istanbul. For many, *that* was the greatest football 'miracle' in memory. Leicester had to do something on the Istanbul scale to be title-winners – but sustained over not 45 minutes but 45 weeks.

Bags of money do assist. Some of the economics against Leicester were eye-watering:

> No team with a wage bill outside its top five had ever won the Premier League and the last winners with a wage bill outside the biggest three were Arsenal in 1998. Leicester's wage bill was in the bottom five.
>
> Leicester's turnover was £104m. Chelsea spent more than twice that in wages. Manchester City almost double on a training ground. Manchester United were soon to pay nearly the same amount to buy one player (Paul Pogba). In November 2015 Arsenal had £159m sitting in the bank.
>
> Manchester United rake in £122m per year from kit deals. Leicester's shirt sponsorship was worth £1m annually, the second lowest in the Premier League, while kit manufacturer Puma handled their arrangement via an offshoot company dealing with lower clubs on Puma's roster like Fleetwood Town.

Then there was precedent:

> Since the Premier League's creation only once in 23 seasons had the title gone outside a cartel of four clubs from two cities and then the champions were Blackburn Rovers – briefly England's best-funded club. In the past ten years the title winners finished their previous season in an average second place and 4.2 points off the top. Leicester were 14th and 46 points off the top in 2014–15. This was like trying to scale Everest, unacclimatised, without experience, directly from base camp.

And then there was pedigree:

> Think of this. Come the 2015–16 season no fewer than 43 clubs had won either of England's major competitions, the League and the FA Cup. Leicester, though 132 years old, were not among them. They were more famous for 'yo-yoing' – bouncing between the top two divisions. Their combined total of 22 promotions and relegations was the fourth highest of any English club.

The old joke among fans was the authorities needed to invent a new tier, 'Division One-and-a-half', because that is where Leicester belonged. James Astill, Leicester-raised Washington correspondent of *The Economist* remembers ''Ow's City, going down are we?' as a standard local greeting from his youth.

Finally, the practicalities. Leicester were still playing 'like a small team', with the league's worst pass success and average possession under 45 per cent – no champion had gone remotely close to letting the opposition dominate the ball like that.

Some said them winning would be like Buster Douglas flooring Mike Tyson, 17-year-old wildcard Boris Becker winning Wimbledon; John Daly driving all night as late call-up to make the US PGA – and then winning the thing. But these were individual sports and one-off tournaments; in team competition, played over ten months, how can you really shock the world? The Leicester underdogs would need to be champions week-upon-week. Try Douglas beating Tyson and still holding the belt 37 fights later, or Daly mounting a long reign as world No.1.

Even the closest football legend had little relevance: Nottingham Forest being English champions in 1977–78. Different era. Financial differences between big and small were not as pronounced – indeed Forest held the British transfer record in 1979. And Forest was the platform for a genius, Brian Clough, a character so outsize Muhammad Ali bantered about him on TV. Ranieri would prove how underrated he was – but genius? That's a description of himself the gentle Italian would never claim.

And Leicester? The city of *Leicester?* A Rugby Union town. Produces the odd snooker player. A cricketer now and then. But football? Aside from an England captain, Gary Lineker, and a couple of legendary old goalkeepers, what had Leicester given the game?

Where was it anyway? North of Birmingham ... no, south ... wait, east ... okay, kind of near Birmingham when you drive from London. Somewhere in the Midlands. A seldom-taken motorway sign. Crisps. Lineker. Kasabian. A cheese.

What else?

'Welcome to Leicester: home to Europe's largest covered outdoor market.'

'Visit Leicester: birthplace of Daniel Lambert, Georgian England's fattest man – come see his big trousers at Newarke Houses Museum.'

Tourists tended to stay on that motorway.

And for Britain in general it was just such a neutral place, with no accent, no character type, no landmark, no quirk, no historical event, to latch on to. A provincial city with the population (330,000) of a London borough. Nah, the remarkable doesn't happen somewhere like that.

• • •

Petr Čech intercepted Schmeichel as he left the field. Hand on Schmeichel's shoulder the Arsenal No.1 told his counterpart how well he had played. Goalkeeper's Union, as they say. If there really was one, Schmeichel would be a shop steward: you won't meet a keeper as passionate about the position, as annoyed when keepers are criticised, as him.

The previous week there had been another nice union moment. After Leicester stunned Manchester City, 3–1, on the pitch at the Etihad Stadium, Schmeichel hugged Joe Hart. Hart, a friend as well as rival, and despite City's own ambitions, said, 'All right, right, come on. If you are ever going to win it [the title], it's now. Get it done. Get it done.'

Kasper is not a fairytales guy. Big, blond and straightforward, he deals with exactly what is in front of him – a pretty useful trait for a goalkeeper. To him, a lot of modern football is fluff. Take the made-for-TV routine of team line-ups and the ref ceremonially scooping the match ball from a plinth. 'I still miss the days when you ran out. I hate walking out with the handshake. I would rather run out,' Kasper says.

The plinth? 'I can't stand it,' he continues. 'I would rather just run out and get ready for the game. All the shenanigans before could very easily be scrapped for my liking.'

Here is how focused Kasper is.

He joined Leicester in 2011 and by the end of 2015–16 had played 111 home matches in the King Power Stadium. There, the 75-year-old ritual is a lone brass player heralding the players' entrance with a haunting tune, the *Post Horn Gallop*. Leicester are The Foxes and (though it isn't) it sounds like a hunting tune.

It is spine-tingling. Absolutely distinctive. Kasper had come out to it 111 times. Does he like it? 'Um, I haven't really thought if I liked it or not liked it.'

His father, Peter, maybe the greatest goalkeeper, has exactly this tunnel vision. Though the two are long sick of being compared there are unmistakable common traits between father and son.

One is dressing room presence. Kasper's gee-up to teammates was typical. *We have been dominant. We have been brilliant.* 'I mean, come on,' says Kasper, 'it was our third defeat of the season. Three defeats all season? That was still amazing.

'I felt we'd been resilient. That it didn't matter about the result . . . and there had been massive injustice in the decision [to send off Simpson].

'Eleven v eleven – we were comfortable. They hadn't had a shot on target at that point. Even with ten men, we were so comfortable.

'Losing the game in the way we did? Seeing Arsenal celebrate as if they had basically won the league against us: that a victory against *us* could mean so much to them? It really showed how far we'd come. Watching them [celebrate], for me, was actually a boost.'

King recalls similar. 'There were people after that game who thought they had won the World Cup! They were on their knees, pointing to the skies, doing victory laps of honour . . . We were like, "hold on",' he smiles.

If Kasper is Mr Positive then King is Mr Leicester. An even longer-serving player, a first-team regular since he was 19, nine years ago, King spreads his bright-eyed love of the club throughout the group.

They sat in their normal places in that Emirates dressing room. At the training ground it is different but for matches Leicester's players are put in shirt number order. Next to Kasper sat Danny Drinkwater, 'Drinky', bluff Mancunian and self-confessed 'moaner' from a tough estate.

And Drinkwater *is* tough. At 5ft9in and 154lbs, he has the build of a welterweight and power to match. In the gym it is he who surprisingly challenges Morgan, Huth and Marcin Wasilewski, in the lifting stats.

Morgan sat next to him. Solid, powerful, never to be messed with but also caring, 'Big Wes' is, said former Leicester striker Andrej Kramarić, 'the captain who never raises his voice'. At half-time, Ranieri lets Wes speak first. When players want something, it is Wes who goes to the manager. 'The boys put some ridiculous requests in. Mainly days off,' he tuts. But make no mistake: 'They are my boys.'

Ranieri called him 'Baloo' and Claudio knows his Kipling. Baloo, in the Disney, is comical and lazy. But in Rudyard Kipling's original *Jungle Book* he is 'the sleepy brown bear who teaches wolf cubs the law'. Morgan, indeed, was nicknamed The Bear early in his career. 'It's a fantastic feeling to know someone has got your back,' he says, of teammates. 'And I have got their back.'

Next sat Huth, 'Huthy'. An ironic, deeply funny German. King was in Chelsea's junior ranks when Huth played in the first team. Once, the kids had to hold out jerseys for the senior players to autograph. 'Huthy signed the shirt then drew on my face. I was walking round the training ground with permanent marker on my face thinking, "What if one of the big players sees me?"' King grudgingly laughs.

Then sat Jamie Vardy, 'Vards'. 'I think if you gave him a lightbulb to hold it would light up,' says Ranieri. Vards is the livewire, the joker, with the shark fin hair and predatory eyes. With the back story – from seventh-tier steel mill team to England hero – that Hollywood loves.

Journalists speaking to Vardy find he answers as he plays: disconcertingly quick, sharp and direct. All lean, fast muscle, he's just a pared-down guy: 6 per cent body fat, 0 per cent bull.

A mild pair, Marc Albrighton and N'Golo Kanté, were at the next lockers. No club can live without an Albrighton. He, 'Sharky', is the good pro, the team man and family guy. He was carrying grief but did not burden anyone. Then Kanté, 'NG', so small, so quiet. A French agent (who we will return to later) arranged to meet him at St Pancras Station in London and there was Kanté, stepping incognito from a second-class carriage with no one bothering him.

Next to Kanté sat Simpson: a much-travelled full back famous for his superstitions like getting his hair cut by the same barber the night before every match, or wearing tape round his left wrist because he did it once as a kid and then played well. A bit OCD? 'Not a *bit*,' says Schmeichel. '[Superstitious] about everything. Every little ritual. Has to eat the same, do the same. I have a little giggle at him. He starts 48 hours before a game.'

Shinji Okazaki next to Simpson. Just 'Shinji' to the lads. Popular and given a standing ovation at the training ground when he passed his basic English language test. His efforts to embrace England have led to a taste for fish and chips. The most underrated footballer in the team, King says.

Then Christian Fuchs, 'Fuchsy'. Goateed Austrian and self-consciously madcap guy. In an office he'd wear the musical socks. From his 'wacky' antics on social media he has even developed a clothing brand from his hashtag #NoFuchsGiven. Nice pun – though so is the German meaning of 'Fuchs'. Appropriately it is 'Fox'. Fuchs' wife and kids live in Manhattan and he wants to quit football in a couple of years and become a kicker in the NFL.

Unlikely career path? Riyad Mahrez knows about them. The last of the starting players at the Emirates, he languished for years at a small team in a Paris banlieue estate, too artistic, too frail, for the mainstream. Skill won out, in the end, and Mahrez progressed all the way to English player of the year in 2015-16 – but his laidback, jokey nature did not change.

Laidback? Mahrez, just Riyad or 'Ri' to the lads, is famous for that at Leicester. So much does he love his sleep that he uses beds in the King Power Stadium for catnaps before some games.

A diverse but tight crew, the way Leicester rallied together at the Emirates was simply normal for them. It meant that by the time Ranieri had done his post-match interviews and arrived to address the group he really had no need to conjure any big speech. 'There haven't been many occasions when he has had to,' Schmeichel says. 'The dressing room polices itself quite well.'

King agrees and puts things rather neatly: 'We kind of manage our own dressing room.'

• • •

Ranieri was impassive, standing arms crossed, buttoned overcoat, Roman mouth downturned, when Atkinson blew full-time. He was so lost in his thoughts he did not notice Arsène Wenger stride over. Wenger had to pat his back to jolt him to turn round for the post-match managers' handshake.

Arsenal 2 Leicester 1. Ranieri, over the season, had silenced the derision that met his appointment and finally won English respect, but the game did seem another hard luck story in a long career of narrowly missing glory.

The game went like this: Arsenal, having overwhelmed Leicester with their attacking in a 5–2 victory at the King Power in September, tried doing the same again but encountered opponents who had very much evolved.

Arsenal worked the ball wide, got down the sides, crossed it in and cut it back, but Leicester's defensive block was well chiselled now. Immovable. Arsenal could not beat Schmeichel and when a Sánchez shot ricocheted off Simpson, Morgan simply held his breath, fixed eyes on the ball and without flinching, let it thud into his stomach.

Kanté was everywhere: stealing, retrieving, driving forward on counter-attacks, and in one of these Koscielny took him out and the ball ran clear for Vardy to hare into the box and trick Nacho Monreal into giving up a penalty. Vardy rammed it in for 1–0 but soon after Simpson was booked for a routine foul on Sánchez, then grabbed Giroud's waist. Atkinson, technically correct, in practice severe, showed a second yellow card and then a red.

With ten men, Leicester stayed dogged but Arsenal began exposing their left side where only a young sub, Demarai Gray, protected Fuchs. Ranieri took Mahrez off to try and stiffen his defence with Marcin Wasilewski. Yet Fuchs was hesitant in getting out to Bellerín, and Gray naïve when tracking Walcott. Bellerín crossed, Giroud headed down, Walcott converted: 1–1.

King came on for Leicester and Welbeck for Arsenal. Schmeichel kept saving. Morgan, Huth, Kanté and Drinkwater kept blocking. Then in the last of four minutes' stoppage time the Leicester discipline finally cracked. The culprit was Wasilewski.

Wasilewski, 'Was', a giant, square, 35-year-old Pole, was loved at the training ground, undisputed king of the weightlifting and clear club record holder for longest stint in Leicester's cryotherapy chamber. The chamber, used for rehabilitation, is set at minus 135 degrees and if you possibly can you are supposed to do two minutes in there. 'Was' has managed five. According to legend, when he played for Anderlecht in Belgium he once lifted a small car.

Wasilewski's cameo offered a rare chance for him to do his bit. As back-up to Morgan and Huth, he had played just one league game all season prior to Arsenal. And so maybe he was too eager. With Monreal set to cross, he charged from the box and ploughed into the Spaniard late and high. Özil, with the most beautiful delivery, pinpointed Welbeck and with the game's last touch Welbeck headed in.

A Valentine's Day cold and grey. Arsenal and Tottenham were both just two points off Leicester now. Romance retreating. 'There is nothing quite like football for filling your heart with joy one minute and tearing your heart to shreds the next,' Lineker tweeted.

● ● ●

Legacy, James Kerr's seminal book about New Zealand's All Blacks, tells of how they 'sweep the sheds'. Every dressing room these great rugby players use, they clean up afterwards. The idea being, no one looks after All Blacks, All Blacks look after themselves.

But, come on, *Fearless* is not about gods of their sport. This was Leicester. They did not tidy the sheds. But they did mess about in them.

They were men together. Nothing more, nothing less. Their locker area was never solemn long. 'There isn't a secret,' Drinkwater shrugged. 'It's just that we are a bunch of lads that get along.'

Turning selfies into banter that becomes motivational rocket fuel? Very them. Speak to players and you get little vignettes that hint at a giant group spirit. Here are three: The Flying Socks. The Fitness Stats. The Driving Fines.

The Flying Socks. It seems Kasper started this. What you do is take used socks at the training ground, roll them up, and soak them in water, then lurk to await the next entrant to the dressing room. Don't walk in there unawares. An arm might rise from the team bath ... and a ball of hard, wet hosiery come flying at your head.

'Childish behaviour,' says Albrighton in feigned disapproval. 'The lads are in the tub, looking to see the next person go past ...'

'If you walk in at the wrong time ...' explains Schmeichel. 'You've got to have a little fake around with the door. Or just stick an arm out and see if something comes flying.'

'Someone else might get three or four,' Albrighton adds, 'though if it's Was the socks don't get chucked.'

'You don't throw at Was,' Schmeichel shudders. 'Or Wes. Then we stay clear. Or Huthy . . . though Huthy is usually in the tub.

'Other than them, everyone gets it. There have been some great hits. Some great, absolute head shots.'

The Fitness Stats. Of course the socks are a silly game . . . but just a silly game or a daft sign of a group that enjoys getting one over, enjoys competing? On a board on the way into the changing room are put all the read-outs from the GPS vests players train in, and stats from matches.

There are graphs showing where everyone stands in different categories. New ones go up each morning and these sheets are among the first things players look for.

'There is no hiding place,' says King. 'If so-and-so has been lower than someone else there is no hiding it. All the lads have a bit of banter. So . . . Huthy knows he is normally [running] 9km a game and if he is 9.5km in the last game he will say to the sports scientist, "Right, 9.5km, if you think I am training today . . ."

'It works. The boys like to see it. The top speeds. Jeff [Schlupp] wants to see if he is quicker than Vards, Vards wants to see if he is quicker than such-and-such.'

The Driving Fines. Another one to ask Kasper about. These are something the group just came up with, and are supposed to be enforced by the three-man player committee of King, Morgan and Schmeichel. But, says King, 'I'm not too bothered . . . and Wes is just too laidback.'

Kasper though, he is draconian. The fines are for driving in late for training. Arrival time is usually 9.30am, so the committee struck an arrangement with the security hut.

The guys in there send stills from training ground cameras whenever someone misses the 9.30 cut-off and these are printed off. No one says a thing, then a culprit walks in and – bang – there on the dressing room wall is the photo. Look. 9.31. Gotcha. Pay up. Usually the offender is Riyad.

• • •

Ranieri walked in on this lot at the Emirates. What had he been thinking when he stood so impassive? Well, he would look back on this defeat as being as pivotal as any victory. As he left the touchline he spoke to his closest confidant, assistant manager Paolo Benetti. 'I said we can do something. Because if Arsenal *suffer* so much, eleven against ten [playing us], we can do something.'

We are still top of the league, Ranieri told TV, still two points ahead: 'We must carry on and smile.'

So, in the dressing room: 'The way you worked out there, I am so proud of you all,' he said. 'Have your week off.'

If you want to escape the box they are putting you in, then why not think outside it?

Unconventional, but this was Leicester. Go on, lads, go and win me the title.

But first, go on holiday.

2 THE BEGINNING

Twelve weeks later, the seventh of May, on a warm, squally Saturday, a young man from Venice stepped off a train at Leicester station. He was dressed as Jesus. He wore a beard, a robe and a crown of thorns – and a Leicester shirt with 'Drinkbeer' on the back.

Walking along Platform 2, he spread his arms and shouted, 'Where are the Italians?' No one batted an eyelid. They sent him towards Victoria Park, where his compatriots were gathering. They bought him drinks in London Road's pubs.

The 'Jesus of Leicester', as he became known around the world through social media, was Edoardo Magro, 21, a student living in London who joined an invasion of Leicester by 1,100 young Italian fans. They slept in their cars, in parks, even under the awning at Leicester market following a 21-hour road trek. They just wanted to be in town on the day Leicester were crowned champions of England.

None, not even Jesus, could conjure tickets for the game at the King Power versus Everton 'but I wanted to see this miracle city,' says Edoardo. The sight of him did not shock locals at all – because Leicester people were well used to the miraculous by then.

But where does our miracle start? Most have tried to explain in terms of Kings. There are two – both longstanding guardians of Leicester fortunes. There is Richard III. And of course there is Kingy – good old Andy King.

The yarn-spinner's version focuses on Richard III. In 2012 the bones of the last English king to die in battle were discovered and dug out from under a car park, off New Street, belonging to Leicester City Council Social Services. They had lain there in the soil since 1485. On 26 March 2015 Richard was reinterred at the city's cathedral. Leicester were bottom of the Premier League at that point, seven points from safety, with nine games left. They had lost six and won none of their eight previous league matches.

But, with Richard's old bones now lying in dignity, they won their next game. Then their next. And then their next. And did not stop winning until they were not only clear of the relegation places but a respectable fourteenth by the season's end. No team in history had ever left it so late to climb off the bottom of the league and then survive. Newspapers branded it the 'Great Escape' and talked of the 'miracle of Leicester' even then.

Survival had been Richard's thank-you gift. Somehow through the supernatural, 'king power' had literally been used to transform the football club. Sir Peter Soulsby, Leicester's avuncular mayor, loved this theory of ghostly largesse. Not to mention the chance it offered to entice people to the Richard III Visitor Centre, suddenly displacing Daniel Lambert's trousers as his city's premier tourist attraction.

In 2015–16, as Leicester closed in on another miracle, the Premier League title, foreign newspapermen and broadcasters beat a path to report on the story – and usually found themselves, sooner or later, in the mayor's office, hearing great yarns about 'king power'.

The football cognoscenti tend to prefer the Andy King version. Anyone who knew the game and was watching Leicester closely during 2014–15 could see that their low league position was misleading. They played well nearly every week – even shocking Manchester United with an uproarious, Vardy-fuelled, 5–3 win early in the season. Nearly all their defeats were a little unfortunate and by a single goal. Steve Parish, the Crystal Palace chairman, told Susan Whelan, Leicester's CEO, that 'You are the best team I have ever seen at the bottom of this league.'

So, even in their parlous position of still being bottom at the start of April 2015, this was a club ripe for an upturn. Its players just needed a confidence boost. That came, on 4 April, at home to West Ham when, with five minutes to go, just on as a substitute, and with an improvised touch, King diverted a mishit Vardy shot past West Ham's keeper Adrián to turn 1–1 frustration into a 2–1 win.

'That kept us in the race and gave us the belief we could win,' King reflects. 'It did feel like a moment, like we had turned a corner; when I look back that is the most important goal of my career.' And, indeed, King's typically quick-thinking finish did seem to spark something in colleagues: suddenly Leicester were a decisive team, grabbing points with late goals and comeback wins and this mentality carried on when the title season began. But . . .

But those who really, *really* know Leicester – including King himself – know there is a much earlier starting place to the journey. 'I think the biggest turning point was actually Watford,' says King. Watford? At Watford, 12 May 2013, Championship play-off semi-final second leg, Vicarage Road.

There. That's where the miracle began.

● ● ●

First scroll back further. Back to August 2010 when after being Leicester's sponsor Vichai Srivaddhanaprabha decided to go further and buy the club. In fact he was called Vichai Raksriaksorn then. Srivaddhanaprabha, granted by the King of Thailand in early 2013 and meaning 'light of progressive glory' is an ennobled surname.

Around a dressed-down football club, in any case, the owner has always been known as Khun Vichai or Mr Vichai. His son, Aiyawatt, youngest of his four kids, is Leicester's vice-chairman and day-to-day boss and goes by his nickname, 'Top'.

Back in 2010 Khun Vichai and Top did what new overseas owners in England tend to do. They backed a big name overseas manager. Sven-Göran Eriksson. And, as tends to happen in these situations, it was an expensive call that did not work.

But then something occurred to suggest these Thais were not just another set of moneyed football naïfs from abroad. Khun Vichai and Top decided Leicester should reappoint its former manager, Nigel Pearson. An unglamorous, even controversial decision. A masterstroke.

Pearson, once a rugged centre-half, is bullet-headed, crew-cutted, straight-backed. He looks like a military man and says he would have joined the RAF had it not been for a football career opening up for him upon leaving school in Nottingham. He is a man's man.

Pearson described, to Henry Winter of *The Times*, how he once went on a walking holiday, solo, to the Carpathian mountains in Romania and was set upon by a pack of feral dogs. He blinded a couple with his walking pole – and dived into stinging nettles to escape the others. He is the type who prepares and had researched the local area, knowing it had a problem with wild dogs that attacked sheep and even killed bears. He had also read that these dogs' sensitive noses could not stand nettles – so in he dived.

Pearson goes in for horseplay and caused a ruckus midway through the 2014–15 season when he grabbed Crystal Palace's James McArthur and put him in a half-joky, half-menacing, headlock. But he is also principled, a deep thinker and – say those who know him – a sensitive man beneath the exterior.

Top and Khun Vichai figured that, as Leicester's last successful manager, indeed only successful manager for a decade, Pearson might have the roadmap.

Pearson's first stint, spanning the 2008–09 and 2009–10 seasons, involved leading Leicester back from the lowest point in their history, the third tier, League One, and King remembers that 'everyone at the club was panicking after relegation but Nigel arrived and he was so calm.'

In the Championship, Pearson's good run continued and the side completed a full calendar year unbeaten. Yet after Leicester lost a play-off semi-final to Cardiff, the previous owner, the fickle Milan Mandarić, jettisoned Pearson.

It was November 2011 when Top and Khun Vichai brought Pearson back from Hull and by the end of the 2012–13 season Leicester were in the play-offs again. They beat Watford 1–0 at King Power stadium in the first leg, then were 2–1 down in the second leg at Vicarage Road when, right at the end, six minutes into stoppage time, they were awarded a penalty.

French striker Anthony Knockaert stepped up to shoot Leicester to Wembley. And missed. Then fluffed the rebound. Watford counterattacked and ten seconds later Troy Deeney was putting the ball in Leicester's net.

Watford's fans were on the pitch, Knockaert was crying, teammates sunk, ruined. 'Lost for words . . . distraught,' is how Pearson's assistant, Craig Shakespeare, described the dressing room.

So what happened that was to mean so much?

Two things.

Remember King's words – 'we kind of manage our own dressing room.' Well, the strong core of players was already there. King. Schmeichel. Morgan. Vardy. Drinkwater. Schlupp. Matty James and Ritchie De Laet, who were all also in the 2015–16 squad. This group avoided tears, calmed down and reassessed.

'We sat around afterwards and said, "We need to stop messing around in this league,"' says King. 'We'd won three games in the last seventeen that season and you don't deserve to get promoted like that. We were way too good to be scratching around and not making it. That was when we had to take note: "Okay, we're getting to a good age here, we have to sort it out and stick together."'

'After we'd lost in the play-offs to Cardiff we'd said, "it can't get worse than this." But Watford was worse. And it was then that I and others said, "Okay, enough."

'I think that's where the character we've built began. We won the Championship in the next season and then in the Premier League were dominating established teams – even if it took that West Ham win to give us the confidence we could also beat them.'

Second thing: another set of people, the team behind this team, regrouped.

Pearson had assembled a faithful group of staff around him. Shakespeare, Steve Walsh, Dave Rennie, Matt Reeves, Paul Balsom – and a couple more. And now he told his staff to drop any thoughts of taking a break or going back to their families: they were to come to his father-in-law's pub in Shropshire.

In Shropshire, they would brainstorm and get to the bottom of all this underachievement.

So, for two days, over pints, amid gentle countryside, the gang conversed: 'it provided a non-threatening environment for us to talk as a group of people,' Rennie said. The outcome was a strengthening of their bonds; a pledge to communicate and cooperate better. There would also be a shake-up of playing personnel.

Changes were made. Over the summer of 2013, experienced, strong-headed players started arriving like that Polish tank, Wasilewski, and Kevin Phillips, still hungry at 40 and a Peter Pan of goals. That helped mentality. But the other issue to address was conditioning. Why had Leicester's campaign petered out?

Emerging from the pub pow-wow was the idea of closer collaboration.

Of sports scientists, physios and coaches working absolutely in partnership to make the key decisions about training and match preparation. The big deal was player-loading. What running should a football squad do during the week?

From now, Rennie, the head physio, Reeves, head of fitness and conditioning, and Paul Balsom, the sports science chief, would have a direct influence on player-loading.

And what they pushed was a little radical for English football. A mantra of 'less is more'.

• • •

Pearson already believed in the integrated and enlightened approach. His coaching education involved a stint with Sam Allardyce at Newcastle in 2007, and Allardyce was pioneer of putting sports science at the centre of English football clubs.

Pearson also spent four months in 2008 managing Southampton in a structure big on backroom staff influenced by Sir Clive Woodward, the former England rugby coach. He had been collecting a high-quality support team around him.

Steve Walsh, the recruitment genius who was soon to bring in Mahrez, was chief scout at Newcastle when Pearson worked there. Craig Shakespeare he knew from playing days and they had been reunited at West Brom in Bryan Robson's coaching team.

Paul Balsom had worked for Allardyce and having been hired by Woodward was at Southampton when Pearson became manager there.

In 2008, when Pearson got the Leicester job first time round, he rounded up Walsh, Shakespeare and Balsom and brought them along.

Now *that* was radical. Leicester were in League One. It is unusual, at that level, to invest in staff. Indeed Parish believes, even at the very top, English football embodies the old business flaw of spending 2 per cent of its efforts on recruitment 'and 98 per cent trying to fix that recruitment's mistakes'.

There was already talent at Leicester's Belvoir Drive training ground when Pearson arrived. Men like academy chief Jon Rudkin, who would become director of football, seasoned youth coach Steve Beagehole, and goalkeeping specialist Mike Stowell. Pearson struck a particular rapport with Dave Rennie, a first-class graduate who spent time in the National Health Service and in rugby, netball and triathlon, before becoming Leicester's head physio in 1999.

In the first few weeks of Pearson's new regime an email arrived in Rennie's inbox.

It was from Matt Reeves, the top student on the renowned sports science course at Loughborough University. Reeves was alone in the halls of residence and, at a loose end, decided to chance his arm by asking for work experience at the local football club (Loughborough is twenty minutes from Leicester). 'Yeah, come in for a day of pre-season training,' Rennie replied. 'A day became two and then the rest of the week. And before I knew it I was a kind of full-term intern,' Reeves recalled.

Reeves had not just brains but an engaging manner with footballers and a decent playing background. A centre-half, he partnered the England player Chris Smalling in Fulham's youth team. They were friends: Smalling actually applied to Loughborough for the same course as Reeves before his transfer to Manchester United. Reeves was quickly in Pearson's inner circle.

In 2010, when Pearson was sacked by Mandarić, Walsh, Shakespeare and Reeves followed him to Hull.

In 2011, when Khun Vichai brought Pearson back, the trio returned – as did Balsom, another part of Pearson's first regime.

Balsom had a proposition: he told Pearson that to make things really work he needed 'ten key people' and particularly to expand his sports science department on the analysis side. Problem. There was only so much money. Beef up the staff or sign a player? Pearson chose the slow-and-lasting fix and backed Balsom.

● ● ●

Interesting guy, Balsom. 'An absolute fruitcake,' says a former colleague. 'But an absolute genius. Cutting edge. Ahead of his time . . .

'And a fruitcake.'

This ex-colleague worked with Balsom at Bolton under Allardyce. Fruitcake? 'He was so full of ideas – he'd have everyone working until 1am or 2am on some project or other then disappear back to Sweden.

'He was the sort of guy who'd walk around the training ground barefoot.'

Balsom improved match analysis and much more at Bolton, developing young, talented operators like Dave Fallows, who became Liverpool recruitment head. Now in his early fifties and from Devon, Balsom was a schoolboy at Torquay United but put his education before playing, studied sports science in Cardiff and then completed a masters degree in the United States.

Writing around in search of work, his most positive response was from

Sweden, the home of exercise physiology. There he joined Stockholm's world-renowned medical university, the Karolinska Institute, in 1989.

Soon – through his Karolinska professor – he was working for the Swedish FA. He joined the staff of Sweden's women's team, married Sussie, its physiotherapist, and became head of sports science and performance analysis for the Swedish men's side. He remained in Stockholm, where he and Sussie raise their four sons, and his English club postings have always been part-time: he visits Leicester one week in every month.

Pearson's barefoot guru had a talent for bringing people together. At Bolton, there was a famous night when Tommy Soderberg and Lars Lagerbäck, then co-managers of Sweden, and visiting through Balsom, ended up in a humble Chinese restaurant with Sam Allardyce and his staff. It was a late, great night by all accounts – the beer, chow mein and football knowledge passed freely around.

Balsom is also good at stimulating others' curiosity. He brought to the attention of Zlatan Ibrahimović the 'Unknown Swedes', a team with learning disabilities, and Zlatan ended up paying for every one of them to go to the World Cup in Brazil.

● ● ●

Inside Leicester the mindset is that you share expertise. Club staff are always attending or staging conferences, doing podcasts and contributing papers. It is a behaviour that comes from Balsom, Rennie and Reeves.

In March 2014 the club ambitiously hosted a Europe-wide football medical summit where Balsom used his connections to bring as keynote speaker Professor Jan Ekstrand, a Swede, and one of Uefa's top docs.

In February 2016 there was a 'Tactical Insights' conference at King Power stadium featuring Roy Hodgson and Sweden coach Erik Hamrén. A few weeks later Balsom hosted a workshop for managers and coaches across Britain, on science and analysis. The title of his presentation was 'the team behind the team'.

Why does this matter? Expertise-sharing is shrewd. Think about it. If you are going to stage a conference and present your work to the outside world . . . well, you'd better make damn sure that it is in order. When you trawl the podcasts and web articles contributed by Leicester's younger staff at Belvoir Drive it is clear the philosophy of perfecting your role and then pushing yourself outwards, ambitiously, is pervasive.

A coach/analyst at Aston Villa ignored an invite to Tactical Insights. 'I thought, "It's just people at Leicester talking,"' he laughs. 'But one of our guys went and said it was fantastic. So I went to the coaching workshop.

'Balsom is impressive. I think he's fundamental there. He wants all his staff to grow and develop. The technician even tries things.

'People inside clubs were saying, before they won the title, that Leicester were something different, that departments were really good and they were striving to be something bigger than what they were. If Man United or Man City held those conferences, you wouldn't be surprised. But you've got little Leicester doing it? I think it's something around the club that's helped them win. They haven't limited themselves. That bigger thinking about what they can achieve.'

• • •

'Culture eats strategy for breakfast,' goes a saying attributed to the management visionary, Peter Drucker.

'Every professional golfer has a separate coach for his drives, for approaches, for putting. In football we have one coach for 15 players. This is absurd,' said Johan Cruyff.

Pearson's take, as Leicester powered to promotion in 2014, was 'it's all quite open here and you have got to be guided by the people who have the specific knowledge. In any working environment everyone needs recognition and the knowledge that the man in charge values the contribution and expertise of those who work for him.'

In spring 2016, Reeves went back to Loughborough to address a meeting of a community of creatives called CAKE. On a screen he projected an image of three men in three sinking boats: each was bailing water into the next boat. His point was about blame culture. How in many organisations, especially sports clubs, departments dwell in silos and vie with each other rather than cooperate. Leicester are the opposite, he said.

An Aston Villa story: at the club, en route to relegation in 2015–16, culture and cooperation were so lacking that one day youth players could not train because the laundry room were not aware of their schedule – and unable to provide kit.

Pearson put his 'team behind the team' at the centre of Leicester's architecture. He made Walsh not just scouting head but assistant manager, a very rare move. This created total buy-in between coaching and recruitment.

At Belvoir Drive the main analysts, Andy Blake and Peter Clark, are based in the same room as the coaches. 'They are our primary audiences, so sharing an office with them makes a huge difference. It means that with just the turn of a shoulder we can discuss ideas and talk things through,' said Clark. 'And it's the same with the recruitment team.'

A Pearson innovation was to have a specialist analysis room built inside the King Power Stadium that is connected up to the changing room while Clark and Blake also have a connected desk in view of the pitch. If a player, for example, keeps losing his aerial duels there will be data and video clips on hand for the half-time team talk.

Further integrated, further strengthened, Leicester were promoted in 2013–14 after a record-breaking run of wins. One key to success was the 96 per cent availability of first-team players, not just for matches but training sessions. Less is more. Schedules were revised to give players more days off and more recovery sessions. The 'light load' of Leicester's training would raise eyebrows nearly everywhere else in the Premier League.

More science came in – like GPS monitoring of players' running distances, intensity levels, directional changes and speeds. But just as crucially there was an upping of the feedback players are invited to give. How was training? Click this iPad questionnaire.

'It's a holistic approach,' said Reeves. 'The coaching department, sports science department and players themselves coming together to really understand what we're trying to achieve.'

Balsom observed, once Leicester were promoted to the Premier League, that 'we couldn't have done it two years ago because the players weren't all the right sort of people. Now they are.' The careful work of Pearson and Walsh in assembling a squad with no bad apples is appreciated by stalwarts like Morgan – who thinks Pearson may be the best he has ever worked for – and King.

'When Sven was in charge there were a lot of players not playing, a lot of sour grapes around the training ground,' King says. 'One week it was him, the next week another guy, disappointed not to be in the team. Nigel got rid of all that.' Morgan, Vardy, Drinkwater, James, De Laet – all arrived in quick succession after Pearson's return. In the summer of 2014 types like Albrighton and Ulloa arrived to further strengthen the dynamic. Pearson also added the midfielder Esteban Cambiasso, Argentine World Cup veteran and Champions League winner, to add big-time fearlessness to the group.

Says King, 'With Wes, I'd played against him. You knew what you were getting. The spine of the players is so important: We have players who care about the club.

'They're good footballers but great people as well and Walshy gets a lot of credit for his scouting. People like Wes, Riyad, Vards have talent that makes you think, "Why weren't they picked up by someone else?" but he also scouts personality, hunger, drive, team ethic. You can have all the unbelievable players in the world – but if they don't want to work as a group you have no chance.'

• • •

After King (Richard/Andy, take your pick) intervened and West Ham were beaten on April 4, Leicester's run to safety over the closing weeks of the 2014–15 season was spectacular. Away at The Hawthorns, where Leicester had beaten West Brom just once in 21 attempts, Pearson's team was behind with ten minutes left but through muscle and willpower forced a goal: Wasilewski heading to Huth to head in at a set-piece. In stoppage time Vardy smashed aside Gareth McAuley and ran from halfway to score a winner.

Swansea were beaten next, 2–0 at home, Ulloa and King scoring.

Next came a visit to Burnley, where even in mid-April the cold gusts swept down off Pendle Hill into Turf Moor, but Leicester braved the conditions and hostile locals and edged a scrappy, real kill-or-be-killed game.

With sides facing relegation it was always likely the loser would go down and Leicester prevailed after a Burnley penalty hit the post and on the counterattack, 59 seconds later, Vardy scrambled an Albrighton cross in.

From missed spot kick to sucker-punch winner: Leicester did to Burnley what Watford did to Leicester on that pivotal day in 2013 and it showed how far they had travelled.

Despite losing to Chelsea, Leicester then dismissed Newcastle and Southampton at the King Power without even conceding a goal. Another clean sheet at Sunderland secured safety. A romp – 5–1 versus Queens Park Rangers – shot them upwards to a fourteenth-place finish.

Seven wins in nine when it counted: there was potential in this team.

• • •

Culture eats strategy for breakfast. But to stay healthy it must be allowed to chew up all threats, even the person behind its creation. Just seven days from 2014–15 ending, Pearson was effectively gone.

After beating QPR on May 24, Leicester flew off on a 'goodwill' visit to

Thailand. Three young reserve players filmed themselves, naked in a hotel room, with Thai women engaging in a sex act. On the soundtrack one footballer was heard making a racial insult. The video found its way into the *Sunday Mirror*'s possession. Their story published on 31 May carried images from the video and the headline 'Club's Thai owner took players on tour to boost links with his country . . . and this is what happened next.'

One of the players involved was Pearson's 21-year-old son, James.

The Srivaddhanaprabhas ordered an investigation and in mid-June came the inevitable news that the footballers had been sacked.

James Pearson was not the player who used the racist language, but in dismissing the trio the club didn't point that out; Nigel Pearson, knowing his son's shame and remorse, felt it should have done. This was a difference that could not be resolved.

A complex manager, Pearson was very nearly sacked after the McArthur incident and the owners expressed concern about his behaviour when, in December 2014, he was fined £10,000 and given a touchline ban after being caught telling a Leicester fan to 'fuck off and die'.

Even bang in the middle of the 'great escape' there was a silly incident when Pearson somehow rowed with a mild-mannered local journalist, Ian Baker, surreally branding him 'an ostrich'. Baker was not bothered but the clip looked weird – and bad – as it zipped around the world on social media.

So, after deliberating, the Srivaddhanaprabhas sacked Pearson on 1 July 2015, citing 'fundamental differences in perspective'. Said an official statement, 'the Club believes that the working relationship between Nigel and the Board is no longer viable.'

The end of a bully, some wrote. But listen to Paul Gallagher. Gallagher, a Scottish striker, joined Leicester during Pearson's first stint and was still there when Pearson returned in 2011.

In April 2012 Gallagher's wife Hayley lost a baby, a boy called Luca James who was one of twins. The Gallaghers found out he was stillborn at Hayley's 30-week scan and Leicester had a game versus West Ham that night.

'I had to ring Nigel and say, "I can't play." And he just said, "Make sure you do what you need to do, make sure the other baby gets here safe,"' said Paul. Gallagher was one of Leicester's top scorers but Pearson granted him compassionate leave to sit the rest of the season out. 'He was the first one on the phone to me saying, "Whatever you need, tell me." He is always saying to lads who have kids that if they need time off to be with them, then take it. He can look very hard-faced but he's one of the nicest people you can meet,' said Gallagher. They kept in touch. And Pearson always asked how Ava, the other twin, was doing.

● ● ●

Culture. When Yaya Touré, Manchester City's £220,000-a-week star fell out with the club in 2014 because it didn't give him a cake on his birthday; when it emerged in 2016 that an international Manchester United player asked the club chef to make him two hard-boiled eggs to take home because he didn't know how to boil them himself; you wondered whether culture was something strong at every club.

Pearson's gift to Ranieri was this. A team, and a team behind the team, and a culture.

'One of the key aspects of our department is how closely everybody works together. We're really good friends and want to help each other and drive each other forward,' said Reeves; doesn't that sound very like Drinkwater's comment about the friendships of the playing team?

Beyond his inner circle, Pearson bequeathed other good staff whom he brought in or developed. Like Ken Way, an esteemed performance psychologist, or Anthony Herlihy, a sure-footed young head of media.

He bequeathed a focus on excellence that in 2016 saw all sorts of Leicester departments and individuals win their own personal titles. Leicester scooped prizes for their medical and physio team, their matchday programme, and the work of John Ledwidge, the groundsman behind the King Power's pristine playing surface and geometric grass designs.

While Leicester's title win was being interpreted by certain figures in the game as some kind of 'old school' triumph, Brian Prestidge, formerly Bolton's head of performance analysis, tellingly tweeted '"Proper Football People" please stay quiet – as LCFC are the antithesis of what you are. Logical, analytical, strategic!'

● ● ●

Openness and knowledge-sharing. Let us talk about Xavi and Iniesta, and José Mourinho, and offer two stories of which Pearson, Reeves, Rennie – and most certainly Balsom – should approve.

Karolinska Intstiute neuroscientists wanted to test their theory that in brain functions like problem-solving, planning, sequencing and multi-tasking, elite footballers would have superior cognitive abilities to lay people. Especially elite footballers associated with 'game intelligence'. But they needed guinea pigs. The great Spanish midfielders Xavi Hernández and Andrés Iniesta stepped forward willingly (and of course the scientists – you should see Xavi's pen fly in the dot-connecting test – were right).

When José Mourinho was at Real Madrid two English coaches visited the club. One was Graham Potter, the go-ahead manager of FK Ostersunds in Sweden, the other was James Ellis, then in charge of the Great Britain Universities team. The pair were welcomed into Real Madrid to view the great club's facilities, meet its academy director and watch Mourinho train the first team. Don't bring business cards, Potter and Ellis were told, bring a book.

The idea being transmitted by their hosts was a powerful one: 'You are coming to us to take away knowledge and so we would like you to leave us with some.' What Mourinho and Real Madrid were saying was: 'Even the greatest can learn.'

Would whoever came in to replace Pearson still buy in to the Leicester way? There was worry at Belvoir Drive. But another Italian, arriving in town, was to prove a pleasant surprise.

3

CLAUDIO

Always a steak, always a glass of good red, and always his favourite subject – talked over lovingly. There are many types of night out to enjoy in Monte Carlo. But Claudio Ranieri favoured just the one.

'We had many dinners and he is great company,' Tor-Kristian Karlsen remembers. 'But,' Karlsen chuckles, 'he is obsessed ... with football. Ha ha.'

Karlsen is a tall, analytical Norwegian and an Italophile who speaks Italian fluently. He regards with affection and some sense of privilege his times spent looking at the waters, watching the yachts, and talking – well, just football, forever football – with a white-haired and charming man in the fine restaurants of Monaco.

• • •

AS Monaco were Ranieri's previous club, owned by a Russian cardiologist turned potash magnate, and the Monegasque royal family. Ranieri was appointed by the Russian, Dmitry Rybolovlev – and had to meet and charm Prince Albert of Monaco before his posting was confirmed.

But he was Karlsen's man. The Norwegian was one of the youngest sporting directors in Europe when Rybolovlev hired him to guide Monaco back to former glories. Eight years previously, the club was in a Champions League final but by 2012 paddled in the French second tier.

Karlsen called Claudio. He was pinning his hopes on a manager recently sacked by Inter Milan but whose body of work he found varied and impressive. Though 24 years apart in age they clicked. They whiled the evenings by the Med at eateries – and Karlsen's laughter is because of the way their chats inevitably went.

'Claudio likes culture,' he says. 'He's lived all over the place in Europe. He follows the news, politics and world affairs. But it's when you talk about football that he really starts to speak without holding back. He's so passionate and makes no secret: I would say during our dinners 80 per cent, maybe even more, of the conversation revolved around football.

'That could range from tactical issues, to scouting, transfers, methodology. He's not the kind of guy who'll sit and show off and tell anecdotes.' Karlsen is speaking down the line from northern Israel, where he is now sporting director of Maccabi Haifa. The success of bringing Ranieri to Monaco helped him rise to be that club's CEO.

Just football?

'Well, what can I tell you about him apart from that?' Karlsen continues. 'Claudio loves his steak. Good ribeye. Especially on the bone. And a glass of red wine. But what makes him tick? I couldn't say anything but . . . football.

'I don't know what you'll make of that. Or if he'll hate me for saying it. But maybe this is part of the secret. That he has this incredible enthusiasm and obsession, and a freshness, about his sport.'

● ● ●

Ranieri, son of a reputed Roman butcher who as a boy delivered meat on his bicycle, is proof that obsessives can come differently jointed and cut. The clichéd successful football manager is a maniac. A true original like Clough. A Machiavelli like Mourinho. Or like Pep Guardiola an obsessive nerd. Or like Ferguson a relentless, almost animal competitor.

Ranieri? 'In Italy we think he's an uncle,' says Edoardo Magro. In England too.

This nice man, this bespectacled, neat, priestly near-pensioner, whose first instinct is to make a press conference laugh, is actually a secret nutcase; as focused and 24-hour about football and as competitive as Clough, as Mourinho, as Ferguson, as Pep.

But he wears it lightly. He tucks his ambition underneath his slightly crumpled blue jacket. To wield power you have to project power? That is one idea with which Ranieri has no truck.

Light-touch ambition. Low-ego authority. For a place like Leicester (city motto: 'Always the Same', university motto: 'Elite without being Elitist') this was a fit.

● ● ●

When it came to replacing Pearson, the club had no dearth of interest nor shortage of targets. Guus Hiddink was approached, but said no. Sam Allardyce was an option, David Moyes got sounded out.

Former US national coach Bob Bradley emerged as a surprise candidate while some witty supporters, in a Pearson homage, put money on the job going to an ostrich. They got 500-1. Ten times more likely, the bookies felt, than the next manager actually leading Leicester to the title.

The shortest odds were on Martin O'Neill, the charismatic Ulsterman who, in a golden age from 1995–2000, was responsible for winning two of the three prizes (all League Cups) that, after thirteen decades of trying, were all that troubled the club's honours board. O'Neill was well known to Khun Vichai and still friendly with influencers at the club such as Rudkin. Bookies closed the betting but loyalty led O'Neill to remain in the Republic of Ireland job.

Ranieri had offers too. After Monaco he scratched a longstanding itch to try international management but his four games in charge of Greece were a disaster. He was sacked following defeat to the tiny Faroe Islands – 'the ... *Far Away* ... Islands?' Mourinho would taunt. But he had done a very good job at Monaco, gaining promotion and then pushing Paris Saint-Germain close for the title.

Clubs in France and Italy were interested, but over lunch at one of his old Monte Carlo haunts Ranieri confided to Steve Kutner, his agent, that he had a yearning to try England again.

He had last worked there in 2004, sacked by Chelsea. Memories (outside but not inside the club) of his tenure there were mixed. When Kutner circulated Ranieri's CV there were no takers, even among Championship clubs. Eyeing the Leicester vacancy, Kutner got Rudkin's number from the

Arsenal coach, Steve Bould, and started putting in calls. He was persistent. Initially sceptical vibes came back.

But Kutner was confident that if he could just get his client in front of Leicester's hierarchy, Ranieri's charm and knowledge would do the rest.

He emphasised the level of Ranieri's previous clubs: Juventus, Roma, Valencia, Fiorentina, Atlético Madrid, Napoli, Chelsea, Monaco, Inter Milan. Finally Leicester agreed to an interview.

Ranieri was in Calabria, by the sea, enjoying one of his regular holidays with a group of his dearest pals. These were teammates and their wives from Catanzaro, a small club where he spent his happiest playing years, and the friendships spanned 40 years. But he bade goodbye to the group and jumped on a plane to Bergamo, then flew on to London where, in a well-heeled street near Chelsea FC, he and wife Rosanna still kept a house.

At this interview Jon Rudkin, Susan Whelan and Andrew Neville, Leicester's football operations director, were impressed and Ranieri struck a rapport with perhaps the key man in the room – Top. Those two talked about Francesco Totti and Gabriel Batistuta as Ranieri enthused about the great forwards he had coached.

He returned to Calabria not really knowing his prospects but a few days later there was another call, another *arrivederci* to buddies, and a second interview, this time with Khun Vichai there. Ranieri hit it off with the owner too. The deal was sealed.

Leicester's players were in Bad Radkersburg, a medieval town in Styria where the Mur River divides Austria and Slovenia. It was where Pearson habitually booked pre-season training camps. Shakespeare and Walsh were taking charge of sessions.

The players had done their morning practice, cycling through town to the training ground and then back to their base. There, at the Hotel Im Park, after lunch came a summons. Squad assembly, 3pm. Introduction to your new manager. But who?

'The club had kept it really quiet about who we would be getting. We had no inkling,' King says. 'Then they were like, "Right, meeting at 3pm, the new manager is here."

'"Okay, are you going to tell who it is?"

'"Well, you will find out in the meeting."'

In a humble function room, 'we were literally sat waiting for someone to walk through the door. Then he walked in. And we were like, "Right, what do we do now? Do we stand up and clap? Do we sit there and whatever?"'

Other players described this moment as like *Stars in Their Eyes*, the television talent show where doors slide open to reveal a contestant made-over into someone famous. The audience is supposed to gasp. 'Basically it was like that, yeah,' says Schmeichel. 'We'd all heard rumours but didn't know and basically it was a case of "Boys, please welcome your new manager," and he came through a door.'

Ranieri was accompanied by Rudkin and Top and each briefly said their piece. 'A couple of words and that was it,' King recalls. Ranieri made a beeline for Huth, his former Chelsea player, and they shook hands.

King had also been at Chelsea during Ranieri's reign but only as a schoolboy and they did not know each other – though he would sometimes be ball boy at Stamford Bridge and get close to the dugout because he loved watching Ranieri directing tactics. He was excited and so were others in Leicester's squad: 'Everyone, even the kids, knew who he was. A well-known manager. A great CV.'

• • •

The outside world was less bowled over.

What? Ran-*ieri*?

Gary Lineker, who when Pearson was sacked asked, 'Are the folk running football stupid?' had an acerbic take. Ranieri, Lineker tweeted to his five million Twitter followers, 'is clearly experienced, but this is an uninspired choice. It's amazing how the same old names keep getting a go on the managerial merry-go-round.'

Tony Cottee, another famous former Leicester striker, said it was 'a huge gamble'. Dietmar Hamann, the former Germany and Liverpool midfielder, tweeted, 'Can't believe Leicester appointed Ranieri – Great club, great fan base but I'm afraid MK rather than Old Trafford season after next.' MK being little MK Dons, in the Championship.

Others, like Harry Redknapp, joined the outcry. Rival fans offered ridicule and Leicester's were divided. Media reception was cool: thinking, as they do, in headlines many journalists simply thought, 'Ranieri? Tinkerman.'

Tinkerman, of course, was the slur on Ranieri when his constant selection changes were mocked at Chelsea. The bookies, after their narrow escape from an ostrich payout, installed Ranieri favourite to be the first Premier League manager sacked.

Whelan would say, 'trust in us', at a press conference the following week. It was dominated by uncomfortable questions about Pearson's dismissal. Sitting beside her, Ranieri said this, 'I don't understand. The first part of the [2014–15] season was not so good . . . but the character of the manager, the players, the fans, made a miracle because the last part of the season was amazing.

'I want to know. Who is the real Leicester? The first or the second? I'm sure the second.'

The sharpness of this answer and his charisma gave sceptics their first second thoughts.

Claudio Ranieri, then: what were Leicester getting?

'When you appoint Claudio, what you're bringing is someone extremely experienced, who has worked in many different countries and cultures and is able to implement what he's learned from working with some of the most powerful and eccentric owners in football,' says Karlsen.

'Someone exceptionally dedicated,' he continues, 'and someone very clear. His ideas are not simple but clear, and he believes in them. He's not trying stuff for the sake of it: he's in his sixties and doesn't need to show off by trying out the latest trends in tactics or management.'

Oh, he adds, and you are placing a bomb inside your club.

A bomb?

'He's an energy bomb. I'm talking about work ethic and enthusiasm, the fact I don't think I've ever seen someone enjoy his work as much as Claudio does. He comes in fresh every morning, very eager to get on with things. I don't know what drives him, whether it's success or the pursuit of something tangible, or just love of football. But there's no faulting his energy.'

Karlsen casts his mind back to the summer of 2012, when he had just appointed Ranieri. The contract was agreed in late May and pre-season began in mid-June and Ranieri was supposed to spend the three-week hiatus on vacation.

'He was on the phone to me every day of his holiday. First thing, 7.15am, 7.30am, I could be sure he'd ring me up, or at the very minimum there'd be a message enquiring about a player or giving feedback on someone he'd been watching the night before on [the video scouting platform] Wyscout.

'It seems to me, he's from dawn to dusk concerned about one thing. His work. And he is really contagious. He is so full of positivity and energy you have to be made of stone to not let it catch on to you.'

• • •

The Hotel Im Park is a four-star, £90-a-night joint; pleasant but not luxurious. The players breakfasted and toddled off to training on their bikes. Claudio's first session, eh? What's he going to do?

The answer: nothing.

On Bad Radkersburg's modest, municipal pitch, fringed by hedging and a row of garages, Shakespeare and Walsh were left directing a practice that included an eleven-a-side game while Ranieri, flanked by Rudkin, just watched. The following day was for recovery and Ranieri spoke little to the players. The next day involved strenuous conditioning and an 18km bike ride. Again Ranieri just quietly observed.

And on it went until the weekend, when it was time to fly home and recommence training at Belvoir Drive.

'We didn't really hear from him for a week after his introduction,' says Schmeichel. 'He just kept his distance and sort of watched us, to see how we and the coaching staff worked. It was a little bit headmaster-ish.

'It was, all the time at training, off the pitch, at dinner; walking around checking everything, not saying anything. You were willing him, "Come on, say something, please!"'

The nice man cometh. Ranieri, like Pearson, does his research and learned in advance Leicester's reputation for having a strong playing group, backed up by a particular structure of staff. But he wanted to judge for himself. At last he spoke.

'He said, "I have been really impressed by what you have done and what the staff are doing. I am not really going to change anything. It will be as you were. The schedule will stay the same." That made everyone feel good,' King says.

It was a victory for culture. The club wanted Ranieri to retain Walsh, Reeves, Rennie and Shakespeare and Bad Radkersburg demonstrated to him the wisdom of doing that. Back at Belvoir Drive, when he saw the science, facilities and working atmosphere, he was completely won over. 'I looked around at the staff, at the fitness side, recruitment, video analysis – everything was amazing. Why did I have to change anything? The organisation was perfect,' Ranieri said.

There were still questions, though. Would the schedule stay the same *exactly*? Would he *listen* to his department heads like Pearson?

The bellwether would be that issue – loading. Ranieri had brought in three of his own men, Paolo Benetti, an intelligent, trusted, high-calibre assistant, Andrea Azzalin, a young fitness specialist, and Giorgio Pellizzaro, a grizzled goalkeeping coach. Pellizzaro was keeper at Catanzaro when Ranieri was centre-half – and one of his Calabrian holiday pals.

Collectively, the Italian contingent's considerable experience involved regimes far more intensive than the mere two days a week of full training that had come to be the 'low load' Leicester norm. Ranieri's instinct was for more sessions, more work. Balsom, Reeves, Rennie strongly put the counter-case.

Shakespeare, the canny but jolly coach, was an important conduit for the players: they did not want change.

'Shakey is one of the most underrated people at the club,' says King. '[His importance is in] sort of managing the players. A funny character, one the players can have a good laugh with. They enjoy his banter. He still thinks he's one of the lads a little bit.

'But the players also respect him because they know he does a lot for us. He makes every session enjoyable and kind of says, "This is how the players like to work." At the start, if the gaffer had said, "no" and Shakey had just said, "okay", well – we might not be where we are now.'

The Leicester Way would stay. At least while Ranieri further observed the results.

• • •

By May, the whole planet seemed to want to know the Leicester Way. The World Economic Forum (WEM) published an article on '4 leadership lessons from Leicester City's unlikely Premiership success' and the first involved Ranieri, identified by the author as a beacon of 'servant leadership'.

Servant leadership was a concept developed by the seminal American management thinker, Robert K. Greenleaf, who argued for a change to the traditional Western authoritarian style. He advocated leaders whose priority was to serve, not dominate, their institutions and underlings. That, said the WEM analysis, was Ranieri.

The classic Italian coach is Fabio Capello, Giovanni Trapattoni, Marcelo Lippi: a strong man, a man of power. That is the type the players feared they might be getting.

'With due respect, Italians have a different way to the British,' says Schmeichel. 'You are thinking it's going to be difficult [for Ranieri] to impose a full Italian mentality. You can tweak things, but to go in and demand British players, or British-minded players, change completely to the Italian way of training two, three times a day, to being in hotels for long periods of time, to staying away from home for days up until a game ... I don't think that would have any positive effect.'

But there is an alternative Italian model. Carlo Ancelotti, the most successful Italian manager of his generation, is relaxed, open, humble, humorous: a servant leader. At Chelsea, Ancelotti flexed his ideas to suit the English culture, particularly with training regimes. Personality-wise – and in their abiding love of food – Ranieri and Ancelotti are similar. When Ranieri started receiving plaudits for his work at Leicester he told *Corriere della Sera*, 'I always thought the most important thing a good coach must do is to build the team around the characteristics of his players.'

Keeping things as they were 'was massive, massive', says Schmeichel. 'Because with the momentum we had built, the last thing we needed was a complete overhaul. We had already lost our manager, a main figure. We didn't need the rest to leave, the physio and footballing staff, the medical and support staff. There was a routine we had built and had success with.

'A younger manager would probably come in all guns blazing, "This is me, here is how I am going to do things." Young managers, new managers, would come in and want to stamp their authority. The experience [Ranieri] built throughout the years helped. Maybe, without rushing in, he would see the bigger picture – and he definitely did.'

The 'freshness' about his work that Karlsen mentions was seen in Ranieri, in his thirtieth year as coach, travelling to Germany to study Guardiola at work at Bayern Munich, Jürgen Klopp at Borussia Dortmund, and see how FC Augsburg, a successful underdog club, operated. He remains open to new ideas.

Wyscout, invented in Italy and a trove of stats and scouting videos of players from all over the world, is now a standard tool for coaches. But very few of Ranieri's generation embrace the technology so enthusiastically. After dinner one of Ranieri's routines is to retire with his iPad to watch clips.

He seemed open to learning as much as he could about Leicester, being quickly seen out around the city and even in country pubs. On his third day back from Austria, Leicester Under-21s were playing in Loughborough against Dynamo, the town's non-league side. And, in the tin shed opposite the dug-out at Dynamo's tiny Nanpantan Road ground, stood a smiling white-haired Italian, mingling with surprised and delighted locals.

Karlsen found Ranieri's 'view on physical preparation, training and science impressive. He's inquisitive and always looking for new input, and the people he works with [like Azzalin and Benetti] are renowned for being progressive.

All in all, says Karlsen, Ranieri is 'flexible, collaborative, a dream to work with. It comes down to his experience and confidence. A manager who is very sure of himself and knows what battles to pick and not to pick, will be open to ideas.

'I've seen in younger managers that they always bring the same team, do the same things wherever they go, have one concept that is, like, a 360-degrees model. They feel they have all the answers. I think this is quite a naïve approach. You can't possibly know everything about man-management, fitness, tactics, scouting, how to deal with the media. Claudio has learned from working at big clubs, where there's a wealth of expertise available, that you take advantage of expertise.

'Basically, he's an intelligent man. And intelligent people are open to ideas.'

More laughter echoes down the line from Haifa. Karlsen does not want to leave the impression Ranieri is too nice to have steel. He tells two stories. One involves a sports psychologist foisted on Ranieri at Monaco. The guy had ideas above his station and wanted to influence tactics and selection. 'He crossed very much into the manager's territory,' Karlsen recalls. So what happened? 'The psychologist ended up working with the academy.'

The other tale involves a player. No names, but this character had 'a very questionable approach to training and discipline'. He was always late, he shunned club events and did not even turn up when the squad organised something socially. Karlsen and Ranieri 'had many talks about that player'. But Monaco were short in his position so Ranieri took the pragmatic decision to keep picking him. Then came a transfer window. 'As soon as he had the chance to replace him, he did.'

Ranieri had a particular talent, Karlsen relates, for making gifted individuals work for the team: 'He managed to fit players in like James Rodríguez – James had his best season in European football under Ranieri. They didn't always see eye to eye and James had to run more than he had ever wanted to, but it worked. Remember, he had his fantastic 2014 World Cup on the back of his fitness regime at Monaco.'

Yannick Carrasco, the young Belgian who scored for Atlético Madrid in the Champions League final, was brought through Monaco's youth system by Ranieri. 'Carrasco was never Ranieri's biggest fan, he complained a lot, but Ranieri made him a footballer with tough love,' Karlsen says.

What Ranieri always did with creative players was devise tactics to let them use their strengths, 'but he won't excuse them and let them get away without doing the basics – their tracking back, their pressing, their work for the team. As you saw with Mahrez. Another flair player, maybe not simple to manage, but Ranieri got the best out of him.'

● ● ●

Tactics and discipline. When these are invloved the Cuddly Claudio routine stops. Ranieri has a very Italian sense that they are the areas where a coach must truly add value.

He had pored over the Pearson tapes, puzzling how a team could play so well and yet fail to record a win between late September and late December; how such a side could be stranded with nine games to go. 'They were strong, very fighting [sic] but I think they need a little more tactics,' he said in his first press conference.

Pearson's 3-5-2, though voguish again in Italy, was not a formation Ranieri ever liked. No side had really won with it in England – except, ironically, Leicester under O'Neill nearly twenty years before.

One conundrum was how fluently and committedly Leicester had attacked in the previous season and yet how relatively few goals they scored. And how, despite a keeper as good as Schmeichel, and defenders like Huth and Morgan, with Cambiasso guarding, they kept conceding. But the basic counterattacking blueprint of the Pearson days: now that he liked.

He did not say much about tactics in his early conversations with players. He just said stuff like 'when we play, I want you to give 100 per cent' ('well of course we do,' said Huth). When Schmeichel asked before a friendly, 'Do you want us to play out from the back?' Ranieri merely replied, 'just do what you have been doing.'

This softly-softly approach was deliberate. Ranieri reckoned a very British dressing room would be 'afraid of the Italian tactics' and resolved his adjustments would be simple and subtle and gradual. 'Always show me everything you've got and every now and again I will explain a little football to you,' was a playful early message to the group.

Tactics were involved in negative perceptions held about his time at Chelsea. Specifically, it came down to the 2003–04 Champions League semi-final. Having eliminated the Arsenal 'Invincibles' team in the quarter-finals, a great triumph, Chelsea were well backed to beat unfancied Monaco.

But in a damaging first leg away from home, when Chelsea were handily placed at 1–1 and with a one-man advantage after Monaco had Andreas Zikos sent off, Ranieri made unfathomable changes. First he took off a winger for a midfielder (Jesper Gronkjaer for Juan Verón), then a defender for a striker (Mario Melchiot for Jimmy Floyd Hasselbaink) and finally, to complete the set, a midfielder for a defender (Scott Parker for Robert Huth). Monaco scored two late goals against his baffled players to win 3–1.

He forever regretted it ('bad Tinkerman!' he later joked) but, as British journalists got reacquainted with him over 2015–16, he explained his mistake had been listening to the players – who demanded at half-time to 'go for it' – and not following his own tactical instincts.

Indeed, he claims to trust just one person in the world in tactical matters. 'My only technical adviser,' he said, 'is my mother.'

● ● ●

Family is as important to Ranieri as it was to Pearson. His mum, Renata, turned 96 in May and he is not ashamed to say that one of his biggest motivations is gaining her approval for his work. At Chelsea, apparently, she was forever on the phone, nagging him to pick Damien Duff.

Claudia, his daughter, and Rosanna – Dr Rosanna, whom he met in Catanzaro – are 'the most important part of my life'. Before managing Leicester, the time when he spent a lot of his life in the East Midlands was when (on days off at Chelsea) taking regular trips with Rosanna to antique fairs in Newark. She owned an antique shop in Rome. He, the butcher's son, would return with Lincolnshire sausages.

'Family' is a word footballers often reach for when trying to describe good set-ups at clubs and you hear a lot of that from Leicester players.

When Ranieri was crowned manager of the year in May he paid tribute to Rosanna, 'a saint'. A young coach in the audience that night was struck.

'He had that amazing line that all married men would like to say one day: "I stayed with my wife forty years." A lot of literature out there suggests that without stability you can't achieve great things. So, when Mourinho replaces him at Chelsea and becomes the Messiah, what Ranieri had was stability, the love of his wife to fall back on,' the young coach says.

'It's something players respect. Young men: they can look up to something like that. Ranieri is a wealthy guy, but he's kept his wife and I know from experience that does carry weight in a dressing room. Players say, "He's a family man." A lot of players are from broken homes, don't have a dad, and that strikes a chord.'

And what a face Ranieri has. Handsome, tragic, mirthful; one that can look close to sadness even when he's happy and happiness even when he's sad.

A good face for a great comic actor – and indeed it is Steve Martin to whom his appearance is often compared. Above all, he comes across as a human being. Wes Morgan was in North America at the Gold Cup when Ranieri arrived at Leicester and he texted staff, principally in Leicester's media department, to ask what the new gaffer was like. Very good, very nice, came all the replies.

Almeto Cristofori, a childhood friend, with whom Ranieri kicked a ball about outside San Saba church near their homes in Via Giotto, Rome, said, 'even then he had an English sense of humour' and it seems Ranieri quickly grasped the banter of Leicester's dressing room.

'He is good value,' smiles King. 'If he says something stupid in a press conference, we might be warming up and someone will shout whatever he just said. And he is, like, "hey, wanker! Shut up!"'

With Vardy, the biggest joker in the dressing room, Ranieri decided to laugh along and join in. They had a routine with each other that carried on throughout the season and made other players crack up. It was basic stuff. Ranieri would say something like, 'Wanker!'. And 'Wanker!' Vardy was allowed to shoot back.

Part of him carrying his ambition so lightly is a willingness to show the public parts of his hinterland. A few days before Leicester's first game, Ranieri did a Twitter Q&A for fans and in this plus a few early interviews he proved willing to share:

His favourite music? The Beatles, Andrew Lloyd Webber, some Classical, 'Fire' by Kasabian.

Beloved pet? A German Shepherd called 'Shark,' who died and can't be replaced.

Best films? *La vita e bella* (*Life is Beautiful*), *Out of Africa*, *Ghost*.

Wait. His favourite film is *Ghost?* No bad thing, it would prove, for Leicester to hire a romantic. In his autobiography, *Proud Man Walking*, there is plenty of sentiment, including memories of his honeymoon with Rosanna in Istanbul where, 'the outline of all the domes and minarets at sunset, there is a certain magic to it all.'

But some issues are cold, hard, ones. Ranieri's most pressing problem involved Cambiasso, whose authority had carried Leicester through their darkest points of 2014–15. The Argentine was out of contract and considering his future. He almost renewed before Pearson's dismissal but when

Ranieri arrived, old stories surfaced of a rift at Inter Milan when Ranieri was manager and Cambiasso captain.

Ranieri asked Cambiasso to stay at Leicester. A contract was put before the Argentine and Ranieri told a press conference, 'I said to [Cambiasso], "I need you, everybody loves you in Leicester, please come back." But we need a yes or no.'

The following day he got his answer.

'No.'

Cambiasso announced he was leaving.

'Ranieri's first failure,' reports were headlined. Could the sack-race favourite, the Greek failure, the Tinkerman, really stay the course – especially with Leicester losing their most distinguished player?

And, given those Italian tactics Ranieri planned, who now would protect the defence, win the ball, and start counterattacks?

He might need to listen to his staff again.

Walsh had been following him about saying something: 'Kanté, Claudio, Kanté.'

4 CAPTAIN MORGAN

He was their secret, the big plodding kid. The youth coaches at Nottingham Forest hid him from the manager.

Day after day, lap after lap, step after step, he ran – hating each and every one.

When the other young players played, he watched. When the other young players rested, he ran. If the manager asked – he was not necessarily with the group.

The rest were budding footballers, a future elite. He was a big kid, with some talent, with more than some spirit, but in no shape at all.

So they gave him added layers to guarantee extra sweat and a programme, well, more a basic instruction: there's the pitch, stay outside the lines, off you go, run.

The fear was Paul Hart. Hart had high standards. Fearsome Hart, manager of Nottingham Forest, their club, might just see him if he played for the youth team and say it would not do. So the plan was hatched. They would keep him and he could train but could not play until he shed pounds. A lot of pounds.

Why go to such trouble? Because they, the youth coaches, principally John Pemberton, the youth team manager, saw something in a hulking boy who came to Forest from college on a one-week trial, that he managed to turn into a month, and now a short contract. Go and do it, Pemberton told him, go run round the City Ground pitch, go lose weight – and then I know you will show everyone you can play.

And he did it. On frosty Saturdays, while the others were in their digs, he plodded round. Over several months he sweated off two and a half stones. Then he was part of the team, a proper part. A big, tough, kind teammate, with a tattoo of a growling grizzly on his arm. All of that led to a dressing room nickname at Forest – The Bear.

'Yeah, I was a big kid,' The Bear (Wes Morgan) recalls, 'I had ability but plenty of work to do on fitness. They didn't let me play, I just had to run and get fit.'

That was in early 2002, more than fourteen years ago, now. He shakes his head at the memory, this big guy, big Wes Morgan. Know something? 'I hate running. I hate it. I really hate running,' he grins. 'I'm not good at running at all ... from when I was 18 until now I've been back of the group.'

• • •

Kanté, Claudio, Kanté.

So here is how Leicester made the transfer catch of the decade; how they trawled football's backwater midfields and fished out a golden minnow.

Nigel Pearson is not just a researcher but a planner too. In February 2015, just after a transfer window closed, Pearson was already thinking about the next one. He realised there might well come a situation in the summer where Cambiasso would move on. To talk replacements he called in Walsh – and the wonks.

In Leicester's scouting team were several of Balsom's 'ten key men' – the analytics guys, the data crunchers with their baggy eyes and laptops, who process football to within a decimal measurement of its life. They have been integral to Leicester's recruitment since the Team Behind the Team reassembled in 2011. Then, Rob Mackenzie, a Loughborough PhD student, was promoted from first-team performance analyst to a new role, Head of Technical Scouting.

Mackenzie's job would be establishing new ways of supporting Walsh and his trusted chief scout, David Mills.

Mackenzie's analytics influenced the recruitment of Mahrez and put Leicester on a trail that led them to Shinji Okazaki. He was so successful Tottenham headhunted him. In February 2015 Ben Wrigglesworth had just taken over in his place.

Wrigglesworth, 24, was a high-flier who even in his teens was coaching for Simon Clifford's renowned Brazilian Soccer Schools in Leeds. Walsh and Mills, meanwhile, were both in their sixties with 80 years in the professional game between them. And yet, young and old, technical and traditional, the blend in Leicester's recruitment department worked.

How to replace Cambiasso? The analytics guys looked at key metrics. They ran searches for who had the most interceptions, tackles and forward passes per 90 minutes across Europe's top five leagues. Iconic and obvious names came up, like Xabi Alonso and Toni Kroos. But also some more obscure ones: a Brazilian called Allan at Udinese, for example. He was briefly targeted.

Another of the lesser known names rang bells. The cross-checking was done and it turned out to be a 'match' – the name, N'Golo Kanté, figured in a report already in the club's record: one of Mills' deputies attended a game involving French second-tier club Caen a few months previously and picked out their midfielder, Kanté.

Further profiling involved focusing on stats relevant to Leicester's playing style.

Crucial for any midfielder playing counterattack is the ability to effect a 'transition' – turnover of possession – and Kanté's numbers for 'ball recoveries' were off the scale: best in Europe's top five leagues in 2014–15.

Leicester's analysts also do their own coding, compiling specialist stats not available through third-party data. Many of these are 'out of possession' variable. Kanté continued scoring well. The Wyscout clips were enticing too. The nugget that Kanté had never suffered a serious injury was encouraging. Walsh and Mills went to watch Caen, now in Ligue 1, and came back impressed.

Kanté, Claudio: 'When I saw him first I thought, "He is a machine, he's everywhere,"' says a French agent close to Walsh and involved in Kanté's career. Walsh saw what the agent saw, but there was one negative: Kanté's build. He is square-shouldered and strong-legged but – come on – 5ft6in at most. Surely not for the Premier League. 'You think,' smiles the agent, 'he's a 15-year-old boy.'

But Pearson went with Walsh and sanctioned the signing though there was a new problem: Marseille.

Marseille wanted Kanté. With Marseilles history and romance for French players, Kanté was drawn. If Marseille had paid Caen the €8m they asked, Kanté would have gone to them. Yet Marseille tried to lowball. The French clubs fell out. And though Pearson was sacked, and weeks passed, here was Ranieri in need of a midfielder.

Kanté, Claudio. Ranieri was sceptical about size – even tiny Claude Makélélé, whom he had at Chelsea, was an inch taller – but Walsh persisted and Ranieri said okay and Leicester offered Caen the €8m (then £5.6m). Deal.

Kanté's circle talked him round. Marseille is a soap opera, they told him, you like your privacy. Kanté came to Leicester with a friend but intermediaries kept calling on Marseille's behalf. Sometimes transfers are heists and suddenly this became like one: Kanté and his pal were stashed in the Leicester Marriott hotel and asked to keep a low profile (not hard for Kanté) and turn off their phones. Walsh's trusted agent would chaperone.

It went like this for three days. Kanté, anonymous in his hotel. Marseille's reps increasingly suspicious of the phone that always went to voicemail. When Kanté was brought to Belvoir Drive, the message to staff was 'this one doesn't leave until he has signed.' Kanté's primary agent negotiated terms with Jon Rudkin while, in the manager's office, using his French and his charm, Ranieri convinced Kanté how much he was needed.

On August 3, for only £5.6m, Kanté signed. Yet he still looked like a 15-year-old to some. One of Belvoir Drive's security men assumed he was over on trial with the youth team. 'Staying in the Marriott?' he said, as Kanté waited for a taxi. 'Aw. It's nice of your mum and dad to put you up in a big hotel.'

• • •

On 21 July, the day of Cambiasso's exit, Kanté's arrival was almost a fortnight away. And Big Wes Morgan was someone Ranieri had heard much about but not even met: Morgan was in the United States playing for Jamaica in the CONCACAF Gold Cup. But Leicester had to play that day, the first of five pre-season friendly matches. All were away from home and this one did not turn out to be encouraging.

Lincoln, that small cathedral city in the flatlands fifty miles north-east of Leicester, was no football hotbed. Since 2011–12, Lincoln City had been out of the Football League and now were rebuilding after another season of fighting relegation. It was a Tuesday evening and the crowd at Sincil Bank was 3,693, with almost 1,400 Leicester supporters travelling, and Ranieri started with Pearson's 3-4-1-2 formation. Fuchs, Huth and Okazaki, Pearson's last three signings, played. Mahrez floated as No.10. A couple of kids – Liam Moore and Jack Barmby – were in the line-up, and after ten minutes Lincoln's captain, Alan Power, converted a penalty.

Though Mahrez side-footed home a rebound to equalise, Lincoln remained the much sharper side until half-time. A television cameraman and a ring of photographers had tracked Ranieri to the little dug-outs and there was publicity for the first match of his reign.

Half-time: 1–1, being outplayed by non-league lads, humble ground – it was not auspicious. 'We were were like, "This is a little bit awkward,"' recalls King of the moment Ranieri came into the dressing room. Calmly, though, the manager made changes – an entirely new XI for the second half with King as captain and Vardy up front.

It was better, not greatly, but better. Kramarić, with a fine shot, and Vardy, close in, gave Leicester victory late on.

The next friendly was a draw at Mansfield of League Two, featuring a lovely, curling finish by Leicester's then most reliable scorer, David Nugent. Next, with Vardy scoring twice, was a reasonable win at Burton Albion, from League One. Then a 2–1 win at Rotherham, from the Championship, with Mahrez now among the goals.

The programme was completed at Birmingham City on Saturday 1 August and journalists on the Midlands 'beat', who truly know their stuff about their clubs, agree this was a key early moment in the Ranieri reign. Again, as he had throughout pre-season, Ranieri started with the Pearson formation of 3-4-1-2. The team was: Schmeichel; Wasilewski, Huth, Chilwell; Albrighton, King, Drinkwater, Schlupp; Mahrez; Ulloa, Vardy.

Physically, Leicester were up to speed now, and from the off their play was vigorous but Birmingham hit them twice: a 'knuckleball' free-kick by David Cotterill and brilliant run-and-shot by (remember the name) Demarai Gray punished Leicester for situations where they failed to deal with counterattacks. The better team in the first half, but conceding goals and nothing to show? All a bit (pre-great escape) 2014–15.

So at half-time Ranieri made his first decisive act as Leicester manager. 3-4-1-2 was abandoned, never to be seen again.

He replaced Wasilewski with De Laet, Chilwell with Moore, and went to 4-2-3-1, with Kramarić playing behind Vardy. And Leicester were rampant. The sun came out at St Andrews. Huth equalised at a set-piece, Drinkwater volleyed in and Okazaki, replacing Vardy, scored a diving header. 'Brilliant second half – they couldn't get near us,' King recalls.

In this formation, Mahrez came alive, floating, flitting and finding good angles for passes and dribbles. He seemed better from a wider starting position than in the centre and created Okazaki's winner after, in his soft-limbed, borderline-casual way, applying incredible control to chest a crossfield ball from Fuchs.

A good pre-season in the end. And carefully planned. The programme involved playing a fifth-tier team, then a fourth, then a third, then one from low in the second tier and finally one higher in the second tier. Step by step, as Ranieri liked to say.

And all the matches were in the Midlands, within an hour's reach by coach. That summer, as everyone else chased from Australia to Asia to Africa to North America to Europe for extra money, only two Premier League clubs, West Ham and Leicester, stayed at home to focus purely on preparation. And conserving energy, we will see, was important to the Leicester way.

'We stuttered into it, maybe, trying to find our feet, trying to play the way [Ranieri] probably thought he wanted without really knowing the players. Still trying to build from the back, still pass, pass, switch,' reflects King. 'But we didn't lose in pre-season, actually. We won every game.'

In the end: 4-2-3-1. Dynamism. Okazaki's movement. Drinkwater prominent. Huth important. Mahrez casting spells. Coming off the field at Birmingham, just in time, Ranieri's Leicester was taking shape.

• • •

Wes Morgan, in some moments, still looks like he should not be on a football pitch. You look at the shoulders, built for barging holes in walls, the meaty haunches, the heavyweight boxer's neck, the forearms made for carrying boulders.

You see the broad chest, the thick legs, the big, solid head. You see a bear of a man who perhaps should be in a different sporting arena. Who could be wearing the green and red of Leicester Tigers and playing at the Welford Road rugby ground, half a mile from King Power Stadium.

Yet Wes is gentle, a peaceful hulk who despite his rugged style somehow went through 2015–16 with only three bookings. 2014–15 was similar. 'Three bookings for a defender, who some might say is a "no-nonsense defender", is a bit low,' he grins. 'It's great.

'I like to think I time my challenges and am always in the right position where maybe I don't make that foul.' Maybe. Or maybe the strikers of England are simply too frightened to go near him.

After that Valentine's Day defeat at Arsenal, when Ranieri sent his players on holiday, and they headed for the beaches and country parks and mountains, here's what Wes did. He stood on a windy field in Nottingham teaching children to play football, even tying their laces sometimes.

After, he played table tennis with them or joined them in the classroom.

On days off, while teammates relax with families, this is what Wes often chooses to do: he drives to Leicester from Nottingham and does a shift at Blue Ink Tattoo, the studio he owns. It's not flash: situated near Argos, across from where all the buses stop on Leicester's Belgrave Gate.

Why?

The tattoo shop is co-owned with Scott Tynan who he met in the summer of 2002 when they were both called, at the last minute, into a Nottingham Forest Under-19 team going to America for the Dallas Cup. Wes had shed his 35lbs and the coaches finally felt he could play. When Michael Dawson, Forest's star prospect got injured, it was Wes they called up for Dallas.

Tynan was a budding goalkeeper also drafted in for the trip. He didn't make it in the end and left football to set up a tattoo venture in his native Liverpool. After making a success there Tynan sought investment so he could move the business forward. Wes stepped in and the pair opened Blue Ink Tattoo in Leicester in late 2014.

Why, in February 2016, was Wes on that chilly pitch with the kids? Because Julian Bennett, a retired left back, wanted a new direction, and they decided the time was right to launch MB Coaching – a 'professional football coaching and mentoring camp'. Bennett is maybe Wes's best friend; they have been that way since before primary school. There is a lovely photo of Wes and 'Jules' in a small back garden, two imps in garish shorts and foolish poses in front of a picket fence. MB Coaching is an idea they'd had for years.

Then there is Gregor Robertson, another pal from the old youth team at Forest. Robertson was still playing throughout 2015-16 but retired at the end of the season to pursue a career in writing. He won a gig with *The Times*. He is talented but Wes gave him a leg up by regularly obliging, when Gregor was starting out, with interviews. These pieces glowed with the warmth between the pair.

Sir Alex Ferguson said loyalty was the anchor of his life. Well, it is the whole ship with Wes.

'The soccer schools, I am involved with them. I help out my friend who is there all the time. I'm in a position where I can boost the profile of things like the soccer schools and tattoo shops ... and Gregor is trying to get into the journalism world, which is pretty difficult, so I've been trying to help with interviews and exclusives for him.

'I like to help people out,' says Wes. 'I look at myself as a person that, if I am in a position to help someone out and I can do it, then I will do it. Where I grew up, loyalty is very important. You don't stab someone in the back. No one would do that in this [Leicester] team either. It's definitely a quality that I find is very important in a person and I like people to look at me as a loyal man.'

Jules is far from the only friendship he has maintained from from way back. 'You know, the friends I grew up with when I was going to nursery, they are still my friends now,' Wes says. 'Absolutely. We still hang around together like we are teenagers.'

Though Leicester's captain, and Nottingham is a rival East Midlands city, he has no intention of leaving his home town. Because his friends live there, his family live there. He is still 'always in the area where I grew up'. Ah, that. Morgan grew up in The Meadows, an estate notorious for guns and gangs; the drug trade and, latterly, food banks.

At MB Coaching there is a reason the boys and girls spend time in the classroom as well as on the football pitch. 'Coming from where we're from we've seen where kids might get led down the wrong path and football's a big thing, a big tool you can use to point them in the right direction,' Wes said when the BBC featured his initiative.

In 2013, Nottingham was statistically Britain's poorest city. In 2000, The Meadows became one of only three areas in Britain to have routine armed police patrols. Wes was 16 at the time. Now, Nottingham and The Meadows are both improving and Wes is proud of the values he carries forward.

'There was a lot of drugs and crime and stuff going off, especially in the area I was from. Some of my friends are locked up. I'm still in contact and good friends with most of them. But it is a good place in many ways, it shaped me into the person I am,' he says.

How? 'You have to fend for yourself, really, with no help from outside and you learn from that. I look at life and don't take things for granted.

'I think it gives you strength of character. I think I have belief in what I want to achieve.

'Growing up in those places teaches you what it's like to go without, so when people see the opportunity to achieve something they take it with both hands.'

• • •

It may be wrong to suggest football kept Wes out of trouble, stopped him from using his muscle for ill purpose. His goodness always shone through, from his young days, writes Robertson in his articles. When you meet Wes you sense a gentle nature, strength of character and a good brain. He was probably capable of keeping out of trouble all by himself.

But football certainly helped. He stayed out late, though not on the street but the gym, the court, the pitch; wherever he could get a game. At one stage he was playing for 'four or five teams': Nottinghamshire Boys, Meadows Colts, South Notts, a semi-pro team, Dunkirk – the latter after being released by Notts County. He went to college and studied business, with thoughts of becoming an accountant. 'I kept my eye on doing something positive,' he says.

The biggest influence was his mum, Diane. She, Wes smiles, was the captain then. She looked after five kids – he has two brothers and two sisters – and ensured they never went without and spent what she had on getting Wes boots and kit and transport to games.

She is a serious football fan, who supported Forest but also Chelsea, because of Didier Drogba – at one point she even had a Drogba shirt. She is the first to text Wes after matches, usually 'well done' with kisses – extra ones now he's doing so well, he jokingly claims.

So that's where it's from. That is why the diverse personalities in Leicester's dressing room, the sock throwers, the shy Frenchman, the wry German, the livewire striker, the casual genius, bright-eyed Kingy, grumbling Drinky, über-focused Kasper; that's why they're all Wes's 'boys'.

He says, 'They are my team, you know, I love them like family. We have been through so much together and we are such a close bunch of guys. Me, as captain, I feel like I lead them onto the pitch and they are my boys. It's a fantastic feeling, to know someone has got your back . . . and I have got their back. It has taken us a long way, that characteristic in the team.'

He is not one who has to demand respect: people give it naturally to someone like Wes.

'There are captains who like to parade and shout before games. Captains who give players a right good kick up the arse and are in people's faces. Me, I look at myself as a captain where I lead by example. When I am on the field, I like to put the first tackle in, do something positive straight away for the team,' he says.

It is from The Meadows, it is from his nature and it is from Diane. 'The way my mum is, is the way I am,' he reflects. 'We are similar people. We are quite caring people and we look after the people, we are always trying to help people. And try to look after people we care about.'

• • •

A football-mad mum and friendships that span decades. Ranieri could relate to that. Yet entering the final week before the season started, Ranieri still had not met the central person in his dressing room.

But he had listened. He had seen the tapes. He had seen, in 2014–15, how Morgan at first struggled with the pace and decisiveness of Premier League strikers, having never played higher than the Championship. But he had also seen, as that season progressed, Morgan learn and problem-solve and turn himself into a formidable top-level performer.

The tapes bore witness to how, as 2014–15 progressed, Morgan adapted and problem solved and slowly turned himself into a top level performer. Indeed, his career was always about grafting and getting better. He acquitted himself well in that Dallas Cup and came home to become a fixture in Forest's reserves, working his way to a first team opportunity the following year.

He took it and by 20 was not only established in Hart's side but had become a favourite of the fearsome manager. By 27 he reached his four hundredth first-team game and assumed Forest's captaincy. A few months later, just after his twenty-eighth birthday, Leicester pounced when Walsh's grapevine told him Morgan was unsettled after Forest made an unexpectedly cheap new contract offer.

Joining for £1m in January 2012, soon Morgan was established both as Leicester's leader and as a fixture in the annual Championship Team of the Year. Then came the season of transitioning to the Premier League. 'I think it's taken me quite a few years to learn exactly what I need to do in my position. Instead of relying on my physicality as my main tool, I've learned how to read the game more and position myself,' he told Robertson in one of their interviews.

Ranieri did not doubt Morgan's importance. At the Gold Cup Jamaica made history as the first Caribbean side to reach the final and before the game, which was played on July 26 against Mexico before 70,000 at Philadelphia's Lincoln Financial Field, Morgan's phone went. It was a text from Ranieri saying best wishes and good luck.

That meant a lot, Morgan says. He felt terrible he was not around when Pearson was sacked: he wished he could have said goodbyes and paid respects to 'the best manager I've played under', who did so much for him as a player and person. And it was 'particularly difficult' that he had missed Ranieri's arrival. As leader of the group he wanted to have been there. Not just for the new boss but to help the other players, his 'boys', adjust to a different life.

But he also takes playing for Jamaica – for whom he qualifies through grandparents – very seriously and the reason he stayed in touch with events in Bad Radkersburg not through teammates but Leicester's media department was to avoid the distraction of being drawn into Leicester dressing room detail. He wanted to stay focused on his national team.

Jamaica lost the final but Mexico were seven-time champions and Jamaica acquitted themselves well. It was time for Morgan to come home and Ranieri told him to have a couple of days' rest then report to Belvoir

Drive on Tuesday, 4 August. Ranieri thought they might just have a chat then Morgan would go off on a break before rejoining the group after the season was underway.

For Morgan's summer commitments had been demanding. Jamaica not only played six Gold Cup games in the heat of the US in July but in June were in Chile for the Copa América. There, Morgan faced Lionel Messi in Viña del Mar in a match against Argentina and there were other tough games against Paraguay and Uruguay.

Surely Morgan would need a holiday, Ranieri thought. From the start of 2014–15, he had played 49 games, each a battle, very few breaks. He was, by August 2015, he admits, as much mentally as physically tired.

But this was more or less the conversation in Ranieri's office.

'How do you feel, Wes?'

'Fine.'

'You tell me what you want, do you need rest? You tell me and I will listen.'

'I am fine. I'm okay. I am okay. I want to play. I want to play.'

Ranieri shrugged. 'So he just went along with me,' says Morgan, 'which was fantastic. It was great to come back and find the manager thinking of me and concerned about me [needing a holiday], but also asking if I wanted to play.'

This was another immediate and key connection, like the one Ranieri established with the owners. 'The message he sent before the final was a nice touch and to come back to the office to see he was concerned about how I've felt . . . that was very good,' Morgan says. 'I definitely felt a rapport.'

But was it wise to insist on playing? Being available for Leicester's opening match versus Sunderland, that was a stretch. There were just four days and two training sessions before then. Just as that big kid on laps of the pitch had done, he would push himself.

'[Playing for Jamaica] literally took me right up to the beginning of the season. So, it has been constant and I have had to manage myself throughout the season and try to get in rest where I can. But it has been tough, it has been tough work,' says Morgan, reflecting at the end of the campaign.

'As a player, I just wanted to be in the manager's thoughts. I wanted to be able to play and prove that I belong in the team. In terms of me going away and taking an extra couple of weeks off . . . I didn't see that as much of an option. I wanted to lead the team out onto the pitch. That was really important to me.'

● ● ●

Ranieri was a captain himself. A defender too. 'He gave his heart and soul out on the pitch. Off the pitch, he was a very open, expansive guy,' said Gianni Di Marzio, his manager at Catanzaro. Ranieri liked the cut of Morgan immediately, though that day they did not actually speak about whether Morgan would remain as captain.

This was confirmed in an odd way. The following afternoon, Ranieri did his Twitter Q&A for fans.

#AskClaudio. 'Will Wes MORGAN remain as your captain for this season' @BertLcfc wondered. 'Yes.' Ranieri replied.

And that was it, no shouting, no parade, probably the way Morgan would have wanted it. In the Q&A Ranieri also revealed Mahrez was signing a new contract. That day, 4 August, was also Kanté's first in full training at Belvoir Drive.

Kanté snared. Mahrez staying. Formation decided. Form building step by step. New signings, especially Okazaki, looking good. Captain Morgan back in business.

Fundamentals were aligning. Ranieri was further buoyed by the capture of Yohan Benalouane, a giant French-Tunisian defender whose signing he had pushed for from Serie A. Ranieri claimed glitches remained. Kanté wanted to be called 'NG' and 'now I have NG and Shinji!' said the manager, launching easily into 'comedy Claudio' act.

More seriously, his old friend Pellizzaro had decided to retire and return to Italy to dedicate more time to his grandchildren. But Leicester already had a fine goalkeeping coach in Mike Stowell, and Pellizzaro's was the kind of decision Ranieri understood.

Overall, he was glad the real season was here at last and told a press conference that while a manager can never be sure of his players' true fitness until the proper matches start, he trusted the work of Reeves and the conditioning team. The fun he could see Leicester had at Belvoir Drive chimed with his longstanding belief: that even the toughest training has to be made enjoyable. 'You can do it all with a smile,' he wrote in *Proud Man Walking*.

• • •

Morgan's first 'transfer fee' was two sets of strips – donated by Forest to Dunkirk. They are a ninth tier club, playing in front of crowds of 100, on muddy pitches, where no scout treads. Back then, Wes was targeting accountancy because he 'wasn't too bad at maths' and 'knew the money was pretty good'. A football career seemed off the agenda. He was not exactly refueling like an athlete then.

And he did always like his food: Robertson wrote of a moment at the Dallas Cup where Morgan walked into the team hotel 'holding the biggest ice-cream sundae you could possibly envisage, one only Americans could make, the plastic spoon in his hand filled with every topping, sprinkle and sauce known to man'. Even the belief of Pemberton – who went potty – was tested by that.

Robertson relates another story from when Wes, then 19, was breaking through with the first team and Forest's spies spotted him out in town. Hart commenced an inquisition.

What were you drinking, Wes?

[The wise answer was lemonade.]

'Just double brandy and Coke, innit.'

Staff and other players were fearfully silent and Hart ... burst out laughing. 'Only Wes could have got away with saying that. There is a degree of innocence in his answer – when many would have simply told a little white lie – that I hope provides a glimpse of the authenticity of his character. He is what he is and Hart simply couldn't bring himself to be angry,' wrote Robertson.

• • •

Leicester would begin the Ranieri era in earnest at home to Sunderland in their first Premier League game of 2015–16. Not the toughest start, not the easiest. The sides met in the penultimate game of 2014–15 and it was an attritional 0–0 draw. Ranieri set the objective for the season as winning one more point than the previous campaign. The owners asked him to avoid relegation and nothing more.

Ranieri had not managed in the Premier League since Chelsea beat Leeds at Stamford Bridge in May 2004. He had gone into that game knowing he was to be sacked. The club had made no official decision but Peter Kenyon, Chelsea's chief executive, had told journalists he was 'Dead Man Walking' – hence the title of Ranieri's book.

That 2004 day was emotionally difficult, Ranieri has said, but with a light moment. Chelsea's owner, Roman Abramovich, had made small talk with him.

'So, when do the players come back now?' Abramovich asked.

'That depends when the new coach wants them,' Ranieri smiled.

Manager and oligarch ended up giggling.

You can do it all with a smile. For the manager's office at the King Power, Ranieri ordered portraits of the other nineteen Premier League managers. These were hung on the wall, ostensibly to make each rival boss feel at home when they visited for the traditional post-match drink. But, as the *Telegraph*'s John Percy observed, the more Leicester won, the more 'they assumed the look of big-game trophies'.

Said Ranieri, looking forward to the campaign, 'I love English football – because I am a fighter.'

He would be waiting for those nineteen managers – beware the smile.

5 TEAM MAN, FAMILY MAN

The songs. 'You listen to the radio and the funeral songs come on,' he says. Maybe that is when it was worst. When he was driving and on the car stereo came funeral songs.

Lee Mason, that big and upright village policeman of a referee, led out the players of Leicester and Sunderland and Ranieri, in grey-blue suit and blue club tie, waved to all corners of King Power stadium.

Mason whistled, and suddenly the real stuff began.

Leicester's first minutes of the 2015–16 Premier League campaign were as discouraging as their first half at Lincoln in pre-season. Morgan made a mistake, playing Jermain Defoe onside and Schmeichel had to save well.

He had to save again from Younès Kaboul's header, and again from Jack Rodwell, as Sunderland threatened from the corner.

But soon, in sunshine, Leicester had a free kick. Albrighton delivered: flat and curling and quick. Vardy flicked his header. And though 10 yards from goal and outside the width of the posts he judged the angles perfectly and his header looped over Costel Pantilimon, Sunderland's giant goalkeeper, and went in.

A goal after just 11 minutes, and the first scored by any side in the new Premier League campaign.

And, suddenly, Leicester were so lively. King and Okazaki were arriving from deep, Albrighton and Mahrez switching positions. Vardy was peeling off markers into space. There was a speed and fluidity in Leicester's attacking that Sunderland's lumpen defenders could not deal with. The clappers sounded. The King Power got going.

Albrighton, this time in open play, put in another unplayable delivery. This time it was Mahrez who glanced home the header. Schmeichel uppercut the air and bellowed a Viking roar.

And suddenly Mahrez slouched into Sunderland's box, ball at toes. For Lee Cattermole, it was like the cup-and-ball trick. First Cattermole saw the ball to his right then, after blurring feet, to his left. He was so baffled he fell on his backside, threw out a leg and tripped Mahrez up. Almost shrugging, Mahrez knocked in the penalty.

Just 25 minutes in and Leicester were 3–0 ahead. The previous season it had taken them until May, and their 35th game, to lead by three goals. Vardy, thrice, Mahrez, twice, almost scored again and the line-up Ranieri had chosen looked good.

No. Back. Three.

Leicester lined up 4-2-3-1 Schmeichel; De Laet, Morgan, Huth, Schlupp; King, Drinkwater; Mahrez, Okazaki, Albrighton; Vardy.

In the second half, Sunderland scored twice – Defoe and Steven Fletcher – but Leicester added their own fourth through Marc Albrighton – 'Sharky'. Ask any player. A team man. An archetypal good lad. The sort who is the quiet glue of any dressing room. His selflessness on the left wing balanced nicely Mahrez's individualism on the right.

Yet, that day, Albrighton had an edge. He was so assertive: 42.2 per cent of Leicester's attacking play came down his flank and now he scored a goal that epitomised his hunger for the ball.

Albrighton sprinted across Adam Matthews, Sunderland's substitute, to attempt to convert a Vardy cross. That was defended but then Kaboul dwelt in possession and Albrighton came back on his blindside and stole the ball, spinning and depositing it in the net.

But after scoring, Albrighton did not smile or celebrate: he brushed aside teammates, pointed to someone in the crowd, and raised both index fingers to point to the sky. In his post-match interview he hinted there had been something going on. 'It's always nice to score a goal but that one felt good today,' he said. 'It was one that I'll remember.'

• • •

The songs. Maybe that is when it felt the worst. When the radio was on and he heard the funeral songs.

Every morning he would say goodbye to Chloe, his partner, and Matilda-Beau and Dollie-Boo, their little daughters. And he would get in the car. And he would drive out towards the motorway. And the songs would come on. And he would lose it.

Marc Albrighton lives in Sutton Coldfield, once a royal town and now an affluent suburb of Birmingham. It is only a few miles from Tamworth, where he was born and raised. It is even closer to the Bodymoor Heath training ground of Aston Villa, the club he supported from since he could remember and with whom he started at the age of only eight.

Sutton Coldfield is forty miles from Leicester. Not far, but the road journey involves three motorways in the busy Midlands network, meaning plenty of time in the car. 'The drive to work for the first few weeks was an absolute nightmare,' Marc says. 'Like, I was breaking down most days. That is when you think about things. You are driving an hour from Birmingham to training on your own.

'You think about things. You listen to the radio and the funeral songs come on. Everything about it is a nightmare.'

Marc, Chloe, their girls and their family suffered an unimaginable loss in the summer of 2015. On 26 June, at around midday, a young man in shorts and black T-shirt appeared on the beach at Port El Kantaoui, a popular resort near Sousse in Tunisia. Apparently, he was smiling. He carried a Kalashnikov.

Thirty-eight sunbathers were killed by the gunman in an Islamic State terrorist attack. Thirty were British holidaymakers. One was Sue Davey, Chloe's mother.

She was a special woman by all accounts. Conor Fulford, Chloe's brother, has written on social media and given television interviews about Sue. He doesn't want her forgotten and his last memory was of him video-calling her from Massachusetts, where he was coaching at a soccer camp, and his mum 'grinning from side to side' as she talked excitedly about her vacation. Warmth seems to have been typical of her. She was 44 and had travelled with her partner, Scott, to celebrate buying a house together.

Marc, Chloe and their girls had just returned from holiday themselves, Disneyland Paris, when news of the attack broke and Chloe called Marc in a shop to say she had a bad feeling. Conor flew to Britain. The family phoned hospitals, hired an interpreter to help, appealed on Twitter and Facebook and FaceTimed people in Tunisia as they searched for information. The British Foreign Office offered little of that. At home, Marc and Chloe kept the TV locked on rolling news. Following two days of this their worst fears were confirmed.

After Sue's death Marc and Chloe kept seeing feathers. Around the house, on football pitches. They were not religious but felt these to be signs of Sue's presence. Conor was living with them. The night before Sunderland he told Marc, 'You need a celebration, you need to do something for my mum.'

In the stand at the King Power had been Marc and Chloe's family and he had pointed to them and then to Sue, right up there in the sky.

● ● ●

Albrighton does not shout about stuff or make big dramas. He did not speak publicly about his bereavement in the run-up to the Sunderland game, although afterwards he did explain to reporters the meaning of his celebration.

Ranieri, in his post-match interviews, was twinkle-eyed. Leicester had perhaps surprised Sunderland with the speed and intensity of their attacking and pressing, he said.

He also spoke about the King Power, his first taste. He not only enjoyed the stadium's clappers, its noise, but especially, hearing the tune played to celebrate home goals: Kasabian's 'Fire'.

It was a choice of music suggested by the players several seasons previously. The bit played at the King Power is the song's rousing instrumental riff. But Leicester's relentlessness perhaps came to embody some of the words.

And I'm on fire . . .
I'm coming, you coming, no hiding

'The Kabasian [sic] are a fantastic rock band of Leicester. I think the guitar man is Italian, no? [Half Italian: Serge Pizzorno's grandfather was from Genoa but Pizzorno grew up in Leicester.] And this is good. I think they love the fighters. And we are fighters,' Ranieri said.

Leicester finished the day top, with Chelsea, the reigning champions, surprisingly drawing at Swansea. Okay, it was only day one of the season but it felt lovely: Leicester had not topped a Premier League for sixteen years.

Sunday should have been a day to wake up, open up the newspaper or website, and bask just a little at that league table. Instead there were difficult headlines.

The *Sun* carried a front-page and inside-spread story about Vardy and an altercation with an East Asian-looking man in a Leicester casino. Vardy, there with his fiancée, Rebekah, and De Laet and Nugent, was playing poker and believed the guy was looking at his cards. He told him to back off using the dreadful words, 'Jap. Yo, Jap. Walk on.'

The incident had taken place a fortnight previously and now Leicester had another crisis to deal with involving racist language and key personnel. The club began an investigation. Vardy released a statement seeking to 'wholeheartedly apologise' and take 'full responsibility' for his behaviour.

The Football Association got involved, since Vardy was an England player, and he agreed to a programme of diversity awareness training. He also asked to meet the guy he had abused and his club fine to be donated to a charity of the victim's choice. 'A massive learning curve', Vardy later said.

David Nugent departed that week. He had been popular and one of Pearson's stalwarts, top scorer for three consecutive seasons in the Championship. But his output dipped in the Premier League and he was not a direct, fast attacker like the others Ranieri wanted to use.

Next, on Saturday August 15, Leicester were at West Ham, who had beaten Arsenal on the opening day. For an always testing away trip, Ranieri demanded 'more concentration' from his players. Slaven Bilić, West Ham's manager, who himself once had a sideline as a rock band guitarist, remarked how much he approved of the motivational use of Kasabian.

• • •

Albrighton was a bit of a sensation when he broke through at Aston Villa. He had not been the most feted prospect in Villa's youth team but proved one of those footballers who step up into a first XI and just seem at home immediately.

Mentality has so much to do with making the jump to senior games and in Marc's head, back then, were just clear blue skies. 'Didn't have any fear of football,' he remembers. 'Didn't fear anything. When you first play, you have the confidence flowing. I had good confidence from the management at Villa. Everything was going well.'

Then? 'Second-season syndrome, which they call it. A few things played a part.'

Martin O'Neill gave him his debut and Gérard Houllier, with a track record of developing youth, took over as coach and made Albrighton a first choice. Albrighton was 19, beating men, putting in crosses, scoring the odd goal, and everything felt so fine. For Villa supporters he was a joy – a kid who loved the club as much as them, performing with a smile.

That was 2010–11. Back then, with his unstyled blond hair, sharp features and skinny limbs, Albrighton looked very much the teenager. Five years on he remained the type a barman might just ID. But clouds had passed across his sky. Two years after being Villa's boy wonder he was chucked out on loan to Wigan and, there, he could not even get a game. At 24, Villa released him.

What on earth went on?

'Injuries didn't help me,' he begins. 'The loss of form. Probably got found out a little bit by defenders and whatever. I think I had five different managers in two years, which obviously didn't help.

'It was difficult. I kept working hard. I didn't do anything different from when I was bursting on the scene and doing well, to when I was playing poor.

'This is football. It's crazy. All of a sudden, Ashley Young and Stewart Downing [Villa's main wingers] had left and I'm getting questions thrown at me left, right and centre – "Are you the player to replace these players?" I had barely played a game. There was a lot of pressure at a young age.'

He remembers the phone call from his agent, two days after the 2013–14 season, telling him Villa weren't offering a new contract. That he was being cut.

'Devastating,' he says. 'I was gutted. He told me not to worry and that he had stuff in place but it wasn't any consolation because Villa were my boyhood club and everything I'd dreamed of doing. I'd been led to believe that there would be a contract [offer] and for the last six months I'd been playing well. It was heartbreaking, and took some time to come to terms with.'

Like any guy who loses his job, he says, he felt a certain shame. He kept the news from people around him. 'I remember being on holiday in Portugal with my family. Villa came out with the list of players they had released and I was on it. So now everyone knew. I ended up being bombarded by text messages saying, "sorry to hear it" and "we wish it wasn't true." For a few hours, I am sitting there reading these texts. And it was terrible. It did get me down a bit.'

• • •

Upton Park, East End of London, another sunny Saturday. This time Ranieri wore a navy suit but his line-up and formation were unchanged.

Again, Morgan began tiredly, heading against his own bar but, again, Mahrez, Vardy, Okazaki, Albrighton were all threat, complementary skills and quick movement. By half-time, West Ham had dominated 63 per cent of the possession. But Leicester had scored both of the goals.

Such counterattacking. Albrighton started a break in his own half, playing down the left to Vardy, who chipped to Okazaki, who volleyed brilliantly, without breaking stride, and then headed in when Adrián, West Ham's keeper, parried the ball high in the air. 1–0. Vardy began another move and Okazaki made good ground before Albrighton took over, beating Winston Reid then cutting the ball back from the touchline. He had seen Mahrez arriving, West Ham had not; a lash of Mahrez's left boot made it 2–0.

This was minimalist, laser-point football: six West Ham players inside their own box had been no match for Leicester's two. Dimitri Payet scored for West Ham but 2–1 Leicester the game finished. Leicester had averaged just 37 per cent possession in their two matches yet began a top flight season with two wins from two for the first time since 1997.

The ball? In Leicester's company, there for a good time, not a long time, as they say.

• • •

Albrighton is sitting at a table in the players' canteen with Schmeichel, a pal, and they giggle as they remember Ranieri in the dressing room at

Upton Park: by that point the players were getting to know their new manager's quirks.

'He keeps team talks short,' says Schmeichel, 'I think that's important: not to drag on with endless messages you end up forgetting. His team talks and debriefs are quite funny. At West Ham he started biting his pen to show that ... he was like a dog [with a bone].'

'Sniff goals, sniff goals!' hoots Albrighton.

Schmeichel: 'He said: "You are like a dog with a bone. You have to ... *grrrrrr* ..." Making like he won't let go of the bone. I was like, *whaat*? and everyone was like, "what is going on here?"'

Sniff goals. During the calendar year 2009, Okazaki was the world's top scorer in international games. Already, his signing seemed another shrewd spot by Walsh.

The analytics guys helped, no doubt. Okazaki was lined up to sign from FSV Mainz as soon as the summer transfer window opened in July 2015, but first targeted a full year before that. Key metrics involved his high work rate and contribution out of possession. He was used to pressing from the front, just as Leicester like doing.

Okazaki was versatile, having played as striker for Mainz, but wide at his previous club, Stuttgart. Walsh's background checks would have revealed a player regarded as a model professional at previous clubs.

Ranieri may have even known that his fellow Italian, Alberto Zaccheroni, regarded Okazaki as a unique member of the Japan team he managed from 2010–2014.

Zaccheroni found Okazaki to be the one player he could give a tactical concept and who would get it immediately – able, without further instruction, to apply it on the pitch and problem solve himself. At Leicester, already in these first two games, Vardy was playing with a freedom not seen before. Throughout the season a hidden factor would be Okazaki's ability, playing behind him, to keep adjusting position and retain the structure of the team.

These were fruitful times for Japanese in Leicester. In January 2016, the granddaughter of Emperor Akihito, Princess Mako of Akishino, graduated from the University of Leicester, after spending two years completing a postgrad degree in museum studies – but the British press and most of her fellow students had no idea of her identity until she was close to graduation.

She had worked, incognito, in New Walk Museum and she thanked Leicester for providing 'such a favourable environment' for her to go about her business. Okazaki would end up saying similar.

Providing the assist for Okazaki's first Leicester goal had been Vardy. The ever-sharp Gary Lineker tweeted, 'Oh, the irony.' But there were no scandals to mar Leicester's weekend this time and they finished it second, sandwiched on goal difference between Manchester City and Manchester United, in the Premier League.

• • •

Belvoir Drive. That is what helped Marc Albrighton. That moment, having left the M69 and followed the A563 south-east, of turning off at Aylestone Road, then into Banks Road, then into Middlesex Drive; and then of driving past nondescript houses and through the modest entrance at the end.

'The last twelve months have been the hardest,' says Marc, in the classroom at the training ground in May 2016. 'The last twelve months of my life, of Chloe's life, of everyone in our families' lives . . .

'When you go through something like that over a summer it's hard to come back from. I am lucky, I used football as a release.' Chloe didn't have that, he says, but 'I could come here. As soon as I step through here and get down to work that is my two or three hours of release. That is a breath of fresh air for me. Whereas, at home, my partner and my family have not got that. It's difficult for them.'

Leicester's success in 2015–16 had a special benefit for the Fulfords and Albrightons. 'This year, with what has gone on, the interest in what we have done this season has made it an escape route for them, if you know what I mean. It has given them something to concentrate on.' Marc and Chloe were about to get married too. 'We have been busy with the wedding as well. At least we have had things to take our minds off it.'

Belvoir Drive.

Manchester United have a £125m title sponsor of their training ground and a £25m hospital (which of course has a separate sponsor) onsite.

Manchester City spent £200m on constructing their 'Etihad Campus,' a superb facility replete with not just training pitches but its own stadium for youth and women's games.

Arsenal no longer allow visitors anywhere near the building players use at their London Colney site; even before then, you were obliged to slip sterile slippers over your shoes because Arsène Wenger worried about germs.

Chelsea's is high-security and in Cobham, one of the most expensive villages in Britain.

At Tottenham's, they'll make journalists wait in the car park out of sight of the main building until just before an event starts; they are not keen on prying eyes.

In the Premier League, even most of the smaller clubs have out-of-town complexes now and of the big ones only Liverpool use an inner-city, traditional site – and Liverpool, in May 2016, submitted a planning application to build a new road, barriers and traffic island, to ensure players are no longer mobbed by fans.

Belvoir Drive? 'When the schools are off you can be half an hour in your car trying to get out,' says King. There is only that one modest entrance and the houses go literally right up to it. When training finishes, players must queue to drive out through the autograph seekers and Vardy's blue Bentley wasn't built for 2mph crawls.

And yet no Leicester player would change it. King shrugs. 'It's not a hassle for anyone.'

The canteen is the hub. Eight tables, all circular, and around a central salad bar: no corners to skulk in here. Staff recall Martin Allen wanted it renamed the 'Command Centre' or something, when he was manager, and was laughed back to his room.

For the vibe is informality. The youngest trainees are invited to eat here during school holidays. The previous season, a wonderful photo was taken of ten to fifteen kids crowding round Cambiasso as he ate, and hanging off the great man's words with saucer-eyes.

There is a big frieze on the canteen walls with happy images of different first teamers, for morale. Key words like NUTRITION, HYDRATION, RESTORE, ENERGY adorn the walls, enforcing messages. The office for the manager and team-behind-the-team are just off this room. If an impromptu meeting is required, Morgan, King and Schmeichel consult the lads, stroll past the coffee machine and go in to see the boss.

The classroom – that is for everything, really. Press interviews, agent meetings, Okazaki's language lessons. Jon Rudkin, despite the seniority of his Director of Football role, often kicks around in training gear: a very visible and friendly presence, representing the club hierarchy.

And then there is Alan Birchenall, club ambassador. 'The Birch' seems forever somewhere near, his laughing, whistling, daft jokes and booming voice always just around the corner and the sunshine of this place. He was a fine player himself, the Andy King of the time when he starred for Leicester during the 1970s. 'You still alive?' someone – probably Vardy – might quip. But all know the value of having him around.

The changing room? Well, don't go in unless the coast is clear of flying socks. It was redone in 2012 and is relatively modest. Each player has a nameplate, locker and four shelves.

The seat ordering is different to the match dressing room, a haphazard one based on which locker was free at the particular time a player arrived. The corner ones are best but, superstitious lot that footballers are, nobody fancies swapping.

In March, a school class from Leicester College was invited here. Their impressions? 'A lot of players have tubs of Vicks and Vaseline in their lockers. Jamie Vardy's has lots of paperwork in it and Riyad Mahrez has a very, very, messy locker, with lots of random things sticking out of it,' was the kids' report.

In the kit room are the international shirts of capped players. The kit manager Paul McAndrew, Macca, is highly popular and enjoyed that by the end of the season the players from the big clubs wanted shirt swaps so they could have Leicester jerseys – rather than the normal other way around.

Macca's association with Leicester goes back two decades – like Sheila Kent in the laundry room. Ranieri brings her chocolates back from Italy and the Swiss-born Gökhan Inler 'the Lindt stuff from Switzerland and it's beautiful'.

Says Jeffrey Schlupp, who first came here as a schoolboy from Milton Keynes, 'We've had the same laundry woman as when I was 12, same kit man, chef . . . we've got pictures in the laundry room of the really old days and we just look at them and laugh [with the staff].'

Chef? Gary Payne, whose team prepare meals as Radio 1Xtra blares in their kitchen, remembers 2002–03 and the period when the club was in administration and there was no money for fancy ingredients. Ranieri, that foodie, actually did not change the menu as Payne had feared. Since Martin O'Neill's days a tradition has been apple crumble and custard on Fridays – hardly *tiramisu* but Ranieri was soon asking for second helpings of this stodgy old English speciality.

Though Ranieri did make one small, significant adjustment to canteen rules: players had to eat and leave together, for unity.

Don't mistake the modest for the mediocre, however. Never do that with Leicester. There is plenty of sophistication inside Belvoir Drive. Anti-gravity treadmills, the cryotherapy, the top-class gym, three perfect pitches, all scoped by cameras for performance review. One pitch was relaid, in 2014, at a cost of £1.5m – just so Leicester could have a practice field with the precise dimensions and same DESSO hybrid surface as the one at King Power Stadium.

Ranieri was agape, when he arrived, at the facilities, especially the cameras tracking training and the number of video analysts at his call. And something else, of which he greatly approved: the wine list from which to choose when entertaining opposition managers at the King Power.

'We must all hang together, else we shall all hang separately,' said Benjamin Franklin. Fun and work are balanced at Belvoir Drive.

'It's a massive mix of characters, as I imagine it is in all changing rooms,' says King. 'The thing that we've got, is that everyone knows how to treat everyone, whether you are a loud character and want to be rash . . . or whether you are the quietest guy in the room, like NG.

'We know that if it's Vardy and he's being loud, he's going to be nice to NG because NG is the nicest guy you are ever going to meet. There's no point shouting something to him. Because what is he going to do with that? Everyone knows how to take each other and accepts who each other is.

'When someone comes into our changing room I never think anything of it. They are welcomed well. If you are not a tight group and you see a teammate doing something not right – if he's out when he shouldn't be, for example – it can cause heat. But, here, you are certain that everyone who comes in to training will give 100 per cent. Whether he's been in America or France the day before, when he gets to that training ground he is going to give 100 per cent and that is all you need to know.'

Huth cannot quite explain how, but when he walks through the side door and into the building at Belvoir Drive, he feels himself click into a work mode that is both intense and fun. 'I know what he means,' King reflects. 'It's not, "Right, heads down, we cannot speak to anyone as we are training." We have a laugh in training. I know it took a while for the gaffer to get used to, the sort of joking culture we have. But when it's work time we are 100 per cent serious.'

Maybe Drinkwater's line – 'there isn't a secret, it's just that we are a bunch of lads who get along' – really is all that ever needs be said. 'Like I mentioned, we are a big family,' says King. 'I know people in football say that and it gets thrown around too loosely. But we properly care about each other's lives.'

• • •

Walsh and Pearson deserve the credit for bringing Albrighton to Leicester. Other Premier League clubs were interested but use of the grapevine helped Walsh and Pearson suss Villa would let him go and Leicester's offer was what his agent had 'in place'.

The Leicester contrast makes you wonder about many aspects of Premier League wastefulness. By 2015–16 only 11.7 per cent of players in England's top flight were club-trained, an all-time low, less than half the proportion in Spain and well below the European average of 19.7 per cent. It costs around £20,000 per year to educate a player at a Premier League academy. That's £200,000 to take a scholar through from age eight to eighteen; every time a kid is discarded, their club is incinerating a pile of money.

Yet teams like Villa (who made twenty, almost entirely unsuccessful, signings in the fourteen months after dumping him) release players like

Albrighton; his is not an isolated case. Leicester, for nothing, picked up a player who in 2015–16 was in the Premier League's top ten for crossing and fifth best Englishman for 'key passes'.

Ranieri demands credit. Under Pearson, Albrighton was in and out, until playing a key part in the great escape. Pearson used him as a right wing-back but Ranieri had the acumen to restore him to the wing – and put him on the left, cutting onto his stronger foot.

And Ranieri helped not just tactically but psychologically. 'When I was younger I remember going into matches where I hadn't played well for a game or two, thinking if I don't play well now, I'm definitely not in the side next week. 100 per cent, I need to get a man-of-the-match today.

'Whereas this year [2015–16], after the first few games when I had got to know the manager and he got to know me, I realised if I just do my job I'll be all right,' Albrighton says. 'I don't need to set the world alight. I just need to be solid in what I am doing. He likes the way I play, so he will give me a chance next week.'

It is funny, because when he came to Leicester they were a newly promoted side whereas Villa were the established power, the biggest club in the Midlands, one that, despite struggles, people still did not envisage dropping out of the Premier League. They were relegated with Leicester five points clear in the title race. Funny that Albrighton feared swapping Bodymoor Heath for Belvoir Drive would be a 'risk'.

He smiles. 'Sometimes you just have to take risks. I felt this was the right club for me. I like to work hard in games and looked at this squad and noticed exactly the same thing straightaway. The work ethic and the togetherness was the perfect fit for me.

'It took some settling in,' he reflects, 'but it was a totally different atmosphere [to Villa]. I just found it so refreshing. The whole place was more relaxed.

'Like no one took themselves serious. Like everyone got on with their business. They came here, worked hard, had fun. I was happy. It was everything that I wanted to play for.'

In June, in Tamworth, almost a year to the day, there was an event in Sue Davey's memory, to benefit a charity helping young people with bereavement. There were stalls and bouncy castles for the kids and Conor Fulford thanked everyone on social media.

He added hashtags, #LoveSueDavey #LoveAlwaysWins.

6

OWNERS

The players were not sure about them and nor were the fans. To the *Leicester Mercury* they had seemed 'cringeworthy in principle'.

That was at first.

Chickah chickah chickah. Chickah, chickah, chickah – what once seemed a cacophony, became an unchained symphony. Those clappers. What could be more representative of Leicester: something that should not work but really, really does.

They first appeared at the King Power in April 2013, before a game with Watford. Leicester lost. They disappeared.

In April 2015, with the club desperate to boost atmosphere amid a relegation fight, the clappers came back. Supporters for the match versus West Ham arrived and each found a clapper neatly tied to their seat, and those who did not make them into paper aeroplanes gave them a clap, King scored, Leicester won.

Yet having stayed for every home game during the 'great escape', the clappers were not certain to reappear when 2015–16 commenced. They did, when the season opened versus Sunderland. But King thinks players were told 'just one more game'. Of course 'we were 3–0 up at half-time,' King recounts, 'and they thought they should keep them for the whole season.'

That noise. *Chickah, chickah, chickah*. Gets in your ears. Should not have been brilliant but turned out to be so. And think about what it is you are hearing. Every time those clappers go, it is the sound of something we'll get to shortly: of karma, of the unique relationship between Leicester's owners and their fans.

● ● ●

Two wins from two, Leicester's best start since O'Neill, best in eighteen years. It meant the momentum of the great escape had not been lost. It eased pressure on Ranieri. 'With the new manager coming, a lot were tipping us for relegation and we knew the importance of a good start. Otherwise the season gets on top of you. You struggle then,' says King.

He mentions something else: 'on paper we had a terrible run of games over Christmas.' Why was this relevant? 'Because we knew we had to be in a strong-ish position going into them, because in general we would probably lose those fixtures, not pick up points for a while, and for the first three seasons in the Premier League it's all about staying up. Forty points – doesn't matter how, just get them.'

Turns out Ranieri's constant talk during the first part of the campaign was no bluff. He banged on about '40 points' even when Leicester were top – but the threat of relegation genuinely still hovered in players' minds. 'I won't lie to you,' smiles King, 'for the first half of the season we were thinking, "Well, we have a long way to fall to get relegated from here." We had 35 points by Christmas and we were thinking, "Hold on, we have to have a *really* bad run of form now to get sucked into a relegation battle."'

Tottenham were not thinking about a title challenge either when they came to the King Power on 22 August. Though fifth the previous season, with Harry Kane breaking through, Spurs had lost their opening game at Manchester United and drawn at home with Stoke. Kane and manager Mauricio Pochettino were suddenly under pressure.

Pochettino had been in his post for fifteen months and the average tenure of the six Spurs managers preceding him was twenty months, so you could not be sure he would get long. Kane, well known to Leicester players after a 2013 loan at the club (he was on the bench that fateful day at Watford), looked tired. There was newspaper chat about 'one-season wonders' and one article talked of 'two weeks to save Tottenham's season – and maybe even Pochettino's job'.

As King says, 'That's how it is in football: you don't take time to gauge.'

Kane struggled in the opening 45 minutes, making just 14 touches, but started improving after half-time and helped Tottenham go ahead. Back to goal, outside the box, he turned Huth and laid off to Nacer Chadli and with a diving header Dele Alli converted Chadli's cross.

Just nine minutes remained.

Collecting Vardy's flick-on, Mahrez glued the ball to his left foot and glided towards the box. Jan Vertonghen backed off. Mistake. Mahrez shifted his weight, feinted with the shoulders and caressed a shot past Hugo Lloris using the space his wiles had made.

Leicester were level just 90 seconds after conceding. This team had a magician – and it also had resolve.

The help of fans too, for when Tottenham scored the volume at the King Power increased. And . . . *chickah chickah chickah* . . . it was from the clappers. These – just like the team – were beginning to make people talk.

• • •

The clappers. Or rather, the Clap Banners – for that is the name used by the company who makes them. Leicester are by no means the only sports team using these. Arsenal, the Irish national side, Bath Rugby Union, England volleyball, ice-hockey in Canada . . . just some of the places the clap banners have been used. But now it is the King Power Stadium the world associates with a curious *chickah chickah chickah* noise.

Clap-Banners Ltd are based in London and run by Carolyn Israel, a Leicester supporter. The company started in 2004 with the idea of producing something lightweight that supporters could hold at an event and use for two functions – noise or display. Hence the 'banner' part.

Clap banners come folded like fans, but open out to reveal artworks or slogans. Leicester's are 340mm by 490mm, on recyclable cardboard, and carry different designs for every game. Israel is delighted by her small role in the success of her team. Her husband, incidentally, is a Tottenham fan.

The clappers are one indication Leicester have people behind them who think in ways different to the traditional English club owner. But that is just what happens at the King Power. Ask the hardcore fans and they will say that it's at away games where this contrast is truly felt.

Follow Leicester on the road, and the club offers subsidised transport – £10 anywhere on a 'Foxes Travel' bus. What is more, you get gifts. Perhaps a T-shirt, maybe a scarf. There might be a free breakfast of a gammon cob (local word for a bread roll) or a catering voucher to spend at the away stadium. When Leicester played at Bournemouth their hosts did not know what hit them, and their food ran out.

Such largesse takes money. As do the clappers: 30,000 are distributed every match at a cost of £12,500 every time. A certain calculation amuses the club's shrewd, but grounded, commercial brains like Jamie Tabor, head of marketing. By September 2016, Leicester had spent more on clappers for their fans than they paid for Mahrez, the footballer of the year.

The clappers were still being raised as a contentious issue in the first club consultation meeting with fan groups in 2015–16 but by the final weeks of the season, when a no-longer-sceptical *Leicester Mercury* ran a poll, 93 per cent of supporters wanted the clappers to stay.

'The club have done a lot to help build the atmosphere and the fans have responded. The clappers have been a huge hit. They give the supporters something extra. They help,' Schmeichel says. 'From the pitch it doesn't sound like there are only 32,000 in there. It sounds like many more.'

What did he think at first? 'It's a different type of noise. You do think, "Will this be like the vuvuzelas [the excruciating fan instrument of South

Africa's 2010 World Cup], where they are just so annoying?" But they turned out brilliantly.'

Word association time. Leicester's owners, what comes to mind?

Helicopter?

Father-and-son?

Long old surname?

Thai?

Good.

But the Professor of Sports Enterprise at Salford Business School – Professor Simon Chadwick – thinks of something different.

Buddhism.

Chadwick has been dubbed a 'guru of sports management' in Britain and worked with Uefa, the International Tennis Federation, world cycling, the European Commission – and plenty of others.

He is also an expert in Asian sports ownership and has a particular interest in how the culture of a business leader tends to define how their enterprise is run.

'I'm a firm believer in the sociocultural embeddedness of management and it is not something we think about enough in the West,' Chadwick says.

'What that basically means is that business is influenced by the place its managers and owners come from.'

This means both the culture and the country/society of the company leader in question.

Chelsea? Russian oligarch owner, a club where money abounds but employees do tend to get fired.

Arsenal? Manchester United? American sports magnates. Very structured, commercially-driven clubs. One reason Louis van Gaal remained popular with the Glazer family who own United, long after performances declined, was his dossiers and clipboard, his strict rules for how different football departments should operate and report. The Glazers could identify with this process- and measurement-driven style, familiar in US business.

Manchester City? They love building things. Construction projects. Expanding the 'City Football Group' into other continents. And aren't their owners from Abu Dhabi, with its skyscrapers, malls and seven-star hotels, and government with blue chip investments around the world?

Leicester? Well, what do you associate with Thailand? Tourism, food, sunshine ... hospitality in other words. Nice people, hosts nearly always willing to smile and go the extra mile. The type who, if their cuisine was less refined, might just offer hungry travellers gammon cobs.

And Buddhism? 'Collectivism. Karma,' says Chadwick. 'Essentially karma is that you send positive energy out, because what you send out comes back to you. If you have a football club and treat the fans like garbage, you'll get garbage back. But send out good karma and good things will come back to you.'

Leicester do not just hand out presents but ask their supporters to have an input – into music choices at the stadium, or banner designs. By being warm and hospitable the Srivaddhanaprabhas are just being 'typical Thais' on one level, 'but Thai society is also a reflection of Buddhism, which fosters a more collective and egalitarian approach,' Chadwick says.

'What Leicester's owners are looking for is not to lead without any input but to invite in others, the fans. That is the Buddhist-collectivist business approach.'

Karma is not superstition, but a way of living. Buddhism has been around longer than Christianity. Eastern ideas are now filtering into a range of Western businesses.

At their headquarters in Mountain View, California, Google offer meditation rooms to employees. Toyota has become a focus of study: how did a once lowly Japanese company supplant General Motors as the world's biggest car-maker?

The now celebrated 'Toyota Way' involves principles like *nemawashi* – decisions shouldn't be made by individuals but as a team, with employees involved in deciding the production system. And *asa-ichi* – morning meetings where management invite suggestions.

Einstein said, 'You cannot solve problems with the same kind of thinking we used when we created them.' So why should the football business not be influenced by a different, Eastern approach? Oh, that's right, with its ticket price protests, sack culture, pomp and transfer wastage, the Premier League's traditional ways work so terribly well.

• • •

Khun Vichai very rarely gives interviews. When he did address journalists, on a club trip to the Thai resort of Phuket in May 2014, he said his aim was for Leicester to challenge for a top five place within three years.

The reporting tone was incredulous and fans were uneasy. On everyone's minds were the pratfalls of other foreign owners who bought small clubs and had big ambitions – like Blackburn, whose Indian chicken billionaires arrived promising Ronaldinho but ended in the middle of the Championship.

And of course Khun Vichai was naïve: two years, not three, was all Leicester would need.

A youthful, dressed-down-but-natty 59-year-old of Thai Chinese heritage, Khun Vichai started a business empire in 1989 by securing a licence for Bangkok's first downtown duty free shop. Then he did something similar in Phnom Penh, Cambodia. Then he opened at Bangkok Airport, then the Great Wall of China. And on he went. 'Step by step,' Claudio would smile.

Top was only 25 when he led his father's purchase of Leicester from Mandarić in August 2010. A good footballer himself, his soft spot for Leicester stems from the first match he saw live in England, the 1997 League Cup final at Wembley, when the Foxes forced a replay with a never-say-die last-minute goal.

For a few years the Srivaddhanaprabhas had an executive box at Stamford Bridge (No.8, a lucky number in Chinese tradition). They came to Leicester, prospectively as sponsors, but bought the lot.

'After spending time studying many clubs, I fell in love with Leicester,' Khun Vichai said. 'One reason was the colours, which were the same as my company's. The other was the fact they were playing in the second tier. If we bought a Premier League club, it wouldn't be challenging enough.'

Now *that's* different thinking.

They seem fun guys too. Khun Vichai owns a polo team which amazed the sport by reaching the final of England's prestigious Gold Cup. Top was its leading scorer. Father and son once played in the same polo team as Prince Charles and Prince William.

Khun Vichai owns a Gulfstream G650 business jet, bought for £43m from the wife of Formua One boss Bernie Ecclestone; another hobby is collecting Buddhist statues.

Wait, what about the Agusta A109S? With its tan, padded seating, royal-blue livery and familiar fox badge on its tail. 'Proper helicopter,' says Steve Parish, Crystal Palace chairman, approvingly.

The Agusta takes Khun Vichai and Top from their London home to matches, landing and taking off on the King Power pitch. It also alights from time to time at Belvoir Drive.

Crystal Palace, FA Cup finalists, have had their own moments of challenging the establishment and Parish – like West Ham's David Sullivan – was among the several owners of smaller clubs to express delight at the trail Leicester blazed.

'The owners stuck with it through thick and thin in the Championship, don't make a lot of noise, embrace the fans,' Parish says. 'There's a lot of negative stuff about foreign ownership but for me they're a poster-child. I love the helicopter on the pitch at the end! Proper helicopter too.'

The boyish and amenable Top oversees Leicester day-to-day. Susan Whelan ('great lady,' says Parish) is CEO. A blonde Dubliner who worked in her family's jewellery company before becoming a buyer in the airports business, she worked in several countries before ending up in Thailand, where she was headhunted by Khun Vichai.

He spent £39m of his $2bn fortune buying Leicester, bought back the stadium from a US pension fund and wrote off £103m in loans, making Leicester debt free for the first time in twenty years. And Leicester's success is not bad for his business either. Think of the 25 million tourists arriving in Thailand each year who pass through Bangkok Airport and might just see a King Power shop and think 'Leicester!'

• • •

On 29 August, Leicester went to Bournemouth, owned by a Russian petrochemicals magnate whose wife once stormed the dressing room and gave the team talk. Let's not deconstruct the sociocultural context of that.

Bournemouth brought Leicester's first moderate performance under Ranieri and his first line-up change. Kanté started and was incessant but a wan Mahrez was substituted at half-time. Callum Wilson scored for Bournemouth but Vardy won and converted a very late penalty. Twitter laughed at Ranieri for his attire: in the rain he borrowed a baseball cap at least one size too small.

There was an international break. Morgan, finally, got his holiday. 'A good week away,' he remembers. 'I got a bit of time off to forget about football, which was important mentally.'

Under a plan devised by Matt Reeves, Morgan had been doing lighter training than the rest to nurse him through until he could have his vacation. Ranieri continued to bend to the established, 'low-loading', Leicester conditioning regime.

'The structure we had was with an international break you always got four days off,' says Huth. '[Ranieri] was like, "Everyone gets four days off?!" Being an Italian he thought we should train. But he said, "Okay, see how we go." I think he had wanted to change stuff – but we just didn't give him the chance.'

Thing is, Huth adds, the players have a habit of repaying leeway shown. 'Our first game back [after Bournemouth] we won. After each break, I think we won or drew. [Ranieri] said in the end, "I trust you guys."'

What you send out, comes back. The first game after the International break was at home to Aston Villa on Sunday September 13. Leicester began untidily. Villa were 2–0 up after Jack Grealish curled home and Carles Gil scored spectacularly on a breakaway. With 18 minutes to go a first defeat seemed likely. But then, for the first time in 19 months, De Laet scored – a fine, flicked header – then Vardy converted Drinkwater's centre after a hypnotic Mahrez run.

And all of a sudden it was 2–2. The clappers went. And in the final seconds Mahrez swung that wand of a left leg and chipped a perfect ball to Nathan Dyer, who looped a header over Brad Guzan. Dyer was knocked out after colliding with Guzan, only discovering he had scored from Dave Rennie, when the physio helped him up.

Header by *Dyer*? He was as small as Kanté. A TV commentator quoted the owners' favourite slogan 'Foxes Never Quit.'

● ● ●

Dyer was a loan signing from Swansea. The deal took place so close to the transfer deadline that Khun Vichai lent the Agusta to helicopter the winger in from Wales. His favours to players are another part of the owner's generosity.

When Schmeichel was on a family break but needed to come back and shoot a club advertisement, Khun Vichai lent the helicopter so Schmeichel could return quickly to his holiday and extend his time with his kids.

After promotion Khun Vichai treated the squad to caviar and vintage wines at an exclusive west London restaurant. Each player and member of staff were then given a £1,000 chip to gamble at a nearby private members' club.

He throws parties for the players. 'The owners look after us, they take us out to places,' Morgan smiles and all that can be said is those parties are good enough to impress young men with seven-figure salaries.

Huth has been around the block. And is the last to gush. But, he says, 'It really does start at the top. The owners, I mean they do everything for us. This filters down to the manager, his assistants and then the players. I have never had so much help from a club.'

Now, look away if you think all this is getting touchy-feely. But here is a social media post from a Mike Rowell, written in May:

> My grandad and nannie have had a season ticket for 36 years now, and I can honestly say they hadn't missed a game to my knowledge in that time. They would literally organise their holidays so they'd leave the day after and be home the day before a game. However, sadly my nannie passed away a few months ago, and as a family we've been stepping in to fill her seat as my granddad is too upset to go on his own. Now is the time of year to book a new season ticket and granddad was preparing to pay for 2 individual seats so he wasn't alone.
>
> However the club (I have no clue how) heard of his loss and have offered to give him the extra ticket next to him free of charge. Now, I know this is 'just a sport' and it's not a huge amount of money; but what a lovely gesture that makes me proud to be a City fan.

Ranieri has worked for Jesús Gil, the sack-happy tyrant of Atlético Madrid who was a convicted embezzler and friend of General Franco. He worked for Massimo Cellino, Vittorio Cecchi Gori and Corrado Ferlaino. Cellino was nicknamed *il mangia-allenatori*, 'The Manager Eater', at Cagliari. Cecchi Gori (Fiorentina) went bankrupt and to prison. Ferlaino was the kind who hired private detectives to check what his Napoli players got up to – the snoop assigned to Diego Maradona must have been busy.

Ranieri worked for others: Abramovich, Rybolovlev, Massimo Moratti. Point is, the Italian did not arrive at Leicester expecting cuddles and roses from club owners. So he was delighted at his rapport with Top and Khun Vichai. 'Without [Vichai], it is impossible. He is the owner but he is very calm,' Ranieri said.

This echoed something said by Nicholas Colquhoun-Denvers of the Ham Polo Club, where Khun Vichai was president. 'Some people in our sport get very wound-up, whereas they are the sort who, win or lose, will say, "Wasn't that fun?" They seem much more philosophical than the others. Whether that comes from their religion, I don't know.'

When the Gulfstream G650 lands at Southend, Khun Vichai's regular airport, bringing the owner back from business in Thailand, often on the plane are Buddhist monks, with amulets and talismans and saffron robes.

These monks are regular visitors to the King Power where, on either side of the pitch entrance, are hung Buddhist shrouds. The monks hang amulets round the necks of players and bless the stadium. Back in Bangkok, at the Golden Buddha Temple in Chinatown, where Khun Vichai worships, are cloths emblazoned with Leicester's name and colours and Leicester artefacts.

Not all intervention is divine. In April 2016, the *Guardian* newspaper reported on a marketing partnership Leicester signed while in the Championship that was being scrutinised by the Football League under its Financial Fair Play rules. Leicester deny any wrongdoing and say they will contest any fine.

● ● ●

The owners gave Ranieri funds to land his prime transfer target in the summer transfer window. Gökhan Inler, a Turkish-Swiss midfielder of pedigree, arrived from Napoli. He would compete with Drinkwater for the role of central, controlling midfield player. Inler had struggled a bit against Villa but started again versus Stoke.

Leicester went 2–0 behind again.

Stoke were yet to win a game. Inler impeded Morgan when Bojan Krkić escaped Leicester's offside trap to score. Then Morgan was unusually timid with a pass back gifting Jon Walters Stoke's second goal. Schmeichel right hooked the air in frustration. This shipping of soft goals could not go on.

Leicester's balance was not right. Resting Albrighton, Ranieri tried Kanté on the left and though his running and retrieving were prodigious as ever, Kanté is no crosser or dribbler and looked much better when Ranieri moved him back inside. Inler seemed to be struggling with the speed of English football and Bojan dispossessed him but missed a lob attempt that could have brought Stoke a third.

Leicester's lifeline was offered by Marko Arnautović, fouling Drinkwater daftly for Mahrez to stroke in a penalty.

Then, a long Drinkwater pass, a flick-on and Vardy was in to steal the draw. Leicester had come back again, but could they really keep getting away with giving the opposition such opportunities?

'It would be a lot easier if we didn't concede two goals every second game,' was Drinkwater's pithy post-match summary.

There was certainly a spirit about this side. Perhaps a nothing-to-lose fearlessness carried over from the 'great escape'. No team had come behind to draw or win in so many consecutive matches (four) since David Moyes' rugged Everton in 2012. Ranieri later said the early season comebacks were crucial to him developing a sense of just what this team could achieve. 'It showed me they were fighters. Like me,' he said.

Morgan reflects, 'There were a few games when we were coming back and showing real resilience. If you have that in your team, you can go a long, long way.

'We have the likes of Riyad and Vards, some real quality in the team. But then others like Shinji, working day and night for the other lads. We have always got a chance. That is in the back of our minds.

'We always have a chance.'

7 LEICESTER

It was love at first sight for Chandu Dave. As a little boy in Uganda, he always wanted to be a goalkeeper.

And when he was 16, something magical came on his family television: the football World Cup in far-off England.

Dave had developed a support for Chelsea – he cannot remember why – but England's goalkeeper in 1966 was about to change all that. 'Gordon Banks,' he says. 'I never forgot Banks, the saves he made.' Through Banks, or rather the club Banks represented, 'I found out somewhere called Leicester existed.'

In that way it can, life sort of clicked into place over the next few years. Dave's family are Gujaratis of Indian origin and life was getting difficult for Uganda's Asians. Idi Amin expelled the population in 1972 but Dave got out early, coming to England in the hope of doing a diploma – 'in computers: they seemed to be coming in.'

He could not find a college place in London but somebody recommended an institution in Leicester; that name again. He immediately thought of Banks and off he went. And remains there; he would never want to live anywhere else. He first watched Leicester City at the old Filbert Street ground, when he was 'the only Asian in the crowd', and he has held a season ticket for approaching forty years.

At games there are fully fifteen of them, Dave's family and friends, all sitting together at King Power Stadium; his daughter Reena, a university worker, volunteers for Foxes Travel. Vishal, Dave's son, an IT consultant, is just as ardent.

And Dave? He did not go into computing but aerospace engineering and still works for a Leicester company. His wife is indifferent to football but when they were on holiday in Thailand she didn't mind being dragged to various King Power shopping outlets. 'I've had good times and I've had bad following Leicester City, probably, until recently, more bad times,' chuckles Dave. 'I've loved it all. Leicester's in my heart.'

Your sport, your family, your city, your club, all meshing to shape your life story: many a fan would relate to that. And many a non-fan would snort.

• • •

Players are settlers too. Few, in modern football, play for their local teams. Many have travelled, sometimes from hard terrains. And maybe Leicester's had travelled further and had a harder road than those at clubs who fought them for the title.

Among the squad, Okazaki and Albrighton stood apart: they were the only regulars never to have been employed by a lower-tier club. (Here, we are not talking about loans but players with permanent contracts who have nowhere else to go.) Drinkwater, Simpson, Ulloa and Wasilewski were almost privileged – they had only gone as low as the second tier.

The others? Third tier: Huth. Fourth tier: Fuchs. Seventh tier: Vardy and Mahrez. Eighth tier: Kanté. Ninth tier: Morgan.

Leonardo Ulloa had come the furthest. His hometown was General Roca, a small city of waterfronts and orchards in the north of Patagonia: next stop south a lot of ice, then the edge of the world, Tierra del Fuego.

Ulloa left home at 15 to traipse 700 miles along the Patagonian coast to sign for an Argentine second division club. He was his mother's youngest son and she suffered.

His first ten years as a pro consisted of small stepping stones: seven clubs in two continents before arriving at Leicester. He never stopped missing home. On his wrist there is a tattoo to honour his grandfather. 'I remember him at *asados*, barbecues. He was at the grill. He is a symbol of the family,' Ulloa said.

One of the reasons he kept moving was he married young and had two daughters to support. When he scored his first Premier League goal there were articles asking, 'Who is Ulloa?' Not just in the English but Argentine press.

'*Ne vale la pena*,' It was worth it, Ulloa says. As Rory Smith, of the *New York Times*, wrote, Ulloa has 'drawn deep from his wellspring of hope'.

But hadn't they all? Kanté – a speck of a player too tiny to interest French scouts. Mahrez – too much a maverick for them. Vardy – dropkicked by Sheffield Wednesday onto the factory floor.

Leicester's players all knew how to draw deep; their manager too. And just maybe that was one of the things that fuelled their comebacks.

But of course waffle about wellsprings is no use if you hand Alexis Sánchez hat-tricks on a plate.

• • •

Well, not a plate. When Arsenal came to the King Power in late September Sánchez was on marvellous form, his finishing sublime. But it is true that the Chilean, having started the season slowly after his Copa América exploits, was helped to get up to speed by Leicester's defending.

Leicester started so well, Vardy hitting a post. Then Kanté, the smallest octopus in history, stretched out a tentacular leg to steal the ball from Aaron Ramsey and pass, pass, bang: a quick break and suddenly Vardy was beating Petr Čech for 1–0.

On another attack Vardy hit the bar but from Arsenal's counter, a progression of perfectly fed forward passes, Theo Walcott scored. Leicester's left flank opened up and Sánchez snatched a goal, then Mesut Özil exploited weakness on Leicester's right to cross for the Chilean to score again.

Arsenal now found spaces everywhere and Sánchez smacked in a beautiful finish for his third. Vardy poached one back for Leicester but Arsenal went back-through-to-front, slicing Leicester yet again with their passing, and Olivier Giroud completed their victory, 5–2. Vardy was disconsolate. 'They just kept scoring,' he said. 'We need to get back to that training field now.'

• • •

Vardy lived in Melton Mowbray, ancient market town and capital for foodies – though he admits to a diet more like that of the up-until-dawn nightclubber.

Morgan had not left Nottingham, nor Albrighton Sutton Coldfield and Huth still lived near his old club, Stoke. Simpson was one of what he calls the 'Manny boys', the contingent of Manchester-based Leicester players.

Schmeichel drives two hours to training, from Alderley Edge. Usually, he drives himself but if tired, if the kids have given him a sleepless night, he will call a driver and take the luxury van, customised with bed and suede duvet, that he keeps in the garage.

So, only about half the squad lived in Leicester itself. There were King and Mahrez, in the leafy Victorian streets of Stoneygate; Ulloa too. Ranieri lived in a peaceful suburb on the edge of the city. And Kanté? Perhaps reasoning he already covered more than enough ground, he just lived near the stadium.

What's Leicester like?

Let's start with *Ratae Coritanorum* (*Corieltauvorum* – spellings are disputed). On the road they built from Exeter to Lincoln, the Romans took over a settlement on the River Soar, where lived the native *Corieltavi* tribe. The Romans built ramparts (*ratae*), baths and belatedly something of a forum. But it never became an important place in their *Britannia*.

On the map, but mostly just on the way to somewhere else: some would say the die was cast for Leicester.

It evolved as a pleasant enough provincial centre and the Victorians reshaped the city both physically and in terms of culture and local character. Leicester became a bastion of the Victorian Temperance movement laying down 'moderation' as strong local value and theme.

The Industrial Revolution had impact without quite defining the city to the extent it did northern counterparts. Leicester's most famous factories were not heavy industry but sound almost jolly: they made hats and shoes and socks. Knitwear too. Garments of all sorts in fact. The old boast was that Leicester could 'clothe the world'.

Not everyone felt the city had much to shout about though. Leicester seemed 'to have no atmosphere of its own ... to lack character' said JB Priestley, the writer and historian, in 1934. Joe Orton, a son of Leicester, suggested it was 'arguably the most boring city in Britain'. Even Terry Wogan could not find whimsy there, lamenting it as 'England's lost city'.

The 'dull' label stuck. In 2003, a seven-year marketing campaign was launched to change perceptions. Martin Johnson, a local and England's World Cup winning rugby captain, appeared in it and there were slogans like 'boring? Who's laughing now?' and (intended ironically) 'Leicester – Nothing to shout about!'

Hmm. Dynamic ways of selling themselves did not seem to come easily to Leicester folk. This is from 'The Leicester Song', from a musical written for the city's 1972 Expo:

> '. . .We like Leicester it's our sort of town
> Not too stuck up and far from being down
> Leicester's full of people, folks like you and me
> This is what makes Leicester such a pleasant place to be'

Not quite 'New York, New York.'

What are Leicester people like? Nice. Really nice. It is very easy to arrive and fit in. Locals don't try and impose anything upon the newcomer: how you speak, behave is up to you. Ninety-five per cent of the time, this is wonderful but five per cent you secretly wish there was a Leicester something – an accent, a saying, a symbol, a personality type, that you could hold onto. The furthest you get is that Gary Lineker once sold fruit and veg from his parents' stall at the indoor market and that before Kasabian Leicester spawned Engelbert Humperdinck and the least-known member of Queen. Oh and the local pronunciation of the name is 'Les-tah'. But is that so very much?

• • •

Next was a visit to Norwich on October 3. The club internet TV channel featured a classic – of sorts. Kanté gave his first English language interview. They tried to get him going about how well he was taking to the Premier League and he mumbled, 'The good start . . . is better for me than a bad start.' And on it went. You don't get past NG.

Ranieri's pre-match press conference was also block-and-parry. He was unusually terse. The Arsenal defeat – which dropped Leicester to sixth – seemed to be still on his mind.

The bright beginning had given way to a run of one win in four and, conceding 14 goals in seven matches, Leicester had the Premier League's worst defensive record bar bottom side Sunderland.

Ranieri noted that all Arsenal's five goals came when Leicester were counterattacked and now another Roman would build ramparts. He made his first major line-up revamp: simple, but radical. New full backs.

De Laet and Schlupp, with their pace and adventurousness, had been raiding forward well but what if he introduced two more natural defenders? Simpson and Fuchs were in.

Fuchs' Premier League exposure amounted to 21 minutes as a substitute – though he had played two League Cup games and, as Austria captain, was experienced. Simpson knew the Premier League very well but had not played in it at all under Ranieri and was coming back from off-field troubles having been convicted, in August, for assaulting his ex-girlfriend. A December appeal hung over him.

But Simpson started on the right and Fuchs the left. Huth remembers Ranieri's message to the new full backs: 'Defend. Pass the ball to Marc or Riyad. Back it up. Only when we are losing can you do an overlap.'

Still 4-2-3-1, Leicester were: Schmeichel; Simpson, Morgan, Huth, Fuchs; Kanté, Drinkwater; Albrighton, Okazaki, Schlupp; Vardy.

Leicester's recent record against Norwich was dismal: six defeats and only one win in eight games and immediately Fuchs almost headed into his own net. But soon he settled and brought not only discipline to his position but a new weapon, a prodigious long throw.

Simpson plugged away. Kanté stole from Jonny Howson and slipped in Vardy, who expertly enticed some contact from Sébastian Bassong to go down for the penalty. With Mahrez uninvolved (for the only league game all season) Vardy smashed it in.

Leicester were back to being the blitzer and not the blitzed. Okazaki robbed Howson to find Kanté, who found Schlupp, and Schlupp finished surely for 2–0. Dieumerci Mbokani headed in for Norwich and a little raggedness crept back in, but Leicester's defending was much better overall and 2–1 it ended.

The neat narrative is that this was the day Leicester changed, for good, into a 'Ranieri team' defensively. But that is not quite true. Next, at Southampton, on October 17, they were 2–0 down again – conceding two set-piece goals to the opposing centre backs, José Fonte and Virgil van Dijk.

Yet another comeback: Vardy headed in Nathan Dyer's centre and, in the very last seconds, belted home an equaliser from Mahrez's subtle pass. Vindication for Ranieri was that he had introduced Dyer and Mahrez in a tactical switch.

Seven points won, now, from losing positions: no Premier League side had a record as resilient as Leicester's. 'We believe everything could be possible,' said Ranieri. 'And I believe in this team. When we are desperate we make more, more, more.'

● ● ●

By 2015 Leicester had come to disprove JB Priestley. It *did* have a distinctive character. It was the first minority-white city in Britain, a place of diversity unmatched anywhere outside London. Stories like Chandu Dave's were everywhere.

Thousands of African Asians, mainly from Uganda like him, had arrived in Leicester during the 1970s adding to strong, older Caribbean, Sikh, Polish and Irish communities and turning Leicester into a centre of migration. The mild local identity, the unimposing local character, suddenly became assets: attractive to incomers who found tolerance and were left to their own customs in their new cities.

The immigrant arrival was timely, as globalisation was killing off the old factories and Leicester's clothing industry was in its death throes by 1970. Many of the newcomers were from metropolitan Africa, educated and middle class, perfect for a future that would see such as precision engineering, retail and the university sector grow to regenerate Leicester's economic life.

Leicester cannot pretend it was always entirely welcoming: in 1972 its Labour controlled city council took out an advertisement in the *Uganda Argus* discouraging new immigrants and announcing its services were 'stretched to the limit.' But generally Leicester took pride in its changing character. As far back as 1958 the local press trumpeted their city as an 'ethnic friendly' place, in contrast to other English cities and their racial disturbances.

If you go down Narborough Road to look for the 'Lost Bar', a pub entirely devoted to Leicester City, you will find it tucked amid a kaleidoscope of outlets, with shopkeepers from 23 different nationalities Narborough Road is dubbed 'the most multicultural high street in England'.

Variety is everywhere. Don't fancy a Lost Bar lunch of a 'Vardy Bomb' (WKD blue plus Jagermeister, two for £5) and cheese-and-onion cob? One of Leicester's excellent Polish bars is just up the road. Although the landlord unsuspectingly drew attention to himself by innocently naming it Forest Bar – Nottingham Forest being Leicester's most hated rivals.

You won't struggle for curry in Leicester. Your problem will be choosing the restaurant: Keralan, Goan, Karnatakan, Punjabi, Himalayan, Gujarati vegetarian – your choice. Leicester's Diwali celebrations, centred round the 'Golden Mile' of Belgrave Road, are among the biggest outside India.

In Britain's 2011 Census, a third of Leicester's 330,000 residents were born outside Britain; Leicester had Britain's third highest Hindu and eleventh highest Muslim (percentage-wise) populations.

A large influx of around 10,000 war-fleeing Somalis arrived around 2000, while Leicester's Caribbean, Irish, Polish and Chinese communities are longstanding. At the end of May, the far right 'Britain First' group set up a stall by the old clock tower on Gallowtree Gate – and were chased out of town by Peter Soulsby, the mayor, leading a crowd of residents.

A friend's grandparents were Asians from Malawi and arrived in the 1960s. His granddad worked in trade and was an Anglophile who loved James Bond and smoked a pipe. The grandparents were welcomed in and an icebreaker was cuisine. In their cramped street, through open windows, you caught wafts of next door's dinner.

The Malawi Asians just could not get their heads – or rather nostrils – around how the food being cooked by the English had no smell, except for fat. For their part, the neighbours were calling round to find the source of their wonderful aromas.

But let's not get dreamy. Not all the stories were like that or Chandu Dave's. People from Leicester's minorities might roll their eyes when newcomers wax too rosily about diversity and the new Leicester.

Leicester is nice, a highly comfortable city to live in, but far from perfect, they might tell you. While communities live in peace they do not necessarily mix. And the friend, a successful office worker, occasionally still gets 'heckled' as he puts it by whites in the wrong parts of town.

Professor John Williams, author, Liverpool fan, and renowned sociologist from Leicester University, could interest you for hours on nuances like that. Until recently, Williams chaired the Foxes Against Racism group at Leicester City.

He says, while striving for improvements, the club could still do more to reflect its community: employ more minorities in key jobs, for example, or start bringing Asian players through its youth ranks. Though compared to other Premier League clubs, he agrees, Leicester does well.

Success helps. Leicester – Buddhist owners, Italian manager, Caribbean captain, Japanese icon, Euro contingent, Muslim poster boy – and whatever warrior planet Wasilewski is from – seemed an example of diversity winning. In the League Cup the club fielded a team of eleven different nationalities and Ranieri merely shrugged – so what?

● ● ●

Crystal Palace came to King Power on October 24, and at last Leicester were back at their new home. There had been no football there for a month. The stadium had been hosting games for the Rugby World Cup.

This was ever-so-slightly delicious for those football fans who always felt slightly patronised by their rugby counterparts. Though Leicester Tigers have been English champions eight times since 1999 and are the country's best-supported rugby club, their Welford Road pitch was deemed too small for World Cup games, so the King Power was co-opted. 'Leicester is an unusual English football city,' says Williams, smiling at the sitting room table of his airy house near the university on Victoria Park. 'It is one divided not by clubs but codes.'

Crystal Palace had enjoyed their best ever start in the Premier League and could leapfrog Leicester by winning. For a third game, Ranieri picked his new defence and Mahrez was back as a starter, supplanting Okazaki. Perhaps it was Leicester's least entertaining home performance of the season. 'It was a tactical match,' Ranieri conceded, 'more an Italian match than an English one.'

The sort of match where one player cracks in one small moment, another pounces, and 90 minutes and a whole week of training preparation are made irrelevant. Palace's Brede Hangeland misplaced a pass and Mahrez slid Vardy through to chip Wayne Hennessey, then followed the ball in.

Vardy counted: one, two, three, four, five, six, seven fingers. He had scored for a seventh successive Premier League game, joining a small elite to achieve such a feat. Drinkwater was superb, making 88 touches, and Leicester survived two Palace penalty shouts to win 1–0. Ranieri celebrated with both fists. It was Leicester's best start to a top-flight season in fifty years.

The new back four was making a difference. 'Jeff [Schlupp] replaced by Fuchs, Ritchie [De Laet] replaced by Simmer, who are both defence-minded – that was important,' says Schmeichel.

'Jeff and Richie going forward are lightning. But when you had both Ritchie and Riyad on the right side going forward it left huge, huge, spaces to be exposed in behind.

'The Arsenal game was like basketball. We attacked, they attacked. There was space in behind for both teams and they took their chances better than us. It was good for us, because we needed to change something. Now we have four *defenders* in there.'

Fuchs, the quote-unquote interesting Austrian: he has a story. On tour in New York with Schalke, he went out partying and 'at some point she was standing there. It was her fault. I don't want to be too sentimental but it just clicked, from that moment it was trouble – positive trouble!' She was Raluca, head of an event management company and former senior analyst at Goldman Sachs. She still lives in Manhattan with their toddler, Anthony, and Ethan, an older son from her first marriage.

Fuchs knows his retirement plan: New York. He now runs a football academy there and dreams of making it as an NFL kicker for the Giants. FaceTime is the godsend that keeps him close to his family, with it impossible for Raluca and the boys to get to Leicester more than once a month. Ranieri, the family man, gives him extra time off to get to Manhattan now and then.

• • •

Leicester's first stars were the 'foreigners' of the day and determined travellers. They were Scots, like Andy Aitken, Johnny Duncan, Jock Paterson, Adam Black. Black was a decorated First World War hero who fought on the Western Front when he was 16, and who also forged an unusual partnership – at 59 marrying a 17-year-old bride.

Leicester City grew out of another club, Leicester Fosse, the 'Fossils', formed by the well-off sons of shoe factory owners: they were literally well-heeled. They were friends from a Bible class and held meetings in the shed of a garden on Fosse Road – the old Roman route.

Before settling at Filbert Street, Leicester Fosse played at Belgrave Road – not yet called 'Golden Mile' – but then Leicester Tigers outbid them for the site. Narborough Road? Between the wars, in club houses, a lot of Leicester City players lived there.

The sockmakers and the shoe manufacturers have all but disappeared from town and on Frog Island the old redbrick factories are used by small businesses; several of these small IT firms are owned by sons and grandsons of immigrants like Chandu Dave. About half a mile from Frog Island, Ranieri took his squad for a pizza.

He was delivering on a promise made in one of his press conferences. He had said – oh, way back, back before the 2–2 with Stoke – he would treat the players to pizza if they managed to keep a clean sheet. Now, against Palace, in Leicester's tenth league match they had at last delivered.

Of course Schmeichel, with his purist tastes, feels clean sheets are something of a media obsession. 'Obviously you want clean sheets. But in that early part of the season we were winning games. For me, "clean sheets" is a silly stat that for some reason is massive in football,' he says.

'In one game we had 33 attempts on goal and absolutely battered them but they got three lucky ricochets and the "clean sheet" is blown. It's a silly type of stat. You don't want to be conceding goals but it's not vitally important as long as you are winning.'

But Ranieri had been ready to see a nice, clean, Italian zero against the opposition name in a scoreline. The squad went to Peter Pizzeria on Welford Place, where a certain Austrian initiated a food fight. ('I think this is the Austrian mentality, we don't give a Fuchs!' Okay, Christian.)

The group enjoyed their day. Dough? Ah, there was a twist. These players: they came up the hard way. Why make things too easy for them?

Ranieri led them to the restaurant kitchen, where was laid out the sauce and the cheese and the dough. 'You have to work for everything,' he said. 'You work for your pizza, too. We will make our own.'

8

VARDY

King Power Stadium, countdown to kick-off. On the pitch a lone brass player sounds the haunting *Post Horn Gallop*. Spines shiver. Air is gulped into opposition lungs. Game time, time to begin the chase. From the big screen one image, burning fox eyes, peer down. On the stadium walls the signs say #Fearless.

Welcome to Leicester City in 2015–16, a time where the impossible became merely quarry. The world's hardest league. A forgotten club. A nearly manager. Team of £400,000 and £1m men. Yet there were Leicester, little Leicester, right on top. Ridiculous. Miraculous. Fearless.

Late November, Manchester United came. Referee Craig Pawson gave his signal and it began. Manchester United had the ball. Leicester had the game.

What United learned was: they steal that ball. They steal it when they need to and – *blink* – it is in your box. They pen you in, they are under your feet. They run off your shoulder, stay on their toes.

Time you thought you had gets snatched away. Those King Power fans with their clappers and flags: they get in your ears and the corners of your eyes. Vardy, circling, scanning, ever there to swoop ... And to think their manager looks kind.

United were thinking about the top: winning would see them leap over Leicester into first place. But soon it became a matter of survival. Leicester were incessant, nipping away, running all over their aged midfield. And when United had a corner Schmeichel caught the ball and rolled it to Fuchs. And – *blink* – Vardy, with that ball, was in their box.

It was time for the question. Four years ago that weekend this striker was scoring in the fifth tier, the Conference, in front of 768 up at Gateshead. Now, one of the great goal records was his to take. Really? Had he really come on that much? Head down, clean hit, he slammed his finish past David de Gea.

And he ran off, screaming.

Screaming, 'All mine!'

• • •

The box – 'Pandora's Box,' he jokes – is chaotic but it is telling that he has curated it. Now Allen Bethel, kneeling on the Axminster carpet in the 1980s-feel committee room at Stocksbridge Park Steels, is going through his print-outs about Jamie Vardy. 'Two from Norway, two from Sweden ... there's Henrik from Sweden ...' he says. 'France. Belgium. ITV News. BBC Sport.

'There's *Marca* from Spain. Wright-Thompson, ESPN – he couldn't make it in the end. Two Japanese. Reuters. *Mail on Sunday*. *Daily Star*. Spoke to him on the phone – the *New York Times*, bloody massive article.

'Photos to Brazil. Brazil wanted photos. Who's this? AFP. French TV. Danish TV.'

Bethel grabs a cutting. The *Wall Street Journal*. 'Look. There he is ... next to [a piece about] Putin!'

Do all journalists ask the same?

'They do – in different ways. The film guy,' he continues. 'We've had the film guy here twice. Someone said to me, "Who's going to play you, you old sod?" *beIN Sports*, they ...

'... oh, just look at that hawk, coming over here ...'

Bethel stands up and stares out of the window. Turns out ornithology is a passion too. 'I do birdwatch,' he says. 'Yes ... hawk. Look, it's quite a way away.'

Coming up the valley, against slate-grey sky, a dark silhouette; there it is, the predator bird, riding an air current and scanning the river below. It is rugged round here, and gloomy today, in this South Yorkshire valley. The opposite hillside is scarred by quarrying and wind turbines; mobile phone masts are staked down across its top.

Beneath, there are thick trees, the river, the town, and what is left of all the mills. On this side is an oasis, a small rectangle of manicured green, the only flat ground for miles. And we are overlooking it: the somehow pristine pitch of Bracken Moor, Stocksbridge Park Steels' home ground.

Bethel, the Steels' chairman, still has the high, engaging laugh of a teenager and moves nimbly. But he is white-haired and 75 now, and long meetings such as the one he chaired in this committee room last night – three whole hours – can be a strain. The meeting was about that ever-pressing non-league subject, finance: but the worldwide attention Jamie Vardy has brought, has brought the Steels a lifeline.

Vardy was here for seven seasons, far longer than any of his other clubs, so if anyone can claim him as their son – and get a few rightful rewards for that – it is the Steels. Outside sits the modest 'Jamie Vardy Stand', which Bethel recently renamed. 'Some people don't know Jamie played here – and those who do know want to see his name,' he explains.

Stocksbridge, nine miles north of Sheffield, is a weather-bitten small town of 13,500 and the average crowd here is 170. Yet the Steels run seventeen teams, including four for girls, and pay their best players up to £130 per week to play in the Northern Premier League. 'Our motto,' says Bethel, 'is "We always pay." We don't pay the most but, unlike many at our level, we always pay.'

Finance comes from working hard to keep local sponsors and being endlessly creative with small initiatives to bring pounds in. Just as well, then, that Bethel is a former credit manager who handled money for the factories and mills that once thrived by the fast-flowing Little Don river. He looked after 'millions and millions' and travelled across Europe, North America – all over. In 1980 he was offered a big job in London.

He came home on the train. 'On a Friday night I went up to the trig point at the top of the hill, I looked at the hills and over to Ladybower reservoir and thought, "I'm not going, I want to stay here."' Bethel says. He has a smile to himself. No regrets. One way or another, he has been involved at this club more than forty years.

Stocksbridge was forged as a town by an industrialist, Samuel Fox, who came over the hills one day in 1842 in a horse and trap – and saw the valley, the fast-flowing river and slopes from which you could very probably dig coal. The factories he built made umbrella frames and crinoline and before long there were steel furnaces, wire draws and rolling mills as well. The old warehouses and works by Little Don river have been refurbished as a development called 'Fox Valley'.

Fox Valley. Where else did you think Jamie Vardy and the arc of his Hollywood story was going to start?

• • •

When Vardy struck against Crystal Palace on October 24 he was suddenly among the elite. He became one of only eight players to score in seven successive Premier League games and many of the others were footballing aristocrats: Alan Shearer, Thierry Henry, Ruud van Nistelrooy. The serious coverage of his backstory started then. Bethel had his first visitor at Stocksbridge – nice chap from the *Daily Mirror*.

The Tuesday after Palace Ranieri tried resting Vardy for a Capital One Cup tie at second-tier Hull. Yet Hull proved difficult and Vardy had to come off the bench. It went to a penalty shoot-out and he missed. Would this affect him?

Bethel:

> We got him from a team the other side of Rotherham. [Sheffield] Wednesday had let him go. A skinny lad, edging towards 17, Jamie

became another member of a decent Under-18 squad we had. On midweek nights I'd be opening up, might be sweeping down the stand, and the 18s would [train] in the far end. This Jamie arrives and, before long, he's joking away. Always sat in the same position. He'd always be first. Sometimes he'd be there already when I was opening up: 'Where have you been?'

He'd carry stuff on t' field. He'd carry whole kit bag down there. All the balls and the bollards for everyone else. And then he'd help take it all back. He was first here and last out – that was the first thing I noticed.

On a Sunday I was walking past the junior fields. It was before they were redone – crap pitches, bumpy, dog shit on them. And I see this kid. He was playing left side. Jamie. I see how quick he is – over five, ten, fifteen, twenty yards he's quickest. He can kick with his left foot, kick with his right foot, head it. He wasn't fazed if someone knocked him on the floor. It weren't a problem. The retaliation – that's another story – came later . . .

Vardy is from Hillsborough, near the stadium, and Sheffield Wednesday was his team. All his mates supported them – as do most people, as it happens, in Stocksbridge, which is on the Hillsborough side of Sheffield. The side the Steels snatched him from was Wickersley Youth, where he was playing amateur football while working in a factory making carbon fibre splints. He kept that job throughout his time at Steels, who had him for seven years. By the end, he was swelling their gate, attracting other good players and drawing a procession of scouts and managers to Bracken

Moor. He remains best mates with former Steels teammates like Brett Lovell, and keeps in regular touch with Bethel. He came back to Bracken Moor not too long ago.

And yet, when Bethel brings out a fundraising wall calendar, and it has two pictures on the cover, and one is, 'Jamie Vardy 2005 Stocksbridge Park Steels U18 Player' while the other is, 'Jamie Vardy 2015 Full England International', it . . . well, it still all seems surreal.

Surreal that for seven full years, riding tackles, dodging kicks and dog shit, paid nothing at first and then even at peak only 130 quid a week, the most lethal striker in England stayed here; surreal that a peer of Henry and van Nistelrooy's played for season upon season on this windy hillside.

What did that produce? Well, in the end Vardy did leave the valley. He left as hungry and sharp-eyed as a hawk.

• • •

Being perched on history did not put Vardy off his game. Nor did the next opposition: bruising West Brom on October 31. Nor did the surrounds: a Hawthorns ground rocking for a Midlands derby. And nor did injury: after cracking two bones in a fall during September's comeback win against Aston Villa, Vardy was playing with a lightweight plaster cast on his right wrist. He needed a bone graft and several weeks' rehabilitation but that could wait until this season was done.

Boaz Myhill, West Brom's keeper, touched an early Vardy effort against a post. Then Darren Fletcher blocked Vardy's shot. West Brom scored, from a set-piece – header by Salomón Rondón – and then Huth got away with barging an arm into Gareth McAuley's neck. Anthony Taylor, the referee, said no penalty. Leicester would admit themselves their season had little lucky – maybe karmic? – moments like that.

One goal down, in this hard place, against such hardened opposition – Leicester's lack of panic impressed. They pushed. A gigantic Huth header sailed to Albrighton, who teased a lovely cross to the back post where Mahrez volleyed smoothly home. One each.

Then Albrighton, from the opposite flank this time, centred and Mahrez stroked another in: 2–1. And then one of those flashing counterattacks: Vardy passed to Drinkwater, Drinkwater measured into his path a delicious return pass, and Vardy raced in on goal.

Moments earlier he had needed ankle treatment but now he was accelerating so freely. Too quick for Jonny Evans to catch him and too free of doubt to do anything else – Vardy smacked the ball beyond Myhill.

Goals now in eight consecutive Premier League games. Only Daniel Sturridge had equalled that and only van Nistelrooy, that Dutch master predator, had ever done better.

Bethel:

> I started watching him closely. I could see how he were in the changing room, how popular he was. How, for some reason or another they all generate [sic] towards Vardy. All the senior pros, even. And this when he was a lad.
>
> Even at a young age, people loved Vardy. Second team, people loved Vardy. First team, people loved Vardy. And he didn't show off. He still took the kit out. He was always bantering. He can gel

people. It's a talent. Some senior players can be quite aloof, but he could gel them.

There was a bloke, Murph. He was a ref and he played over-35s. Passed away. Well, Murph was always around the place and he was here when Vardy was.

So Vardy came [to Bracken Moor] two years ago. He wore a tracksuit that I'm sure cost a fortune but it wasn't Stocksbridge. It was greyish. He was chatting to the lads in the stands and people were taking photos when Murph walks on: 'Oh fucking hell, Vardy. About time you turned up. What the hell have you got on, you look like a fucking plonker!'

And Vardy was laughing, 'Heheheh, oh Murph.' I mean, if he'd become a snobby type, nowadays, he'd have gone off or something, but he loved it. I can see Vardy laughing there, now, everyone else in the stand pissing themselves. I think he's had his downs – but he hasn't had many downs – and look what he's done . . . and he ain't altered.

It helps a team (as shown by Gareth Bale and Wales) if its star has the affection or at least respect of the others. At Leicester Vardy had buckets of both. Yes, he had his spiky side and on his day could easily knock Drinkwater into second in the moaning stakes.

But, in general, he was regarded as a great teammate. Someone you wanted to be around. And now Bethel wants to show a framed picture on the committee room wall. It is the Stocksbridge first team from 2009 and, in the front row, as everyone poses solemnly, some skinhead youngster is sending up the whole thing by letting his hand rest on the coach's knee. Vardy. The dressing room gellist.

When Leicester travel away, Vardy sits at the back of the bus, at the centre of a card school. 'Vards and Was are always playing,' says Schmeichel. 'Sometimes Kingy will join in, Leo [Ulloa] too. Ritchie De Laet will always play.'

'The season before,' adds Albrighton, 'it was [David] Nugent, Ritchie and Vards.'

'Yeah,' says Kasper. 'Nuge, Vards and Sean St Ledger, they were always the main culprits. St Ledger was the mood spreader. He always created a good atmosphere. Nuge and Vards are similar.'

De Laet was Vardy's sidekick, Butt-Head to his Beavis (check the resemblance). They arrived within three days of each other in May 2012 and although De Laet came from Manchester United and Vardy just non-league Fleetwood Town, they found much in common. Principally, silly humour. At Fleetwood, on the poor chef's birthday, Vardy wrapped the guy's car entirely in cling film. That was right up De Laet's street.

In January, journalists for Belgian publications *Het Nieuwsblad* and *Fan* were at Belvoir Drive interviewing De Laet, and got a taste of the double act. Unscheduled, Vardy strode into the room. This from *Het Nieuwsblad*.

> 'He's crazy,' said De Laet.
>
> 'Just a little bit,' answered Vardy.
>
> De Laet: 'Vards and I signed on almost the same day for Leicester. Since then, we were always together: together on the bus, roommates for away games.'

Vardy: 'At the hotel, we always have our PlayStation 4 with us. We play *Call of Duty*. He doesn't need a lot of time to shoot four guys. Ritchie is too good. Frightening.'

De Laet: 'We're continually joking. We throw tracksuits in the bath, pick a painting from the wall and put it on someone's door. At training camp in Austria we invaded the room of two teammates and threw their mattresses through the window. And nobody has ever dared to take revenge.

'In the locker room we have two large baths, a hot one and cold one. Vards and I crawl in there, together with all the socks. Our arsenal of wet socks. Yesterday, there was a player from the Under-18s – who actually are not allowed in our dressing room – and his body looked as if he went to play paintball. Full of red spots after we started throwing socks at him.'

Vardy: 'Someone must keep the mood of the team up, eh?'

De Laet: 'We're equally crazy in training. The manager understands that we can't face each other on the training pitch. It will end up by one of us being injured. Two years ago, we were one-on-one. It ended with a motionless ball in the middle, my studs at the back of his head.'

Vardy: 'And my studs on his knee.'

Being liked can be worth its weight in goals. Leicester's next match was at the King Power on November 7 versus Watford – 'our mirror', Ranieri had said. He admired the work of Quique Sánchez Flores, who had produced a compact, effortful, counterattacking side, similar to his. And Watford's main attackers, Odion Ighalo and Troy Deeney, were a mirror of Vardy and Mahrez in terms of lethal early-season form.

Watford were better, initially. Ighalo hit a post. Only staunch work by Morgan foiled Deeney. Albrighton was Leicester's threat player but could not quite beat Gomes, Watford's keeper.

But then Gomes had the kind of brainstorm to which he is prone. Kanté did cause surprise by taking his shot early, with a short, stabbing backlift, but it still rolled straight towards Gomes who missed it and scooped up fresh air, like a man grabbing in vain at a fly.

One–nil Leicester and now came Vardy. Twice he had torn through on Gomes and failed to beat the keeper but Morgan bumped Ighalo off the ball and, with a long pass, played Vardy clear again. Gomes, head gone, tripped him. Penalty. The chance to extend the scoring record from the spot.

One problem. Mahrez was Leicester's designated taker and the Algerian sauntered towards the mark with ball under arm. Just as he was about to place it Vardy called over, maybe more in hope than expectation. But Mahrez stopped, turned, smiled – held out the ball and said, 'Go on.'

Vardy rattled the penalty high into Gomes's net and ran towards Mahrez, gratefully pointing. The pair hugged and five or six players joined in.

'Vards has blossomed of late,' Morgan reflects. 'I don't think anyone guessed he'd do it, but he went five, six, seven games and suddenly the record was in sight. The boys were right behind him, just willing him to achieve it and we all wanted to help.'

Van Nistelrooy was the only one, now, to have ever exceeded Vardy's new mark of scoring in nine consecutive Premier League games – in 2003 the Dutchman's run extended to ten.

Bethel:

His final match for the second team was against one of the mining villages in the county senior cup final at Rotherham. Vardy had ripped them to bloody shreds, I mean ripped them to shreds. And they weren't a bad side. They tried everything but couldn't catch him.

I have to say, when he was younger I did wonder how long he'd keep his speed but there's no sign of it going. He must be the quickest 29-year-old in t' world! You know, I saw him at Fleetwood doing the same as he did with us: lolling around on halfway line then – whumph – going down left side. And then, I saw him do it in the Championship. Exactly the same. I thought surely if he ever gets to face the top sides they'll do something to stop him. But they never do. I'm not sure they can.

The musculature of sprinters is familiar. The fast guys have biceps, glutes, abs and quads; a visible power-to-weight ratio. You can see their engines. They look like Jeff Schlupp, whose Leicester data shows him to be Vardy's only rival when it comes to speed (though De Laet used to be champion over the longer distances).

Schlupp is beautifully muscled. Not skin-and-bone and all sharp points, like Vardy. In the museum of quick men and explosive athletes, Vardy is going to need his own room.

His body fat has been measured at 6 per cent – marathon runner stuff – by Leicester's sports science team. 'Vardy's physical profile fascinates me,' says Chris Davies, a coach formerly at Liverpool and now at Celtic. 'He's so wiry and slim. No muscles on his legs really.' By June it was fascinating all of England. After Vardy scored at the European Championship every English paper's sports pages and even the *Daily Telegraph* news section carried stories about his unique approach to 'athletic preparation'.

Vardy admitted to staying away from the gym as much as he could, to guzzling caffeine drinks and using an ultra-strong brand of *snus* – oral tobacco pouches popular in Europe but almost unheard of in the UK. 'The last time I lifted a weight,' said Vardy, 'was probably that can of Red Bull the other day.'

• • •

The Lost Bar, Narborough Road, home to 'Vardy Bombs – 2 for £5!!' It is a low-ceilinged, brightly lit, industrial place – like boozing in a lock-up garage – and the drinkers are blue collar. Near the entrance there is a poster of Gary Lineker as Indiana Jones but it is clear someone else is their superhero.

It is not just the Vardy Bombs, or even the framed special edition 'Vardy Salted' Walkers crisps. *He* is the one who, on the ball, gets guttural encouragement from the lager swiggers who shout at the Leicester game on the pub's TV. And a dad brings his ten-year-old boy to the bar because he has a party-piece for the barmaid. Go on son: 'Jamie Vardy's having a party . . . bring your vodka and your charlie!' squeaks the kid to general mirth. 'Charlie' being slang for cocaine.

And it goes on. Every so often the kid shouting out 'Jamie Vardy's having a party' and the barmaid going 'bring your vodka and your charlie!' in a special Lost Bar call-and-response.

Left: The Cockerel and the Fox: Wes Morgan outjumps Harry Kane. Leicester's win at White Hart Lane proved pivotal in the title race.

Below: 'To come away with a point was fantastic.' Captain Morgan scores at Old Trafford to leave Leicester on the brink of glory.

Above: Moment of Huth: in both boxes, Robert Huth, here scoring at Tottenham, made key contributions.

Above: Hunting as a pack: no team matched Leicester for collective defending.

Above: Sock thrower and shot-stopper, Kasper Schmeichel was central to success off and on the pitch.

Above: Great Danes. With father, Peter, assorted family, his wife, Stine, and their children, Isabella and Max, Kasper Schmeichel celebrates with the Premier League trophy.

Above: Fact: 70 per cent of the planet is covered by water, the rest by N'Golo Kanté.

Above: Kanté wins the battle, but Leicester lost a war at the Emirates Stadium, going down for a second time to Arsenal. Could they bounce back?

Above: The Sorcerer of Sarcelles: Riyad Mahrez scored a hat-trick against Swansea and found the net again against the Swans at King Power.

Above: Leicester's Special One: Mahrez's brilliant strike against Chelsea put Leicester back on top but spelt the end for Jose Mourinho.

Above: When he knew it was on: Leicester's incredible performance away to Manchester City, where Mahrez scored their third, convinced Ranieri they could be champions.

Above: More history: Mahrez was the first African to win PFA Player of the Year.

Above: All F***ing Mine! Jamie Vardy beats Ruud Van Nistelrooy's Premier League scoring record – appropriately against Van Nistelrooy's old club.

Above: The magnificent 11. The jumbo screen at the King Power stadium congratulates Vardy on his new goal record.

Above: Who could keep up with Vardy? Not Everton's Bryan Oviedo.

Above: Vardy Party. (l-r) Fuchs, Inler, Wasilewski, Schlupp and Hamer join their host in the title revelry at Vardy's house.

Above: Seismic moment: fans at the King Power celebrated so loudly when Ulloa scored against Norwich it was measured on the Richter scale.

Left: The underdogs were full of unsung heroes, none more so than Shinji Okazaki, here scoring a brilliant overhead kick against Newcastle.

Above: Mr Leicester: Andy King, the club's longest-serving player, has won the Premier League, Championship and League One – the only footballer to complete this unique set of honours.

Above: Angels: celebrating the title with his family had special meaning for Marc Albrighton, pictured here with daughters Matilda-Beau and Dollie-Boo.

Above: Full backing: Simpson and Fuchs provided great support to Morgan and Huth in Leicester's solid back four.

Right: 'The most influential person in the Premier League' according to Sir Alex Ferguson – assistant manager and super scout, Steve Walsh, now Everton's Director of Football.

Right: The blueprint: Nigel Pearson was controversial but laid down the strategies for success.

Below: Pizza party. Ranieri delivered on his promise to take the squad for pizza once they kept a clean sheet – the twist was they had to make their own.

Above: '*Vincero!*' Andrea Bocelli serenades the new champions of England.

Above: Emperor Claudio: after a career of near-misses, Ranieri was finally a champion.

Above: Family business: owner and chairman Vichai Srivaddhanaprabha with his son and vice-chairman Aiyawatt.

Above: 'Proper helicopter.' Leicester's owners were the envy of many Premier League rivals.

Above: Belief. A Buddhist shrine in Bangkok where Leicester are blessed.

Above: Higher power. Monks visit Leicester's stadium to add their blessing.

Above: Those fantastic Foxes. Fans, city, stadium – and club – were one as Leicester hunted down the title.

Above: A 5000–1 miracle and a triumph over football's established institutions that will never be forgotten.

The Jamie Vardy song spread nationally and even internationally from hardcore Leicester supporters as did a Facebook status update he posted as a non-league player in 2011. 'Chat shit get banged,' it said.

The post was retrieved by a fan going through his social media pages and as his exploits grew so this enigmatic shard of Vardyian philosophy assumed cult popularity, making its way onto T-shirts and stickers. It became a default schoolyard or Twitter admonishment to someone talking out of turn. 'My team/phone/dog is better than yours . . .' 'Listen, mate. *Chat shit get banged.*'

• • •

The gym-avoidance and Red Bull is manna to Vardy's 'lad' appeal. Sparkies and white van drivers could never imagine being David Beckham but Vardy is not far from who they see staring back when they look in the mirror. And Vardy *was* one of them, for so long. A factory guy with burger habits. Sometimes Stocksbridge played teams a hundred or more miles away and Bethel tells how Vardy might leave his prosthetics plant at 4.15pm to get a lift up north for a 7.45pm kick off and have only a sandwich on the way.

Even when Vardy moved slightly up the ladder from Stocksbridge to Halifax Town, his regimen remained chaotic, he admits. 'If I had training [that evening], it was up at 7am, in for work, finish work at 4.15–4.30pm, straight in the car to meet up with the other lads and not getting home until 10 or 11pm. Then straight to bed,' Vardy says. 'It was dinner at the service station, whichever fast food shop was there. That is just how it was.'

At Fleetwood, where he went after Halifax and ripped through the

Conference, scoring 31 times in 36 games, he seems still to have lived . . . well, like a lad.

The house the club found for him was full of pizza boxes and the odd vodka bottle when he moved out. Vardy credits his partner, Becky, whom he met in early 2014, for improving his habits, and having kids around now means earlier bed times and keeping the packets of sweets and crisps locked away.

But still. When you see those bony sprints it feels as surreal as seven seasons at Bracken Moor. Vardy's stats: top speed in training of 9.6m per second, fastest player measured in the Premier League in 2015–16, an exceedingly high average of more than 500m sprinted in every game. And great stamina numbers too.

It was De Laet who introduced Vardy to *snus* and his now-favourite Jupiler beer. And more. 'Vardy was in Belgium last summer,' De Laet said. 'He ate French Fries two days in a row. The first day with stew sauce, mayonnaise and a *boulet*, a giant mince ball. He liked it so much that he ordered three pieces of meat again, without fries.

'He always asks my parents if they can't bring along some of the typical meat they serve in the "Frituur" [Belgian chip van]. Vards can eat whatever he wants: pizza, crisps, two bags of candy, he doesn't gain any weight. I wish I could say the same.'

• • •

After an international break, on November 21, the speed freak – or maybe just freak – went to Newcastle and the country was watching now. In the first half he had chances and executed well but defenders and the home goalkeeper, Rob Elliot, were blocking everything. Then, at the start of stoppage time, began a Leicester counterattack.

Ranieri waffles a lot of stuff about his players that make great headlines. One is a description of his forward line as 'my RAF'. He wants Vardy, Mahrez, Albrighton, Okazaki, Schlupp if he is playing, to fly forward in each other's slipstream in a coordinated blitz. But now came a breakaway that was almost Arsenal-style: delicate and refined.

Drinkwater, having a terrific match, found Ulloa, who found Albrighton, who returned the ball and Ulloa nudged it into the box and Vardy took it on. Veering inside Moussa Sissoko he cocked a leg and jackknifed his body, foot cutting across the ball. The shot skimmed unanswerably inside Elliot's near post. Ten games, scored in every single one: he was level with the great van Nistelrooy.

In the second half, after Vardy hit the bar and fluffed a one-on-one with Elliot, Ranieri figured there had been enough spindly miracles for one day and retired him. Ulloa, with a decisive header, and Okazaki, close in, fleshed out the victory: Okazaki scored after he missed the ball when it looped off Elliot but it then landed for him to knock home with his knee, and he ran off laughing.

Vardy was 'very, very close' to not playing at all, Ranieri revealed, because of a hip injury. Vardy put an eleventh-hour recovery down to Dave Rennie's physiotherapy – and the dreaded cryotherapy tomb. No, he did not feel pressure to beat van Nistelrooy's record he said. Ranieri gushed: 'Jamie is an easy boy. He don't think about expectation. He's a worker for the team. I love him.'

Enough to indulge him. In the dressing room, with affectionate mocking, Ranieri called Vardy to stand in front of the group and make a speech. So Vardy turned the tables. 'Obviously I couldn't have done any of it without you,' he began, 'and the gaffer's just said he'll put beers on for the plane.'

Ranieri's eyebrows twitched. He had promised nothing of the sort. But he did get his boys one bottle each at Newcastle Airport. Chat shit get beers, Vardy possibly mused.

Bethel:

> He got kicked, knocked down and didn't respond for many years but then we went to the Northern Premier [League] Premier [Division]. And you get much more ruthless bastards in that division. Some very good players, and guys who have been around a bit. And I think it got to the stage where Vardy flipped a bit. He started with the two-footed tackle. He'd be dribbling along, left side, see them coming, show them the ball and then – boom – go over the top of it. There were no malice. It was his way of looking after himself. But he had four sendings-off that year and three times it was when Sheffield United were watching. That put them off.
>
> The tag? He were so good that we just wanted him to play. The thing was to try and get a goal early on, then get him off and put on a defender. And he usually got that goal and it worked. Where he lived in Sheffield was rougher than here but it wasn't rough. He had a group of mates and had one bit of trouble – but he hit someone that was hitting someone else.
>
> Look, all the players at this club go in bar after [with the

directors]. You spend long drives on buses. If he were a prat, I'd tell you. Because my philosophy is that you send the truth down the middle, then you can't get caught out. A spade's a spade. But Vardy wasn't a prat. I feel a lot of affection for him. We don't have time for bullshit here.

Vardy played for six months, at Stocksbridge, wearing an electronic prison tag. When he was 20, in 2007, there was a confrontation outside a pub where Vardy says he 'stuck up and defended' a deaf friend who had been mocked for his disability. Vardy 'did not start the fight, but he ended it,' Bethel put it.

So, for afternoon games, Vardy would kick off, try and get his goal, play the first half or maybe 60 minutes – then sprint off and jump in a car. The driver, often his mum, who worked in a law office, would speed him home to make his 6pm curfew.

In the build-up to the Manchester United game, on Saturday November 28, van Nistelrooy posted a good luck message on Instagram. You can score so long as United (van Nistelrooy's old club) win, he wrote. Van Nistelrooy, a master lurker and poacher, based his game on advice by his first coach, Foppe de Haan, who told him to 'be like a lion, waiting in the sun.'

Vardy was more the swooping bird. When United began at the King Power the first inroads Vardy made were through his vicious harrying of their defenders, especially youngster Paddy McNair. The King Power was raucous that day, baying for big-club blood, willing special things to happen. It got its wishes.

On 24 minutes, United took a corner. Schmeichel caught. With vision a midfielder would have been proud of, he spotted space for Fuchs and made ground before hurling the ball into Fuchs' path. Fuchs was in unfamiliar territory for him, the right flank, but he sped away with purpose. Vardy was ahead, coming in from the left.

Vardy moved across United's back line before slowing into a pocket of space and then pointed where he wanted the ball. Fuchs fed it there brilliantly, even throwing his eyes in the wrong direction for a 'no-look' pass. And then there was Vardy, alone against David de Gea.

He eyeballed the goalkeeper and looked straight into the face of history. And then, with zero doubt, smacked the shot in. He finished running when he reached Fuchs and leapt on the Austrian and the team leapt on both of them.

This was the first moment, covering Leicester, that you felt a twinge: maybe something was happening beyond the small-club-on-a-good-run scenario. Just maybe, this might lead somewhere other than the inevitable slump, the seventh place and the wan 'well-done' that usually came the plucky small club's way.

Morgan admits something stirred that day and reckons 'you can never take that achievement away from Vards. I am not sure if it will ever be done again – well, in my playing career anyway or while I am watching football.' United scrapped back for a point, Bastian Schweinsteiger scoring at a corner, but it was telling that their manager, Louis van Gaal, had altered his formation to combat Leicester's breaks (a 'big club' changing for a 'small team'!) and it had not even worked. Telling, too, that Ranieri and his players were disappointed just to draw.

They were beginning to expect a lot of themselves. In the dressing room Vardy was presented with a shirt signed by the players. And in Los Angeles a film producer, Englishman Adrian Butchart, reached for his phone. Butchart started watching the game over breakfast and got hooked. 'There's a movie in this,' he thought. Bethel should play himself, the inimitable sod.

Bethel:

> Vardy goes to Crewe for a start-off. It was January 2009, his first year in the first team. Me and [manager] Gary Marrow take him and, if I think right, he has two spells there on trial, with a break, because there was snow in between. The Crewe No.2, who had seen him nine times and arranged the trial, said not taking Vardy was the biggest mistake Crewe ever made . . . and he said that before all this happened. Because Jamie could kick it with both feet, he could head it and no one could catch him. Fearless.

Bethel still has Crewe's letter, signed by their chief scout, thanking Stocksbridge for their 'professionalism and co-operation' but saying no thanks to Vardy. There had been a communication breakdown. Dario Gradi, their legendary coach, had been sidelined and Gudjon Thordarson was managing the team.

Thordarson, an Icelander, had been testing out Vardy as a right winger 'and that was a waste of space. He can't play right side. No good at all,' says Bethel, grimacing at the thought. Thordarson 'was a nice bloke' but said he needed an experienced right winger. 'Well, Jamie wasn't experienced and he wasn't a right winger, so that were that.'

They are used to good things ending in the valley. Bethel used to look down at the town from his home near Bracken Moor and see all the glowing fires from the furnaces and the smoke drifting up to the hills, but that is all gone. And Vardy: several clubs, including Rotherham, chanced their arm with cheaper offers but Halifax beat off the competition to strike a £15,000 deal.

Halifax were in the same seventh tier as Stocksbridge, but far bigger, and after scoring there Vardy went to Fleetwood – for a Conference record £150,000 – a season later. Southampton sniffed. Peterborough, Crystal Palace and Cardiff bid. But it was Leicester who got him, making Vardy the first £1m non-League player. The fee seemed an amazing gamble – given the previous record was £200,000.

Nigel Pearson, who lives locally, knew about Vardy from his Stocksbridge days and Steve Walsh was sold after seeing Fleetwood play Mansfield in the FA Cup, where Vardy gave an ex-Premier League defender, Alex Baptiste, the runaround. Andy Pilley, Fleetwood's chairman, suspected Vardy could go high, real high, and insisted Leicester agree a 25 per cent sell-on clause. Another believer was John Morris, Vardy's sparky agent, who signed Vardy up at Halifax, telling the scrawny non-league lad that one day he would play for England.

And so, in June, there Vardy was. An England scorer at Euro 2016. Wayne Rooney's son wanted a Vardy shirt. In a group interview, Vardy told journalists his life now felt as if he had suddenly climbed aboard 'a travellator' that was moving him ever forwards. He did not want to fall back off it.

In the room, close up, you noticed the sleek, black, expensive watch and diamond-laden wedding band. But, those apart, how unchanged he looked from the unafraid factory lad in Bethel's pictures: spiked hair, buttoned polo shirt, skinny, wiry arms, and grey-blue eyes that darted.

• • •

King Power Stadium, countdown to kick-off. On the pitch the lone brass player sounds the haunting *Post Horn Gallop*. Spines shiver. Air is gulped into opposition lungs. Game time, time to begin the chase. From the big screen burning fox eyes peer down. The stadium walls say #Fearless.

Manchester United came. They had the ball. Leicester had the game. Leicester penned them in, were under their feet, off their shoulder, always on their toes. Advantages United assumed they had were snatched away.

Those fans were in United's ears and the corners of their eyes. Vardy, circling, scanning. Schmeichel caught the ball, rolled it to Fuchs and – *blink* – that ball was in their box.

And Vardy. The question: could this guy, this Conference footballer, really take one of the great goal records?

Head down.

Clean hit.

He beat De Gea.

And ran off.

'All mine,' he screamed. 'All fucking mine.'

9 RIYAD

Stop. *Juste une seconde.* No rush, *tranquille.* Let us chill. Let's have a laugh, dress down into something relaxed.

Jogging bottoms, T-shirt, hoodie? Good. A kickabout? Now you're talking. Let's saunter into Riyad Mahrez's world.

But first:

Drawing with Manchester United took Leicester one point closer to the magic 40. Reaching this total and, with it, likely safety from relegation, remained the prime objective for the season. After celebrating Vardy's record-breaking, Ranieri reminded journalists of the fact. 40 points: Leicester now had 29.

Manchester City replaced them at the top of the Premier League, beating Southampton with Kevin De Bruyne starring. De Bruyne cost them £55m: 55 Vardys. Or 157 of Mahrez. City were the bookmakers' favourites to claim the title, Arsenal, United and Tottenham next. Leicester, even then, were 100-1.

Chelsea, though fourteenth and lurching into a fresh crisis every game – it seemed – were still shorter odds, at 80-1.

It had not been the Premier League people expected and nor would it continue that way. But at that point, the end of November, just swapping Chelsea and Leicester's positions in the table would have ended any disorientation.

Chelsea, after fourteen matches, had lost seven times – more than in the entirety of José Mourinho's first two seasons back in England – and Mourinho's whole brand, that of ruthless winner, seemed to be falling away completely. His team were getting beaten – and well beaten sometimes – at places like Everton, Crystal Palace, West Ham, Stoke. Southampton and Liverpool humiliated them at home. Mourinho's press conferences were getting ever wobblier and more bizarre. And he was doing odd things – like sending on substitutes, then withdrawing them 25 minutes later. A shambles. Soap opera.

When Leicester hold their future title reunions will they send an invite to Eden Hazard? He made two big interventions on their account.

The second – his goal versus Tottenham – finished the title race off. But did the first start it, its whole unlikely nature? In Chelsea's opening match at Swansea, in stoppage time, he called for treatment and Chelsea's doctor, Eva Carneiro, ran on. Mourinho erupted.

The rules meant Hazard would now have to leave the field, reducing Chelsea to nine players – Thibaut Courtois had been sent off – and Mourinho vented his fury upon Carneiro. On the Monday she was removed from her duties, sparking a saga deeply destabilising to Mourinho and his club.

City had also been strange. They started with five wins, not even conceding a goal in those matches, but soon started dropping points.

An ageing team with a hangdog manager (Manuel Pellegrini) whose future was in doubt: sometimes it looked like losing would not greatly affect their stars' £10m-per-season, Louis Vuitton lives.

Liverpool were transitioning after sacking Brendan Rodgers as manager and importing Jürgen Klopp. Manchester United seemed to be going places but slowly. Results (then) were improving under Louis van Gaal – although their football could be as static and telegraphed as the neat little diagrams on Van Gaal's clipboard.

Arsenal and Tottenham did look contenders, albeit Arsenal still couldn't shake a long-held habit of losing in unlikely ways – such as at West Brom, where they led, had 73 per cent possession and missed a penalty . . . when Santi Cazorla fell over in his run-up. Spurs, after starting the season so sluggishly, were emerging – their ferocious work ethic, their young players and young manager, Mauricio Pochettino, impressive.

So, on 1 December the top of the table was this:

1. Manchester City — 29 points (+16 goal difference)
2. Leicester City — 29 points (+8)
3. Manchester United — 28 points (+10)
4. Arsenal — 27 points (+12)
5. Tottenham — 25 points (+13)
6. Liverpool — 23 points (+3)

• • •

Chris Waddle. A slope-shouldered king of English wingers, old World Cup star and legend of Marseille. When Waddle was interviewed for a popular podcast series by the journalist Graham Hunter, in the summer of 2015, he picked out Mahrez as a dark horse to follow.

'I'll tell you who could be a big star,' he predicted. 'Mahrez at Leicester. If they can keep hold of him . . . because this guy, he's, what, 24? He's got better, he's felt more at home in English football. And if you put him in Barcelona's team he wouldn't look out of place. Because they'll get the ball to him, he'll go one on one and "whaay" watch this. By the end of the season [big clubs] will want him. Oh, it will be big bucks.'

Chris Waddle, king of English wingers. Nobody listened.

Pat Nevin. Scottish wing master. Early in 2015–16 Pat went to broadcasters he works for and asked if he could do a special on 'the most skilful player in the Premier League'. The player was Riyad Mahrez. Pat didn't get to make his programme.

Pat Nevin, Scottish wing master. Nobody listened.

Fourteen games into the season, Vardy was top Premier League scorer by four clear goals and beginning to gain acceptance from the wider football public. But the form of his sidekick was still seen as a flash in the pan.

Mahrez was high in the charts, both for scoring and assists, and no attacking partnership had been involved in more goals than Vardy–Mahrez. Vardy travelled to Swansea needing another strike to tie Jimmy Dunne's 1932 all-time top-flight record and it was not to be – but Leicester became top scorers in the Premier League and it was thanks to the genius that the men who know their stuff, Waddle and Nevin, picked out.

Mahrez, though it was unseasonably warm in South Wales (12°C), wore black gloves and a short-sleeved shirt. Attire-wise and football-wise, he does his own thing. His first goal had him giggling: Albrighton's corner looped over Ulloa and bounced in off his body. His second goal had him glancing at the linesman, for when Kanté found him and he calmly beat Łukasz Fabiański he was actually offside.

His third goal had him sucking his thumb. It was a silken finish, from Vardy's pass, on another break. His celebration was a tribute to his daughter, Inaya, who had been born five weeks before.

It was the first time a player from North Africa or the Middle East had scored three times in a Premier League game and Mahrez, in his post-match interview, spoke humbly of 'the first hat-trick in my little career, my small career'.

But so little was humble about his talents. His second goal: yes, good fortune with the offside, but how about the touch he took before scoring? As Kanté's pass dropped he had stunned the ball with the most casual nudge of the outside of his left boot.

And the third goal: his movement and relaxedness. So liquidly he had arrived on the overlap and so loosely he had just knocked the ball in. Some players, like Vardy, are staccato. But Mahrez is a continuous, alluring note.

In that post-match interview at Swansea, all grins and pride, he was far more animated than is habitual. Mahrez's usual mode, before the camera, is sighs and shrugs, pauses and drawling. His voice stays low and his eyes downturned. Sometimes it feels almost as if the TV crew has surprised him on the doorstep in his pyjamas.

Ah, Mahrez's world. Maybe we should start with that relaxedness and his pre-match routine. 'Riyad?' King chuckles. 'For a 3pm (away) kick-off, we have a meal about 11.30am in the hotel, a meeting at maybe 12.50pm. Then leave, say, 1pm. Riyad will come down, maybe 11.30am, eat some Nutella on toast, a bowl of cereal . . . and then go back to bed again.'

Home games? 'They have beds in the stadium. And he will go back there. Maybe not to sleep, but he will lie on his bed with the laptop.'

And maybe, yes, to snooze, sometimes. 'He wakes up in the changing room,' King smiles, 'does a few tricks, a few "around-the-worlds", a few keepie-uppies . . . then goes out and does his thing.'

Mahrez. Meet Mr-Take-It-Easy Genius.

● ● ●

St Matthew's, inner city Leicester. Approaching 2pm, after Friday prayer. From the mosques they come. Tall men, short men, stout men and thin. Bearded elders. Boys, racing down the pavement – or what's left of the pavement given all the cars parked up on the kerbs.

They wear their *jellabiya* and *khamiis* robes. They wear their *koofiyad* caps. Some head back towards work, some chat and laugh on the street corners. The coffee houses – Kilamanjaro Café, Daar Dheere Café, Island Dishes Coffee Shop – are filling up. No one walks alone and this is what you notice most, the sociability: how in this moment nobody is without a family member, colleague or friend.

St Matthew's is one of England's very poorest spots. But in community, in life, in warmth, in fight, it seems very, very rich.

Ten years ago certain indices identified St Matthew's as the most income-deprived area in Europe. But it is coming up and Taylor Road, the local primary school, is Oftsed 1 – marked 'outstanding' for the performance, behaviour and attendance rate of local kids.

The 'paradox of the ghetto', some educationalists call it: how children from the poorest areas sometimes do the best. It happens when the families behind them are strong and instil ambition. St Matthew's is an immigrant place, home to many of the 10,000 Somalis who came to Leicester, fleeing civil war, fifteen or sixteen years ago.

It is a small estate. Four- and five-storey maisonette flats are adorned by satellite dishes and fabrics airing on their balcony railings. Where Christow Street meets Everest Court, two boys kick a lightweight blue football and the skill is avoiding the bin bags.

And it is here that one of the best footballers in the world's richest sporting competitions could be found hanging out. Mahrez comes here, to hard-bitten St Matthew's, for haircuts, to see friends and pray at the mosque.

'Mahrez? Mahrez is a normal guy,' Alli says. Alli is in his early twenties and hanging with his mate Saeed on the corner of Britannia Street. They have been to mosque and Saeed is dressed traditionally, but Alli? Black-and-gold tracksuit, leather jacket. 'You can speak to Mahrez,' he continues. 'Yes, you see him here often. He's fast, isn't he?'

He is indeed.

Especially when you play with him, adds Alli.

What?

'Yes, one of Mahrez's best friends would bring him along,' he explains. Turns out that there is a regular indoor game in a sports hall up in Highfields, another immigrant-dominated, deprived area. Mahrez came and played in it now and then, with all the guys, before his Leicester career got so serious.

A superstar knocking a ball around a community centre, trying to avoid tackles from the guys on the poorest estate? Alli and Saeed are not sure Leicester knew about the extra football in which their stellar acquaintance indulged. But maybe Leicester did, and did not mind. For Riyad, he just goes out and does his thing.

● ● ●

Riyad Mahrez was born to Ahmed, an Algerian electrical engineer, who fixed traffic lights, and Halima, a Moroccan, who both came to France and settled in Sarcelles – one of the vast *banlieues* (suburban estates) around the rim of Paris. There was Wahid, his older brother and, after his parents split up, stepsisters, Dounya and Innes.

He grew up with a ball at his feet (or his knee, his neck, or shoulder, or chest – for he would juggle it all day and his control was extraordinary). He was 15 when a longstanding heart condition took Ahmed, at the age of just 54. Mahrez has always felt Algerian on account of his dad and said there was never any question of him playing for France. And it tickles him, now, as a Leicester player, that the Algeria national team are *Les Fennecs* – the Desert Foxes.

He got more serious about football, he admits, after his father's death. He played for the local team, AAS Sarcelles, up through the age groups with certain brilliance. And yet every year when the scouts came it was the bigger, more muscled, kids that they took away to the professional academies. There is now even less on him than Vardy. So when friends and peers left for Paris Saint-Germain, Toulouse, Guingamp . . . Riyad was always left back in the *banlieue*.

An agent put him on a plane to Scotland – and that ended farcically. At St Mirren, in Paisley, he played four reserve friendlies and scored seven goals, but the club made him wait. There was snow, and the uncertainty drove him mad. One day he skipped his hotel, racing down the back stairs so the landlady would not spot him. He jumped on a bus, reached Glasgow airport and took the first plane home. At last, at 18, Mahrez was offered a trial in France. But it was at Quimper – a medieval town, stuck right out on the arm of Brittany, 300 miles away. The train cost 160 euros. Halima, a cleaner, had to really scrape the money together. 'Don't worry, I'll pay you back,' Riyad said. One of his proudest moments was enabling his mum to give up her cleaning work.

Quimper liked him. But they were a tiny team. Sorry, no cash, no contract, they said. Mahrez called his mother, heaving with tears and Quimper's president, seeing the kid's hunger, found enough to stump up for a modest deal.

In Quimper, he lived 'like a student'. He shared a flat with Mathias Pogba – brother of Paul – living on takeaways, bad meats, fries. The apartment was so messy he was ashamed to invite his mum to come and stay and there were long months between his visits home to Sarcelles.

And here was another thing. Pogba told him that though he was good he just had to build himself up, but though he tried, no amount of eating could make him gain weight. And even though the coaches tried to teach him not just tactics but also about simple disciplines that he struggled with – like staying onside – his game didn't change. There are no offsides in street games, Mahrez points out, and 'dribble, dribble, dribble' was his default.

And his nature stayed the same. He moved to Le Havre, where there was more tactical development and a gym programme to finally improve his physique, but entering 2014, at nearly 23, Mahrez remained, essentially, a shrugging waif whom coaches doubted. Le Havre were only in Ligue 2 yet, with his contract in its final months, were silent on the subject of an extension. 'Is he a five-a-side player?' was the view in France. The offer from Leicester, that January, was pretty much his only option.

How did they know about him? Steve Walsh, back in July 2012, watched Le Havre play Arles-Avignon with another forward in mind, Ryan Mendes. But Mendes 'didn't tick enough boxes'. However, the shrugging artist playing on the other wing had caught his eye. Walsh put David Mills on the case and Mills' further scouting reports were positive.

Rob Mackenzie crunched the numbers, unearthing great indicators in some of the offbeat stats categories Leicester use (like positive attacking actions attempted). Walsh 'met the boy and kind of bonded with him'. The transfer was made for €450,000 (then £350,000). De Bruyne's was 157 times as much.

• • •

At Swansea, on December 5, Ranieri lost the plot. He surprised the players. They went in at half-time 2–0 up and expected smiles but their manager ranted in the dressing room. 'He does [that] when we are not expecting it,' says Albrighton. 'Away to Swansea: The lads were thinking, "Oh brilliant, we are winning 2–0, let's keep doing what we are doing." Then, all of a sudden, five minutes later, he has walked in and raised his voice and said it wasn't good enough.'

This is the Ranieri who, despite the nice guy image, once strode into Jimmy Floyd Hasselbaink's hotel room and ripped out the TV connection to stop the striker staying up. Who once threatened to imprison his Chelsea players in their dressing room and make them watch tapes of all their mistakes unless a performance did not improve in the second half.

Signor Nice has his moments. 'He told us we needed to be compact,' Albrighton recalls. 'And in the second half we were, and we got the clean sheet.'

Chelsea at home on December 14 were next for Leicester, a game with a personal dimension for Ranieri. It was Mourinho who took his job at Stamford Bridge in 2004 and who, when they were rivals in Italy, mocked him mercilessly. 'He's almost 70 years old and hasn't won anything,' Mourinho goaded in 2008. And then there was the 'Far Away Islands' comment.

Ranieri had always ignored the bait and, perhaps because of his own troubles, Mourinho was conciliatory and complimentary in the build-up. Hazard was supposed to be the Premier League's wing star but he had not even scored yet, while Mahrez (like Vardy) had now been directly involved in exactly 50 per cent of Leicester's league-high 32 goals.

For Chelsea, John Terry and Diego Costa were recalled as Mourinho fielded the best XI he could in a last bid to save himself. Ranieri went for what was beginning to seem his first-choice team: Schmeichel; Simpson, Morgan, Huth, Fuchs; Kanté, Drinkwater; Mahrez, Ulloa, Albrighton; Vardy.

After half an hour Hazard was holding his hip and wanted off after a collision with Vardy. Mourinho threw a look to the heavens that confirmed his exasperation with his Belgian, and made the substitution.

Mahrez was bewitching. Setting off on one of those dribbles when, even as he twists and stops, the ball sticks, almost seeming part of his foot, he turned César Azpilicueta, Jon Obi Mikel and Terry inside out. Accepting Ulloa's pass, he dinked in a delicious cross and Vardy converted ravenously.

Now, over the course of 2015–16, Leicester scored 68 league goals, plenty of beauties among them. Storming headers, fabulous volleys, overhead kicks, works of counterattacking art. Yet two goals lived on a higher plane. The other, a Vardy jaw-dropper, we will come to. The first one Mahrez scored now.

Let us pause to consider César Azpilicueta. If the Premier League has seen a more earnest, improved, effortful full back in the last decade, then suggestions please. And here is how Mahrez buried César.

A cross from Albrighton, out of the floodlights, through the dark sky, floated his way. And Mahrez stunned it, moving the ball to Azpilicueta's right.

Azpilicueta went right.

Mahrez moved the other way and made to strike but he was faking . . . and merely waggled his foot above the ball.

Azpilicueta went left and into a half-crouched blocking position.

Mahrez did not shoot and instead went to Azpilicueta's right again.

Azpilicueta went right.

Now Mahrez went to Azpilicueta's left.

Azpilicueta went left.

Now Mahrez shifted right.

Azpilicueta shifted right.

Mahrez went to shoot.

Now, where is Azpilicueta? Not sure by now? Well, nor was he. The Spaniard went half-down into another blocking position, but he no longer had his bearings, and his body was actually in place to stop very little. Through the lovely, clean avenue of space his trickery had opened up, Mahrez spun the most gorgeous shot into Courtois' net. Azpilicueta threw his arms up and sank to his knees in utter anguish, like a man watching his winning lottery ticket float off in the breeze.

Loïc Rémy headed in but 2–1 was the final score. Leicester went top. Abramovich axed Mourinho.

King played most of the match, typically energetic, having replaced an injured Drinkwater after 17 minutes. He picks the win as a watershed. 'We had started the season well,' he explains. 'But Chelsea showed it wasn't just a "good start". We were actually a good team.

'We had beaten a top side for the first time. They were last year's champions. We won 2–1 but it could have been 4–1. We played really well. And before there was the hype of Mourinho versus Ranieri. The gaffer was brilliant, dealing with it and taking pressure off the lads.'

• • •

Take the train from Gare Du Nord, *Ligne H*, and head north-east through Saint Denis. You can be there in fifteen minutes. Another world. Somewhere North Africa, West Africa, Arabia, Israel, the Caribbean, and most of Asia meet. In streets between brutalist Le Corbusier flats, a community throngs.

Sarcelles.

Take it in: the robes, the headwear, the cars, the concrete, the sheer *community*. And then it is obvious. When Mahrez parks his 4x4 on the kerb in St Matthew's and throws open his door, he is finding himself a little Sarcelles, a home from home.

He has two regular barbers, actually. One, Suez Canal Hairstylz, St Matthew's, Leicester: where Naji, in a white *jubba* robe on which he has printed the club badge, gives him a cut. The other is Nassim Coiffure, Sarcelles, where the eponymous owner, his lifelong friend, jokes he's 'the Cristiano Ronaldo' of this *banlieue*. Mahrez's mother and aunts and friends are all still here – and so is he, when time allows.

There are 110 different nationalities in Sarcelles (population 60,000). It is the most multicultural town in France, just as Leicester is the most multicultural one in England. And there are sports halls too, sports halls galore. It was there the unique style of a laidback genius was formed.

'He was always playing football in the gyms, he moved from pitch to pitch in the area. He was even on the rugby pitches perfecting his technique and he went out there every evening, often on his own,' says Boubakar Coulibaly, treasurer and general manager of AAS Sarcelles.

He has known Riyad since he was six years old and there was less of him than a pin. Sometimes Mahrez would stay out in those gyms until 4am. Sometimes he would play on concrete, or on Astroturf when it was snowing. The knocks you take in street football, said Mahrez, 'I had pizzas for thighs.'

All that practice honed the supernatural manipulation of the ball he commands. The French use one of their football sayings for him: 'his foot is a hand'.

'I see him on TV now, dribbling, exactly the same as when he was tiny,' Boubakar says, smiling. 'Riyad was too skinny for the academies. He preferred to play than eat! But, then again, if he had gone to an academy they would have trained it all out of him.

'His style is very much a Sarcelles thing. Many play that way around here, dribbling all the time. It's street football. Or, if it is raining, in the gyms. One of the favourite games for kids is to have a goalkeeper, a ball, and it is everyone against everyone. Everyone is marking you! Another is called "qualification" – ten players, one goalkeeper, you've got to dribble the ball past everyone. That's the way Riyad improved.'

Sounds like the football of South America, that of Lionel Messi and Luis Suárez when they were small. 'Yes, exactly like that,' Boubakar says. 'No one passes the ball very much! In France, the best dribblers are ones who grew up in *Les Quartiers* [estates].'

Boubakar is a laughing, friendly, guy – but razor sharp about football. He can reel off, year by year, the winners and finalists of European Cups, going way back – that kind of stuff. He always knew Riyad's talent was gigantic, as did Mohamed, his brother, one of Riyad's first coaches. 'He's as good as Messi,' Mohamed told all the scouts who kept ignoring his protégé. 'Now they're gutted!' Boubakar chortles.

And the love of napping – was Riyad always like that? Boubakar is really chuckling now. 'Yes, yes, exactly. Always the same, chilled out and then came to play football. Sleeps after the game. Relaxes, hangs out with friends, never in fights, never went to clubs.

'Guys from here went to watch him last winter. He told them to come back to his house and then they all played PlayStation, even though he'd just scored two goals in the Premier League.'

You look around Sarcelles. It is obvious, when it comes to planning decisions, this place is bottom of the pile. When the jumbos take off from nearby Charles de Gaulle airport they are not routed over the pretty towns of Picardie to the north, they are sent south and Sarcelles' way. Overhead, as Boubakar bids goodbye outside the clubhouse of AAS, loom jet after thundering jet.

And when the French national grid needed to find somewhere to place its network of power lines, the giant pylons marched right this way, right through the centre of Sarcelles. The community does get challenged and there were riots here, described as anti-Semitic, in 2014, when a Palestine demo spiralled out of hand.

But, like St Matthew's, Sarcelles spawns a ghetto paradox. AAS, a multi-sports club, have an extraordinary set-up, with 5,000 current athletes, 950 of them footballers. This place has spawned Olympians, tennis stars, rugby internationals – and more than twenty footballers currently at French club academies. Wahid Mahrez still plays here.

But there was only ever one Riyad. He visits when in town, coaches the kids, gives out footballs, offers Leicester kit, watches games. The mayor is giving him a civic medal and AAS are opening a pitch bearing his name – but he still does *maman*'s shopping when he's back. He is so normal, says Boubakar. So relaxed.

• • •

When his agent suggested Leicester, 'I thought it was a rugby club, honestly!' Mahrez told *L'Équipe*. And in his first game, when a substitute at Leeds, 'I stayed on the bench. Better I didn't play ... it was ... intense. I would have got myself killed, for sure!'

He fancies himself as a joker. Like a dressing room Jamel Debbouze, he says. Debbouze is a French-Moroccan comic, with a cheeky, street-guy shtick. Mahrez likes to talk in *verlan*: a witty *banlieue* slang that involves inverting the syllables of words and creating puns.

Mahrez disclosed to *L'Équipe* that he ribs Ranieri. 'I tell him he's old fashioned and laugh at his shoes but, even if he smiles, he'll talk football. He says, "Oh, oh, focus on the match!" He likes to tell us, "Be smart, you are Foxes."

'He organises mini-matches where you're allowed a maximum three touches except one player who is "free" [ie not on either team]. We take it in turns. I say: "Eh, Boss, I haven't had a go at being the free player." I always want to be the free player, the one who can improvise.'

Ranieri and the example of teammates finally got him embracing defending. 'At Leicester, the guys will battle for every ball,' Mahrez told *L'Équipe*. 'When you see them doing this you can but give your all.'

And his manager? 'Riyad is our light,' said Ranieri post-Swansea. 'When he switches on, Leicester change colour.'

• • •

Last game before Christmas: December 19, Everton away. A win would leave Ranieri's team top over the festive period – historically an indicator of who will be champions. Goodison Park, though, was somewhere they had not won at in thirty years. Wasilewski started; a day for strong men, and in lashing rain, Mahrez wore his gloves and short sleeves again.

Romelu Lukaku, close in, and Kevin Mirallas, turning, scored Everton's goals. But these were in vain: the home side were always chasing the game. Leicester were so sharp across the sodden ground, so determined – and the partisan stadium did not intimidate them.

Shinji Okazaki's strike was Leicester's best. King, seamlessly replacing Drinkwater again, closed down Seamus Coleman, won possession, and fed Vardy, whose pass Okazaki controlled with his right, before finishing with his left. That was Leicester's third.

The first two goals in their 3–2 victory were Mahrez penalties. For the first, there was a stuttering run-up and a precise, side-footed strike. For the second he sent Tim Howard the wrong way. That was 13 goals for the season – as many as Mahrez had previously scored in the entirety of his league career.

So, top at Christmas. In 11 of 23 previous Premier League seasons, the side top at Christmas won the title. Ranieri was still talking about 40 points – he now had 38 – but did promise Leicester would not stop there. 'Why can't we continue to run, run, run. We are like Forrest Gump. Leicester is Forrest Gump,' he said.

Such guff is a gift for the media. The Christmas presents Ranieri gave his players were too. At the end of a team meeting at Belvoir Drive, Ranieri handed round little boxes. Inside was a brass bell engraved with each player's name – a joke, because of Ranieri's way of jolting slackers in training by shouting 'dilly-ding, dilly-dong'.

Says King, 'Mine's still in my locker, to be fair. You sometimes hear them ringing around but most lads keep them in their lockers.' Mahrez? You could try and jolt him with Big Ben but you suspect he would just shrug, slope on and continue just doing his thing.

Leicester is indeed his home from home, says Gregory Dakad, an agent who assists him. 'Riyad took some persuading to come, and stayed an extra week at Le Havre to play a "big game" against Metz. But once he got here he realised Leicester play a big game every week. "Why did I wait?" Riyad always says,' Dakad smiles.

He could not let Rita pass by. He said he was never into girls, just football, before, but their romance was whirlwind. Very soon after meeting Rita, they were planning a wedding and married in a small Muslim ceremony in a private hall in Leicester in summer 2015. Inaya arrived soon after, and by next spring Rita was pregnant again.

Mahrez eats better – well, he eats – now, because of Rita, he says. Not far from St Matthew's is a favourite restaurant of his, on London Road, a Turkish grill. And yet, although he is 5ft10in, he still weighs less than ten stone: he makes Vardy look like Wasilewski and is even lighter than tiny Kanté. And you can see why: the forearms, glimpsed between the gloves and sleeves, at Everton, looked like pipe cleaners. The legs the same.

He is another who, physically, bucks convention. The burly Premier League is not supposed to welcome waifs. And yet, as Leicester pressed on, bucking convention every week, it became harder to remember those old so-called rules.

And also, if you can glue a ball to your toes and move with supple control, maybe a zero physique becomes advantageous; you slip like a willow of smoke between defenders. And if – let's cut the floweriness now – you are simply as damn talented as Mahrez, then maybe, as Chris Waddle suggested, you can play on any stage.

He wants to be the best, say friends, his dream is to play for Barcelona one day. The academies missed him and Kanté, and Vardy – *L'Équipe* said to Mahrez that it was as if they were exacting revenge on behalf of the '*pied nus*'.

The *pied nus*. It means street guys, guys who play in dust, on concrete, in gym halls, without fancy boots: literally 'the barefoot ones'.

'We were not trained up to become professional football players,' Mahrez agreed. 'We can play with a certain insouciance. I laugh about it with N'Golo. It's unbelievable, our story.'

Pied nus.

'I like that image,' Mahrez had smiled.

10 THE OUTLIER

Last question, Robert. Same one that is being asked of all the guys.

This Leicester team ... you know ... you're going to be meeting for reunion dinners in ten, twenty, thirty years' time. You'll be on some pitch together, waving to the fans, when you are old.

What do you think?

Isn't that nice?

How do you feel about these guys?

'I am not going to give you some inspirational quote now,' Robert Huth says. 'This is work. It always has been. I have worked at other clubs. And that ... is pretty much it.'

Oh.

'As I said, we don't have a great socialising. It's just work. We get to work. We get on. In ten years' time we will get invited to the club dinners.

I am sure we *will* get on, have a few beers and talk about it. If I woke up tomorrow [and all this was over], it will be fine.'

Not quite the party line.

'Outlier' (noun). A person or thing situated away or detached from the main body or system (Oxford English Dictionary). Yup, that sounds like Leicester. But if Leicester stood apart, offering a different view of football then, inside the club, a tall, wry, square-jawed German stood apart with a different take too. Robert Huth, 'Huthy', meet The Outlier's Outlier. But roll that poster back up. Put that nice slogan away. After all, we're not doing inspirational quotes and hugs.

• • •

Huth hails from Berlin but doubts that has anything to do with his drollness. Then again, when the word 'Berliner' also means 'jam-filled donut', then maybe you have to know how to raise eyebrows and thinly smile. He is a giant. Strapping is the word for it. Six foot three and more than 14 stones of long, lean, stony muscle.

He is great company. Intelligent, unsentimental, analytical. At Stoke he was Jonathan Walters' friend and that is no surprise. Walters is another who does not think like your average player. With both, you enter the room and leave bullshit at the door.

Huthy did not even set out to be in this business. Or, as he puts it, 'I didn't really want to go down that route of becoming a footballer.' *That route*. The wryness has started right there. Malcolm Gladwell, in his seminal book *Outliers* says we must study those contexts where people of different ability are formed. 'We've been looking at tall trees, and I think we should have been looking at the forest,' Gladwell argued. But Huth is just the giant, lone pine. Chuckling at the sycamores on the other hill.

Berlin probably does make better jammy pastries than footballers – generally anyway. The list of great players from Germany's capital and by far biggest city is thinner that it should be. Jérôme Boateng, Bayern Munich's World Cup-winning centre-half, is a rare example of a Berlin football son reaching the top.

Huth's first pro club was not, like Boateng's, Hertha, Berlin's established powerhouse. Instead it was Union, the cult team, traditionally favoured by a boho and creative set. But Huth will not look to that for meaning either. 'I think they were in the third division anyway, and I was too young to even make that decision,' he shrugs, on joining Union aged 15.

In any case the place he really started was a little suburban team from Biesdorf, a leafy fringe of old East Berlin (the Wall came down when Huth was five). Fortuna Biesdorf, they are called, and when Leicester won the title its players honoured Huth with a 'Fish & Chips Party' back at the Fortuna clubhouse.

They billed it exactly like that, by the way, not using German but English – 'Fish & Chips Party' – presumably for ironic effect. Huth among such guys? Yes. Now we are getting somewhere.

'I was quite good at judo and at other sports when I was younger. So it was only when I went to Chelsea that I thought this [being a footballer] is actually pretty good. Before that, I went to a sports school in Berlin. Did rowing, football, handball. The whole spectrum really. But never thought . . . my life was never set up like that.

'You speak with a ten-year-old now and ask what they want to be, they say: "I want to be a footballer.' That was never my attitude,' Huth says. 'Only when I went to Chelsea and it got a bit more professional did I really put all my eggs in one basket.'

'Football was never going to be my career path – Union Berlin wasn't even a professional team. It was semi-pro. The set-up wasn't that great. But then I moved to Chelsea and saw all the players there I had seen on TV, so I got slightly more and more involved.'

That is not exactly how the Biesdorf guys remember him. 'Robert can be very proud of his career,' said chairman Steve Hornig. 'He was very determined and ambitious, while we preferred to watch girls.' But, no matter, Huth proved pretty successful once he put his mind to it at Stamford Bridge. He was 17 when he made his Chelsea debut – under Ranieri, who wrote in *Proud Man Walking* about this 'plucky and enthusiastic' German kid who 'I am sure will have a future in the team.'

He kind of did and he kind of didn't, it transpired.

Huth had four full seasons at Chelsea but the most relied upon he got was in 2003–04, Ranieri's last season, when he made eight league starts. Mourinho used him for a while then moved him on to Middlesbrough and he even struggled there: not in terms of ability but through persistent injuries.

He had a stint for Germany but, despite establishing cult popularity, got discarded. Joachim Löw ditched the big man after succeeding Jürgen Klinsmann as coach and pushing the *Nationalmannschaft* towards an ever more skilful, touchy-feely, 'new Germany' vibe. Huth was Huth, in contrast to all of that. Uncompromising. No Entry. *They Shall Not Pass*.

At Stoke, where they loved him, he really fitted in and the fans chose an obvious nickname: The Berlin Wall.

As Club Player of the Year when Stoke got to the FA Cup final in 2011, Huth would have happily stayed. But a knee injury in late 2013 changed things, as did the switch from Tony Pulis to the more idealistic style of Mark Hughes. By January 2015, Huth was falling out of the picture and he was 30, with 18 months on his contract. Stoke would be open to cashing in on him.

The strategy was to loan him out in the January transfer window then look for a permanent sale in the summer. Though Leicester were reasonably convenient in terms of geography, it was not he who made the decision to go there. 'I felt like I could still play. I just didn't have the chance at Stoke,' says Huth, 'and Stoke made their mind up that I was only going to go to Leicester. There wasn't another option.

'There was other interest but because we had played Leicester twice in the season already, and they were bottom of the league, there was no threat to Stoke of improving a team that might go ahead of them in the table. So it was very much a case of: "You are going to Leicester for six months and then see how you go." Obviously, I have never looked back.'

• • •

The day after the 3–0 win at Swansea, the Leicester players had a bash. Not a Fish & Chips Party, but a full-blown lads' extravaganza in Copenhagen to celebrate Christmas early.

Schmeichel was the organiser. Everyone wore fancy dress. Drinkwater,

King, Matty James and Ben Hamer – four close buddies – were Teenage Mutant Ninja Turtles. Schmeichel was Mr Incredible.

Vardy was White Power Ranger. Schlupp was Black Power Ranger. Okazaki was Bananaman. De Laet was Assassins Creed.

Simpson was Spiderman and Morgan was Pac-Man and didn't stint on the costume: the yellow head was so enormous it barely squeezes into some of the pictures taken that day. The trip was not shy Kanté's scene. And Mahrez was also absent, staying at home with his new baby.

The players made the most of it, the majority remaining in a nightclub until 4.30am: champagne and £1,000 bottles of vodka were involved. Vardy, reportedly, challenged one clubber to a pull-ups competition and opened beer bottles with his teeth.

It was another example of, against all his Italian instincts, Ranieri trusting the group – and being rewarded, for Leicester's ensuing performance, versus Chelsea, was their best of the season to date.

Ranieri loves Christmas Day itself, writing in *Proud Man Walking* about all the treats Rosanna makes and the Italian card games he organises. But, though Claudia and the grandchildren visited, there was little scope for enjoying this one because of the fixture calendar. A difficult away trip awaited on Boxing Day – to Anfield, to meet Liverpool and Klopp.

Leicester were not really at it: maybe the only game of the season where that was the case. Philippe Coutinho was getting space outside their box to try shots. Adam Lallana hit the side netting. Emre Can went close. Divock Origi went close.

Vardy looped a header over the bar and Mahrez floated through to test Simon Mignolet but, really, all the pressure was Liverpool's. Huth got fed up with Lallana's feints and turns and pulled him down and, from the free kick, Liverpool built a prolonged attack that ended with Christian Benteke volleying in.

Three points and 1–0 to Liverpool, who finished with 26 goal attempts. Leicester had not quite been themselves, losing challenges and wasting breaks. Over a glass afterwards, Klopp said to Ranieri: 'Come on, go for it, why shouldn't Leicester be champions?' Ranieri silenced him. 'Stop talking. There's no chance'.

On 29 December, Manchester City visited the King Power and Leicester were much better, injecting into their game the old grit and breakaway adventure. City were terrific too and Huth and Morgan needed to be imposing. Schmeichel made several good saves, from Kevin De Bruyne, Nicolás Otamendi and Raheem Sterling (twice).

Mahrez curled close, after a weaving, soft-footed, dribble. Vardy knocked a shot over, Kanté one just past the post and Albrighton could not quite reach Fuchs' excellent cross. Though goalless, a stalemate, Leicester fans enjoyed it. 'WE ARE STAYING UP!' was the ironic slogan on the clappers laid out for them and when Agüero was substituted, they sang, 'You're just a shit Jamie Vardy.'

Bournemouth, at home on January 2, was concerning though. Leicester's first game in 2016 was against a rookie Premier League side that managed not a single attempt on target and won just one corner. Leicester, for once, had the majority of possession; Bournemouth's captain, Simon Francis, was even sent off. But: another nil–nil. Mahrez missed a penalty, won by Vardy. His body language was unusually timid and his shot at an easy height for Artur Boruc to save.

Vardy and Morgan missed sitters and, indeed, the better opportunities went Bournemouth's way. Arsenal won at Newcastle and Leicester lost top spot. 'Questions will be asked: Is this the start of the decline expected by many?' mused the BBC.

Ranieri, judging well the need for some positivity, even of the fabricated sort, hailed a 'fantastic effort' and promised 'champagne for my players' – for Leicester had now reached those magic 40 points.

But questions *were* being asked. Having scored in 18 consecutive league matches, having been top scorers in the country, suddenly Leicester were goalless in three. Vardy had not hit the net since scoring against Chelsea four games ago. And Mahrez was, out of nowhere, missing penalties.

And their rivals seemed to be cranking it up. Manchester United's form was in tailspin but Manchester City were ascendant – now just one point behind Leicester after a good win at Watford. Tottenham were marching too. Three straight victories and then a comeback draw at Everton had shot them into the top four. Bad time to lose momentum.

For Leicester, a hero was required.

• • •

Huth dressed as Batman when the players went to Copenhagen. 'Perfect for him,' said Simpson. And, well, Huth's Twitter profile did say: 'Centre-half for @LCFC. A small head for such a strong jaw line.'

He is probably the funniest of all footballers on social media.

He tweets seldom but, when he does, nearly always has the Twitterverse sniggering and furiously retweeting. Sending up his own famously rugged style his post, upon signing permanently in June 2015, was 'Now the sexy football show rolls into Leicester!!'

When Leicester made certain of a top three finish in late April his line was 'Yes! Champions League guaranteed! Better start practicing [sic] my Rabonas.'

They are mates, but maybe you would say his humour is . . . *subtler* . . . than that of Fuchs, who smashes eggs on teammates' heads or goes, wait for it, 'Drinking Water with Danny DRINKWATER' in zany social media videos (hey guys, No Fuchs Given!)

He and Huth did shoot one such film together entitled, 'Red Ass Challenge'. In it, Huth does not flinch even slightly when Fuchs batters the ball towards his body. 'Pain is weakness,' Huth, deadpan, observes.

Of course Germans buck the cliché Brits have about their supposed lack of humour. Comedians like Henning Wehn are very funny. But Huth thinks his personality is hybrid anyway. 'I am half English, certainly,' he says. 'I have been here for such a long time. I am very much involved in the whole culture. My wife is English. My kids [two sons] were born here. So it is very split. Clearly, I am German, I will forever be . . . but I have been here so long.'

He is just one who does not like easy definitions. Football does not determine who he is. 'I feel very much this is a job. I don't think: "Oh this is great." I see it as a genuine job, obviously one which I like doing, but everything I do from day to day is because I have training and I have a game to work towards. It's not,' he says sarcastically, '"Oh mate, do you want a game of football? Brilliant!"

'It's my job. Hopefully I'll do it for another few years. And then see how we go from there.'

So, Huthy is the antithesis of Riyad: not just in physique and playing style but spirit too. While one is carefree, the other is acutely conscious of the impersonal business football can be.

Huth signed for Pearson, just before he was sacked. And then the first signing Ranieri pushed for was a rival centre-half, Yohan Benalouane. So Huth prepared for the worst. '[Pearson] would have been one of the main reasons I came here and, you know, sometimes a manager comes in and doesn't fancy you or brings a different player. And [Ranieri] brought in Yohan.

'You did think, "Here we go again,"' says Huth, 'but it worked out.' Something every player in the squad appreciated was how Ranieri had no favourites and always seemed to pick teams on merit. He may, as his marquee signing, have recruited Gökhan Inler – yet because Drinkwater showed better form, Drinkwater played. The same occurred in terms of Huth staying in ahead of Benalouane.

● ● ●

Tottenham at White Hart Lane came next, in the FA Cup, and Ranieri rested all his regulars except for Kanté and Schmeichel, who started, and Okazaki and Albrighton, who came off the bench. Against a stronger Spurs side it turned out to be a good day: Demarai Gray, Leicester's highly rated new 19-year-old, a £3m signing from Birmingham, caught the eye and Wasilewski and Okazaki turned the game around after Christian Eriksen's early goal. Spurs needed a late Harry Kane penalty for the draw and to avoid embarrassment.

Ranieri was far more bothered about the league than cups and Leicester's next match was also at White Hart Lane – this time in the Premier League. It was no classic but it proved critical. One of those games that is instrumental without being symphonic.

Ranieri started with the selection that may well come to be celebrated as 'Leicester's title-winning XI' at those reunions in years to come. Yet, despite this, 20 games into the season, Ranieri had only used it as a starting XI just the once – against Manchester United.

With Vardy back from groin surgery and Okazaki winning his chance thanks to his cup goal, Ranieri went: Schmeichel; Simpson, Morgan, Huth, Fuchs; Kanté, Drinkwater; Mahrez, Okazaki, Albrighton; Vardy.

It was Wednesday evening, 13 January.

Leicester had now gone 291 minutes of league football without scoring. Okazaki at Everton, almost a month ago, was their last league scorer. Who could step up and break that barren sequence?

Not Vardy, who went clear only for Hugo Lloris to save at his feet. Not Drinkwater, despite a terrific volleyed attempt. And not Kanté or Okazaki, who both missed on an early break. Not Mahrez, who was quiet. Not Ulloa, who came on as substitute but could not penetrate.

Spurs were profligate too and Schmeichel, with utter brilliance, denied Kane. His save – standing up, spreading his body, batting the close-range shot away with an outstretched arm – was a stop (and maybe they will allow the comparison for once) in the vintage style of his dad.

So, another 0–0 seemed likely and by the 83rd minute Leicester had reached well beyond six hours without a goal. But Kanté's persistence won a corner. Fuchs' delivery was wonderful, and the ball arced under the floodlights right to Huth, who was level with the penalty spot on the far side of the box.

'A good old-fashioned, plant your feet, arch your back and get your neck muscles going header from Huth. Look at the power. Boof,' was Alan Shearer's description. Shearer, a former master with his head, was right to drool.

Standing planted, putting his head right through the sweet spot, Huth sent the ball arcing though the floodlit air.

Over Toby Alderweireld it went.

Over Dele Alli.

Over Ben Davies.

Over Harry Kane.

Over Jan Vertonghen.

Over Lloris and Lamela, who was trying to guard the post.

And in it dropped. Batman delivered from the skies.

'I just remember thinking, "Where is everyone?!" Everyone was on the floor. I literally had so much time. You know, sometimes, when you have so much time . . . well, maybe it was going to hit the top of my head and go straight out,' Huth smiles. 'I had too *much* time. But I caught it perfect. I was buzzing with that.'

Leicester closed out for 1–0 and won at White Hart Lane for the first time since 1999. With 43 points now, they had surpassed their points total from the whole 2014–15 season after just 21 games.

● ● ●

Huth returned to Twitter and his line was retweeted nine thousand times. 'It's not often having a square shaped head comes in useful!!' he wrote.

Commonly, his posts involve sending himself up. He is fond of jokes about his throwback 'old-school defending', his ruthlessness.

This is how he goes about it in the penalty box: like a nightclub doorman bouncing queue-jumpers and invaders on their backsides.

Playing Manchester City, he had simply picked up Nicolás Otamendi, supposedly City's tough guy. Jon Walters' son wants to be Huth and Walters posted a picture of his boy in a Huth shirt with the hashtag #youwill-meettheoccasionalforearm.

Leicester's defending was another convention-busting thing about them.

Modern playing ideas about building play from the back have led to a generation of centre-halves who are smooth athletes, good on the ball but moderate in the key defensive arts, as Sunderland manager David Moyes notes. Defenders who can supposedly 'play football' go for fortunes. Otamendi cost City £38m and had a very mediocre season. Defenders who can, um, 'only defend'? £3m is all Leicester paid for Huth.

'I enjoyed watching Huth and Morgan every week, defenders who do the old-fashioned basics,' says Moyes. 'And was it any coincidence that Leicester had an Italian coach?'

• • •

Yes, you will meet an occasional forearm playing Huth. You might also encounter the odd limb dug into your body, perhaps the odd grab or even hair-pull. They say he and Morgan have a similar mentality and Big Wes agrees, initially: 'You don't want anyone to have an easy job when they're playing against you,' he says, considering the proposition.

But then Wes smiles. 'I don't think I am as bad as him. If he has to get nasty ... he will get nasty,' he adds.

Huth also grins when asked: Robert, your approach to defending, can you just sum it up? 'Not always legal ...' he replies.

On the edge? 'On the edge. The way I see it ... I mean, you could score a header, but you couldn't score a header if I am this far away from you. Or if I have your hand. That is the way I see it. So, I try to make it as difficult as I possibly can.

'Everyone can be a good footballer ... but not under pressure, not when I am trying to kick you, to nick the ball off you, pull you, punch you. Well, not punch you. But you see some players and they are like, "What? Is he tackling *me*?" Well, yes, because it's a game and I want to win.

'What I try and do is not always possible, clearly. There are better players out there, who can turn and score a goal. But I try to stop that.'

So it is the simple idea that whatever happens in this game, against me it won't be comfortable?

'Yeah. I always look across the line and go, "I am going to get it today [sic]. If you score a goal then it's fair enough. But not because I wasn't doing my job." That's the way I see it.'

Troy Deeney, Watford's big, robust forward, has his own way of putting it.

'Huth is the toughest opponent I have faced. He is horrible to play against, in the most complimentary way. He heads it, he kicks it, and he kicks you – anything – he does not care, as long as the ball does not go in.'

• • •

Toughness comes in different forms. On January 16 at Villa Park, Okazaki scored his fifth goal for Leicester and all five had come away from home – tribute to a strong mentality. He followed in when Vardy, with a nimble leap and fine outstep touch, lobbed Mark Bunn. Bunn scrambled back and clawed the ball off his line but Okazaki slotted the rebound in.

But it was a mixed day for Huth, who made an error with a back pass and was well-beaten in a one v one by Jordan Ayew. He tried the dark arts and got away with an arm round Libor Kozák's head. His block on an Ayew overhead kick – simply hurling himself face-first at the ball – was typically brave. Yet, with 15 minutes left, Rudi Gestede, Villa's own heavyweight, held him off and equalised Okazaki's goal. Leicester had to settle for a draw again – and Mahrez missed another spot kick, sidefooting straight at Bunn.

Arsenal returned to the top the following afternoon and Leicester fell back to second.

A week later Huth's old gang from Stoke then came to the King Power. In an interview, the club's internet channel tried to get him going about the 'banter' he might anticipate with Walters and co., but he stonewalled: 'It's just another game.' He does not go on the pitch for laughs, even against friends.

The game proved full of treats. First, Drinkwater broke an unusual duck. Leicester, though second-top Premier League scorers, were the only side not to have scored from outside the box. This was thrown at them but, when you thought about, the stat was actually testament to the precision of their attacking.

In any case, Drinkwater put them 1–0 up by driving in off Marc Wilson from outside the area.

Then Drinkwater played a pass to savour, managing to find Vardy with a weighted volley despite being off balance. Vardy rounded Jack Butland and caressed in a finish from a difficult angle. 2–0. Vardy's first goal for ten hours and 17 minutes of playing.

Then Mahrez embarrassed Philipp Wollscheid to such an extent that you thought Wollscheid would perhaps be dialling Azpilicueta's number to form a self-help group. Mahrez showed Wollscheid the ball and then – boof – suddenly it was through Wollscheid's legs for a nutmeg. Mahrez mishit his shot but Ulloa diverted the ball in for 3–0.

The fans at the King Power made something beautiful by lighting the torches on their smartphones and raising them, to fill the stands with constellations. But Huth produced the very best sight. There was not a #NoFuchsGiven challenge that could produce such comedy.

Leicester had a free kick, right on the edge of Stoke's area and Fuchs and Drinkwater were over it – but so was Huth, unexpectedly. Fuchs stepped away and Drinkwater went to run across it and maybe Huth misunderstood: whatever, his shot, slicing almost horizontally, like a novice golf shot, produced hysterics. Even the referee, Mike Dean, laughed. Though Ranieri was stony.

'Nine times out of ten they creep inside the top corner . . . Honestly ;) #throwin' was Huth's arid tweet.

• • •

Steve Walsh picks Huth as one of his highlight Leicester signings, one that shows recruitment is not just about the undiscovered gems but sometimes recognising obvious old diamonds right under everyone's nose. Anyone could have bid for Huth but it was Leicester who snatched a Germany World Cup player, with proven mentality, imposing physique, and a track record of popularity in every dressing room he has graced. For just £3m.

£38m for Otamendi? £42m for Eliaquim Mangala? £20m for Baba Rahman? Especially with defenders, you wonder what big clubs have been thinking in the market recently. Cost of Leicester's whole back four? About £6m. 'Everybody knows some players. [With Huth] we knew what we were getting, so it was seeing that he would fit in to what we want to do,' said Walsh. 'That is another skill.'

Fellow players will tell you how crucial the addition of Huth and the creation of his partnership with Morgan was to Leicester's success. His 2015 arrival helped spark the survival miracle. He walked into Belvoir Drive and found something 'a bit odd', and something that really suited him. A vibe. 'The place was so happy even though people were fighting relegation, so relaxed,' he says.

'When I came here, I thought "These guys are really *good*." We lost 2–1 to Arsenal [in 2014–15] but we were *good*. It's easy to sometimes go, "We're bottom of the league, losing at Arsenal, let's just get to 90 minutes." But not here. Not in any game.

'Since I've been here, no matter the score – we could be 4–0 up at Newcastle and it wouldn't change – everyone was exactly the same. We would still go 90 minutes and be chasing down clearances.'

Ranieri remarked the difference between Leicester and other teams he has managed is that most teams play with seven or eight players really 'at it' on any given day: Leicester always play with 11, plus the guys on the bench, plus the crowd, Ranieri said.

'I agree with that, yeah,' Huth nods. 'I know that every game it will be a nine or 10 attitude from the players. Sometimes, when I was at Stoke, I didn't know what I would get from certain players. Are they going to play today? But here we all turn up.'

The contrast with Chelsea, when he was part of title-winning squads (in 2004–05 and 2005–06) was 'with Chelsea [success] was expected. They had big guys. Go through Leicester's team and we don't have a £200,000-a-week player like Chelsea did. Or Didier Drogba for £24m. Damien Duff. Glen Johnson. No: "Right, we are here, we are the richest club, we've spent money and now we going to win the league."

'Here we are very much the opposite story. You think about it: I didn't get a game last year. Drinky didn't get a game last year. [Nor did] Simmo [Simpson]. It shouldn't work. But it does. For some reason.'

It shouldn't work but it does. Huth had been struggling with that thought from the moment he stepped through the gates of Belvoir Drive. 'It's really weird,' he says. 'At Stoke we had a really great social life. With the wives. We would usually go out for dinner. Often the lads would meet up. Here, we don't really do it.

'I mean ... I don't live in Leicester. A few do. Mahrez does. But the majority don't really live in Leicester. I don't really know their wives. We don't have them over for dinner. Or nights out. Nothing like that. Yet when we step into this training ground, it just works. It's really weird, I have tried to explain it. Normally when you need to be strong as a group, you need a sort of social life. But here, nothing.'

And so speaks the outlier. The Outlier's Outlier. Other players wax about the social life they enjoy, like Copenhagen at Christmas, the owners' parties, the odd birthday on the town (like Fuchs threw in April). Or trips, like when Morgan arranged tickets for a Carl Froch fight in Manchester.

But Huth thinks the social diary is fine but nothing special. He really likes these guys but, well, you won't be getting any inspirational quotes from him.

What is special about Leicester, he says, is that chemistry that occurs when they all go to work – not when they go to the bar. Like Albrighton, he mentions pulling through the entrance of Belvoir Drive at 9.30am and something falling into place.

• • •

The Outlier's Outlier. A while back, during a break period between games, a fellow journalist and friend was travelling north from London by train. It was a late Sunday morning, the train was packed, and he sat on the floor between the carriages and by the toilets.

He was recovering from a night out in the capital. Across from him was a guy who looked to be doing the same, who had a plastic off-licence bag and a can of lager. Normal-looking guy. No airs. Cap pulled down. Except he was tall and had a certain jaw. No way would you ever see a millionaire footballer like that. Strange, then, that the friend could have sworn it was Robert Huth.

NG

11

Three Big Tests.

Three Big Tests. And, what? 'There'll come a time when they have to look at us as genuine contenders,' Wes Morgan sighed when the 'tests' theory was put to him.

Entering February, newspapers were discussing a UK teacher shortage. But here was another crisis. Sceptics were running perilously low on ways to write off Leicester.

By hammering Stoke, Leicester went top of the league again and thereby disproved yet another doubters' theory – that once the little team lost first place they just would not have the belief to claw all the way back to the summit.

Well, the blow of being knocked down the table by their scoreless post-Christmas run had very much been dealt with: a month on, Leicester had clambered back above Arsenal and Manchester City and goals were coming freely again.

Other predictions of a Leicester downfall had been:

wait until December, small sides always blow up then
they haven't played anybody yet: the big teams will sort them
they won't cope if Vardy stops scoring
they will lose their best players in the January transfer window
injuries will come and they don't have the squad to cope.

None of these cataclysms had come to pass.

While the injury situation could not be taken for granted, there was clearly something special about Leicester's sports science, with Ranieri able to choose from a full squad almost every week – in marked contrast to Arsène Wenger and Manuel Pellegrini.

While there had been interest in several players, particularly Vardy, the Srivaddhanaprabhas were owners looking to invest, not cash in, and no one left in January; indeed Leicester added Gray and Daniel Amartey to the squad.

December had been navigated. Leicester had now played all the big sides, including Tottenham twice. A long, long run (617 minutes) without Vardy scoring passed and, you know what, the team was still standing and the King Power had not crumbled into the sea.

So the naysayers were almost out of ways to say nay. Then along came 'Three Big Tests'.

Leicester's next games were Liverpool at home, Manchester City away, Arsenal away. All in the space of twelve days: a horrible run. Surely Leicester would not be top after that. This was when, at Belvoir Drive, sitting down in the classroom sometimes also used for press one-on-ones, Wes sighed and said, look, the players just did not listen to that kind of stuff.

'We're keeping ourselves in a bubble, focusing on what we can cause from inside,' he said. And, listen, in these three games and in the rest of the campaign, remember this: 'Whatever happens, our spirit won't be broken.'

Those fixtures *were* tests though. Big ones. Leicester were going to need Vardy and Mahrez. And their little man.

● ● ●

There are four keys to N'Golo Kanté: his intelligence, his running, his size and his silence, and people are struck first by the latter two. So small that when he arrived at Belvoir Drive he was mistakenly sent towards the schoolboy players, he was also so quiet that engaging with the new teammate proved an impossible challenge.

'I tried to speak with him in French,' laughs King, 'I have a small, very small, bit of French. When Riyad arrived we already had [French striker] Anthony Knockaert in the dressing room and if I spoke to Riyad, and it wasn't a proper sentence, they would know what I was trying to say and you'd get somewhere: "you mean this" and so on.

'With NG, I'd say something and he would reply – briefly – in French and that would be the conversation finished. I wouldn't have a clue what he had said. I think he liked that.'

Kanté's old flatmate when they played for Boulogne, Faycal Nini, recalls him as prone to going hours on end without saying a single word. N'Golo was '*gentil*' but you could not draw him out. Even on faith; though an observant Muslim, N'Golo preferred not to 'bother' housemates by talking about it. Meals and car journeys passed silently.

At JS Suresnes, Kanté's first club, it was the same. He joined when he was nine 'but until the age of 17 or 18, the boy just didn't speak. He was so quiet, so unassuming,' says Pierre Ville, Suresnes' former head. Ville is talking by phone from the little Stade Maurice Hubert, in Rueil-Malmaison, near Versailles on the north-west edge of Paris and home of the tiny suburban club.

Ville is a white-haired man with kind eyes and a caring tone whose greatest pride about N'Golo is not his playing career, but rather that Suresnes could help the retiring boy pass his *BTS* exams. A *BTS*, a *Brevet de Technicien Supérieur*, is a vocational degree and Kanté's was in financial management. After gaining it at 19, according to Ville, his confidence changed. 'He said, "I'm going to be a professional footballer. Now I can do it,"' the old club *dirigeant* (chief) recalls.

Over time, Ville reveals, it did prove possible to work out Kanté's nature – and in the silence there was nuance. 'You might think he's shy, but this isn't the right word. Because he knew what he wanted,' Ville says. 'It was simply that he didn't talk.

'I'd rather not say he was an introvert, just someone who didn't speak a lot. But it wasn't shyness. If you're shy you're a bit submissive, if you see what I mean? You lack daring.

'With him, we spoke and he'd look at us with those big eyes, so we weren't sure if he'd heard us or if he'd understood the message. But over the following days and weeks, in his behaviour, in his attitude, we realised he was putting it all into practice. So he *had* listened. He was unassuming but the messages we passed on, he was processing them all and taking in anything he could use.'

And, at Suresnes, at Boulogne, at his next club Caen, a particular set of instincts and emotions developed towards this gentle but determined little soul. Alain Caveglia, Caen's director of football, coined the defining phrase. N'Golo, he said, was *'le petit chou-chou du vestiaire'*.

Vestiaire equals dressing room. A *chou-chou* is a pet. And that seems to have been Kanté, wherever he has played: the one in the group who, intuitively, others both love and want to protect. And now it was like that at Leicester. 'The nicest guy you are ever going to meet,' King says.

Ville explains it. 'Those of us who spent time with him: we know, with his personality and the way he carries himself, how much affection he inspires in others. Here, he was the dressing room favourite. When he was young, he was half the size of the others yet on the field gave everything.'

Half the size. An expression, right?

Well, not really. Not in Kanté's case. Ville emails some photos and when you click them open, you gawp. *Half the size* ... Ville was barely exaggerating. He is diminutive now but, *wow*, as a child ... In the team-line-ups and celebration shots there he is – reaching literally to no higher than the lower ribs of the bigger kids.

One particular picture actually breaks your heart a little. You check the date: Kanté is about 12. The rest of his team are lifting a trophy. And it is *his* trophy – for player of the tournament.

Little N'Golo is smiling but he is so tiny that just to see what is going on he has had to retreat a step and stand apart from the group.

And, in their excitement, the other kids appear to have forgotten he is there, because they all have their backs to him.

A small boy, who did not speak, unable to be in the thick of happiness he created. Ach, it is just a picture. But sometimes it is hard not to see metaphors.

'What you need to know about N'Golo is that until he turned 15 he was tiny, absolutely tiny,' Ville continues. 'But the thing is, his size was never a problem when he played. That's why he was so exceptional. He never stopped running. He covered so much ground, and very intelligently.'

Ranieri joked about Kanté having 'batteries in his shorts' and Steve Walsh came up with a good one, a gag he liked to repeat. At Leicester we always play three in midfield, said Walsh, 'Drinkwater in the middle and Kanté either side.' Says Ville, 'We already knew [about his energy]. In the local area, there's a cross-country race for primary school children, for five- to eight-year-olds. And when he arrived, we already knew he had won that race.

'It's a cross-country race involving all the schools and about 400 children take part. And N'Golo, all 1.20m [four feet] of him, won it.'

Mahrez faced Kanté in Ligue 2, when Le Havre met Caen in the feisty *derby de Normandie* at Caen's Stade Michel d'Ornano in September 2013 (Walsh had a scout there, naturally). And Mahrez warned Leicester's guys when Kanté signed: 'Riyad said, "This guy runs everywhere, wait and see,"'

King recalls. 'But NG was so small. We were looking, thinking, "How is *he* going to be in the Premier League? This is a big physical league."

'But he has flipped that on its head, hasn't he?'

● ● ●

Against Stoke, but not unusually, Kanté's numbers were ridiculous: 11.24km covered, five tackles, five interceptions, eleven recoveries of possession. One of the hidden bits of cleverness about recruiting him was the club he came from, Caen, had been almost a French mirror image of Leicester in 2014–15.

A promoted team, Caen were bottom of Ligue 1 at the halfway stage and saved themselves with an amazing rally. What is more, their playing style was intense, fast and based on counterattacks: indeed the cerebral DeepXG football analytics site ranked the highest-paced teams in Europe (in terms of going from one end to the other) as Leicester (4th), Villarreal (3rd), Darmstadt (2nd) and . . . Caen (1st).

Another thought-through transfer: Kanté was fitting seamlessly into a set-up very like the one from which he came. Liverpool were about to experience just how scorching a Leicester counter could be.

It was Tuesday night, under lights, 2 February. Liverpool's form was hard to make sense of. Klopp's new high-intensity game brought outstanding wins at Chelsea, Manchester City and Southampton – where they won 6–1. And yet Liverpool had just conceded four goals at Norwich and so far in 2016, every single team Liverpool met scored with their first on-target shot.

Ranieri went with the now-favourite line-up: Schmeichel; Simpson, Morgan, Huth, Fuchs; Kanté, Drinkwater; Mahrez, Okazaki, Albrighton; Vardy.

And . . . oh my.

Nigel Pearson's insight about Vardy is that while other strikers have pace, Vardy has '*aggressive* pace'. He charges straight at goal, he accelerates into tackles, he explodes onto the ball. In other words, it is speed allied with belligerence. And that is such a potent mix.

Vardy was about to demonstrate his aggressive pace against Liverpool but in fact the phrase would characterise Leicester's entire performance that heady evening. Boosted by a ten-day rest since their last game (thanks to being out of the FA Cup), Ranieri's players simply unleashed themselves.

There was Drinkwater, storming Liverpool's captain, Jordan Henderson, to rip away possession and launch a counterattack. There was Mahrez, snapping onto loose balls and smacking vicious first-time shots. There was Okazaki, rushing up and down the centre of the pitch, never stopping. There was Fuchs overlapping. There were Huth and Morgan thudding into foes.

There was Schmeichel, with one of his point-blank, stiff-arm saves. And, after an hour of this relentlessness, there was an extraordinary Leicester goal, the only strike to surpass Mahrez's versus Chelsea.

First: *Emre Can dribbles into Leicester's box but is hunted by Morgan, Simpson and Drinkwater. Drinkwater takes the ball. Unbelievable collective defending.*

Then: *Drinkwater's clearance loops high off Can and – how does Mahrez do this? – he buys time by heading it back upwards then finds space with a divine touch as it lands. He doesn't look up. He knows where Vardy is. He strikes a long, arcing pass – 50 yards – that drops right in front of Vardy. Incredible artistry.*

Now: *Vardy is perfectly set and throws his foot right through the sweet spot of the dropping ball. From 25 yards, over Simon Mignolet it arches and in. A strike beyond superlatives.*

Remember, Leicester had only scored one goal all season from outside the box before then. Vardy, in more than 120 matches for the club, had never converted from outside the area. And Roy Hodgson, the England manager, was watching. And Butchart, the Hollywood producer, was in Vardy's private box.

Vardy, eh? In his goalmouth Schmeichel tutted.

'To be fair, he had actually been trying . . . I don't exactly know why, but (Vardy) had been trying to take early shots all week. In training. I remember having a little pop at him: "What are you doing?"' Schmiechel recalls.

'Typical he did that. He had not hit a single one all week in training and then it comes to the game and just hits a beauty. What a goal. Well, he is the guy for the big stage.'

And weren't Leicester turning out similar? They upped their game further. Okazaki, fouled by Mamadou Sakho, really should have had a penalty. But then Sakho was blitzed when Mahrez arrived upon him, Vardy thrust a boot in and Okazaki took the ball.

Mahrez overlapped to create space, Okazaki shot; a mishit, it rolled Vardy's way. Coolly, he lob-wedged a little shot over Mignolet. What group attacking. Ranieri's RAF.

Vardy explained that he had been watching Mignolet leave his line all match and that, though he struck his volley 'blind' he knew the keeper would be stranded. 'Unbelievable. Unbelievable. Unbelievable. Amazing, amazing,' Ranieri gushed.

Within a few weeks, Vardy had a new contract, was negotiating a book deal and bought a £168,000 Bentley Continental GT with personalised plate. There came confirmation his movie would start production in September. And a Leicester fan got 5,000 signatures on a petition for his girlfriend to name their baby daughter 'Vardy'.

Vardymania was at its peak. But not all heroes are extroverts.

● ● ●

The Rash. That's what Drinkwater called his partner. The Rash: Those poor opponents, Kanté gets everywhere. Against Liverpool he had made six interceptions (the most in the game) and somehow, at 5ft6in, against a Liverpool midfield of six-footers like Can, he won four headers. A couple of weeks later Sir Alex Ferguson, speaking at a Cheltenham Festival lunch, called Kanté the best player in the Premier League 'by a long way'. Vardy T-shirts were more prevalent but discerning fans at the King Power wore a different one.

It said,

'Fact: 70% of the Earth's surface is covered by water, the other 30% by N'Golo Kanté.'

Some other Kanté 'facts' (according to the memes):

N'Golo Kanté decided to cycle home and accidentally won the Tour de France.

When N'Golo Kanté lost his virginity ... he won it back again.
The PFA Player of the Year awards are suspended. Kanté has just intercepted Mahrez's trophy.

If planet Earth was ever under threat from an asteroid, Kanté would intercept it (copyright Gary Lineker).

It was Kanté's very nature that encouraged these jokes. He did not do interviews. He did not advertise anything. Most people did not even know what his voice sounded like. They just saw, every time he played, the blur. All this made him nearly one-dimensional; like from a comic book.

And, in an era of players being 'global ambassadors' for blue chip companies, of having their own fragrances and clothing lines, was it not nice that one of the best in the Premier League was such a throwback?

'My main worry for him was the media, when they first started talking about him, because that's a hurdle the young players have to overcome,' says Pierre Ville. 'But he took it all in his stride. Some blow a fuse. He just says: "It's only football."'

Kanté came to Suresnes with two brothers who also became players there. His family is a big one, nine children in all to parents who arrived in France from Mali in 1980. Like Mahrez, Kanté's mother was a cleaner but Rueil Malmaison is no Sarcelles: Kanté's old apartment block, on Rue des Geraniums, looks much too smart.

But JS Suresnes are even lowlier than AAS Sarcelles: eighth-tier, amateur, with a small membership. Size is one obvious reason Kanté was not picked up, and with Leicester's three stars lies a theme that indicts youth scouting both in England in France: Vardy, Mahrez and Kanté were all overlooked for lack of stature at an early age.

Ville identifies another reason that seems just as damming. 'I'm not going to criticise the academies,' he says. 'You've got 14- and 15-year-old kids arriving from all over and the academy has to make a decision. But they saw N'Golo ... well, we knew that, for all his great qualities, he's not a spectacular player.

'He plays for the team. I took him to numerous trials. If he goes for a trial somewhere, he's never going to be the most eye-catching because whether he's being scouted or not, he'll always play the same way. Always with great tactical awareness, with discipline and with intelligence. For the team.'

So that was little N'Golo, saying nothing, smiling and not complaining, helping other boys succeed at his expense by selflessly making them look good in the try-out games.

When Boulogne eventually took a chance on Kanté it was only after a French 400m champion, the late Jean-Pierre Perrinelle and a Suresnes president, hustled them into letting him join their reserves. There, Kanté would get to training on a kids' scooter. He played in France's third tier.

Upon joining Caen, one league up, he traded in the scooter for a Renault Mégane. 'A second-hand car with miles on the clock,' Ville recalls. 'Even though he could have bought a Mercedes.'

For a time, after joining Leicester, Kanté lived in a very humble hotel on the edge of the St Matthew's estate – where he joined Mahrez as frequenter both of his barbers and his mosque. Kanté was *chou-chou*, especially to Mahrez. The Algerian, remembering how Knockaert had helped him settle in, made it his mission to aid his fellow Parisian the same way. Mahrez, at least, got close to 'NG'. 'He comes round to mine. We eat together. We play pool, too. He's shy,' Mahrez told *L'Équipe*.

Piotr Wojtyna, one of Kanté's old Suresnes coaches, still laughs at something. Before one summer break he told the kids, as a joke, 'Over the next two months I want you to do keepie-ups without dropping the ball – 50 on your left foot, then 50 on your right, then 50 on your head.' Of course just a few weeks later N'Golo reported back and quietly demonstrated he had learned the routine.

Obedience, feels Ville, has been both a blessing and curse. 'Listen,' he says proudly. 'You can watch all the videos of N'Golo, since he started playing. If you see one example of him arguing with the referee, or reacting aggressively after being caught by another player – just one example – then you have to send it to me. And I'll give you a thousand pounds for it. He must have only been booked just once in the whole ten years he spent with us.

'But it was also a flaw. His main flaw, since he was little and up 'til now. For it's still the case that he'll always back down in the face of others. He'll always respect orders and he'll never argue. He's there to play and only to play. To follow the instructions of his coach and to respect the referee. Watch the videos: when he gets caught he just gets back up and gets on with it. And just looks at the referee then gets on with it. Even when he could win a penalty.'

• • •

What on earth were Arsenal doing? From being top of the league, they started blowing games. The latest was a home draw versus Southampton when they had 22 shots but could not score. The previous match, their biggest of the season, versus Chelsea, they were led out not by a recognised captain but Theo Walcott – to celebrate Walcott completing ten years at the club. What, was this a testimonial match? They lost.

The Gunners, now winless in four, had slipped, leaving Manchester City as Leicester's closest challengers when the teams met at the Etihad Stadium on Saturday 6 February. The table was this:

1. Leicester — 50 points (+18 goal difference)
2. Manchester City — 47 points (+23)
3. Tottenham — 45 points (+25)
4. Arsenal — 45 points (+15)

All four teams had fourteen games left.

For eleven previous Premier League seasons, the side in first place at the start of February went on to be champions but Leicester were still third favourites according to the bookmakers. City were even money.

Then on February 2 something strange happened: almost as a throw-away at the end of his press conference Manuel Pellegrini, their manager, announced he was leaving – and the club confirmed Pep Guardiola would replace him. This created a strange dynamic for Leicester's visit, City's next home game. And what strange weather. On a torrential day in Manchester there were glowering, slate-grey, biblical skies.

And welcome to the apocalypse, Premier League.

Everything modern football believed about itself was razed in this match. *It's a squad game*. Well, for the fifth time in a row, Ranieri used the same XI and, with freshness, with fearlessness, that XI humiliated City.

It's about money. Mahrez was the superstar, yet he cost £350,000: what City had agreed to pay Guardiola every eight days.

It's about an elite of managers. Well, it was the day that proved Ranieri at 64, after sixteen jobs and seven moves of country, had suddenly found a home and a way to truly contend.

The fun and incredulity of a tweet from Leicester's official Twitter feed, with 30 minutes remaining, said it all: 'So, if you're just joining us . . . #lcfc are leading 3–0 and Robert Huth is on a hat-trick!'

Everyone worked forward, every man worked back. Ranieri's clever game plan involved testing City's weak flanks with quick switches of play. Leicester's energy was unanswerable and their focus unbreakable.

Schmeichel and the back four stood strong and Vardy, Albrighton and Okazaki were tireless but it was in two key departments that Leicester blew City away. First Mahrez: a mobile torture unit who went across the line, tormenting each defender – City had no answer to him. And Drinkwater and Kanté demolished City's midfield. Giant Yaya Touré could use Wasilewski as a toothpick when fully roused but Kanté, through some weird physics, kept outmuscling the big man. After 52 minutes the towel came in and Touré rumbled off for an early shower.

Huth got the first. Mahrez tricked Aleksandar Kolarov to win a free kick and deliver it low for Huth, outmanning Martín Demichelis to turn the ball in off the Argentine.

There was City pressure to absorb – Schmeichel was marvellous – and then Mahrez scored a memorable second.

Kanté led a breakaway, riding a challenge, cutting inside Fernandinho then finding Mahrez. Mahrez let Otamendi commit, then whisked the ball away. He feinted and stepped over the ball, sending poor Demichelis in the wrong direction: another for Azpilicueta's growing self-help group.

Facing Hart, Mahrez shaped to shoot right but drove it to the left of the keeper. Majestic. 3–0 arrived when Huth was again too strong for Demichelis and headed past Hart with precision. It finished 3–1 after Sergio Agüero brought City late consolation.

In the press room afterwards, Ranieri played things down but inside nursed an exciting new feeling: *we can do this*.

'I was so satisfied that day,' he reflected in May. 'It was an unbelievable performance. Maybe then, they started to believe in something. We can win, we can fight until the end. I never spoke about it after. If I get crazy I transmit the nerves.'

But he did not need to tell the players something big had happened.

'The City game was special. The way we did it, you know? We didn't dominate possession-wise but we dominated by being absolutely ruthless on the ball,' Schmeichel says. 'Riyad was phenomenal.'

King agrees. 'I think Man City was when everyone felt "hold on . . ."'

Says Morgan, 'Man City was the game. We'd done well up to that point. Yet people thought the wheels would come off. That was the performance that silenced people the most. That was the performance where I felt we saw how good we can be.'

And The Outlier? Even Huth is on board. 'The second goal, I was running off to the supporters and they were going: "What the fuck's going on here?! 3–0 up." And I'm, literally, "I don't know." I mean, it's Man City. You don't go there and be 3–0 up with 30 minutes to go.'

Mahrez's sublime strike was his first in more than 11 hours of play and made him the only player in the league into double figures for both goals and assists. Kanté's eight successful tackles at the Etihad made him the first in the Premier League to reach 100 successful tackles for the season.

Ranieri did say in December, after all, 'Look . . . there is Kanté and he recovers all the ball in this stadium and the other stadiums, everywhere!'

• • •

Kanté kept racking up stats. Soon he became the first Premier League player of the season to make 100 interceptions. He ended 2015–16 with the most tackles and interceptions in Europe's top five leagues – by a huge margin. But stats can be reductive.

Watch Kanté. Enjoy the footage. You are seeing more than just someone functional. You are watching a unique phenomenon. A one-man counterattack, a ball-winner who does not just win it and simply offload, as academy coaches would have no doubt, to his detriment, taught.

No, he is the ball-winner who then springs forward freely and becomes something entirely new. Even Didier Deschamps, the France manager, used the English phrase: a 'box-to box' player.

Kanté is always running into space. And he almost never fouls – with timing and dexterity he picks possession away. He can pass too. Ronald Koeman, when Southampton manager, said, 'What a player. He is clever in every ball position.'

The marvellous German tactics site spielverlagerung.com observed how Kanté waits, always in the right position, reading the eyes of opposition passers – 'similar to a linebacker or safety who reads the quarterback's eyes'. Breaking down Kanté's game into actions, with great detail, spielverlagerung.com concluded here was a footballer 'who does all the little things right. Kanté is basically an assistant all over the pitch. He has a hand in all things that happen.

'To put it in a nutshell, Kanté is football.'

During Euro 2016, French TV was debating whether Kanté is the new Claude Makélélé – extreme praise, given French pride in how Makélélé was credited with redefining the defensive midfielder's game. There are indeed similarities. Makélélé was also small (5ft7in) and a Parisian *banlieue* boy of Central African heritage. And he blossomed under Ranieri (at Chelsea).

But for Huth, who played with both, Kanté is the upgrade. 'He is the caretaker,' says the German. 'His energy is like nothing I've seen. I don't think I've seen him lose a tackle. He always gets his foot on the ball. Always. Even when he shouldn't he somehow gets the ball.

'Makelele "invented" the position. But this guy is just unreal.'

And his enthusiasm is echoed by King. 'NG gets credit . . . but still not enough. He has played like no one else I have seen before. I still don't know how he does what he does on the pitch. I can't get my head round it. With everyone else, when they tackle someone the ball ricochets. But if he tackles, the ball sticks to his foot.

'Or, if I wanted to tackle someone over there I would have to slide. He doesn't slide. He just sticks a leg out. The ball stays still. The other player will run off. And NG will run off with the ball.

'Or, if you smash the ball and it hits me, it has to rebound. Smash the ball at him . . . and it seems to hit him, land back at his foot again, and before you can run after it, he has dribbled off. I don't know how he does it.'

Ranieri spoke of doing video analysis and finding himself and his staff just saying 'Wow!' as they watched Kanté chase the ball. And in training, if someone ever tried to beat Kanté, a mocking cry of 'know your players!' would go up among the lads. Meanwhile a quiet little leg would confiscate the ball.

● ● ●

Arsenal. The grand, pristine Emirates Stadium on Valentine's Day. The Third Big Test. Leicester arrived five points clear. If they won, any last questions about them would disappear.

Their line-up was again unchanged. Their performance was the same. The relentlessness and fearlessness of it mirrored the Liverpool and City games. In a very rare interview over the summer, with *L'Équipe*, Kanté revealed one aspect of his psychology. 'Fear? No. It's not about that. Whenever I've got to a new team I've felt "I've arrived. Now shit's got real." But always told myself I'm going to give it my all and see.'

At the Emirates, as usual, Kanté sweated for others. He ran, he stretched, he stole, he stopped, he passed, he backed up, he supported. The pitch looked like it had measles when you saw his 'touches map'. Spots all over. The Rash indeed.

Vardy headed very close. Morgan blocked Sánchez. Drinkwater defended well. Ramsey knocked on the door. A great game, with so much to enjoy, but discerning eyes kept being drawn back to Leicester's little 14.

It was Kanté who broke, too quick for Koscielny, to give Vardy the situation where he won and scored Leicester's penalty.

After Simpson's red card, it was Kanté who, with six tackles and six interceptions, led the incredible harrying effort that, for a long while, held Arsenal at bay. 'Right now Kanté is the best tackler/retriever of the ball on the planet,' said a watching Rio Ferdinand.

Stop the tape at 90 minutes. 1–1. Three Big Tests. Leicester have passed them all. And N'Golo Kanté is king of the Emirates. But, of course, the tape winds on, and Welbeck scores, and Arsenal win 2-1. Kanté's mighty performance gets forgotten.

He drove not a blue, personalised Bentley in and out of Belvoir Drive, but a white Mini. Pierre Ville says, 'What I always say about N'Golo is imagine you've got a chemical solution that doesn't quite work. And you need it to work. You put a molecule in it and, all of a sudden, there's a reaction. That's N'Golo. You put him in a team and he'll bring it balance.'

A mighty molecule. That's as good a summary of Kanté as you could get. 'NG', it even sounds like a vital element in the periodic table. What a player. The *chou-chou* of anyone who likes their heroes understated.

But that photograph, of the little lad on the fringes of all the happiness he has created, is hard to look at without feeling a pang.

12

CONDITIONING AND RECRUITING

Jamie Vardy went to Dubai and fed a tiger from a baby's milk bottle. Of course he did: what else would you expect of a white van superhero?

Drinkwater and Matty James joined Vardy on his break (but not the trip to the zoo) and Simpson was in Dubai too. Gökhan Inler went on a long country walk. Fuchs saw his kids and Mahrez had his Sarcelles mates over. He posted videos of them all juggling a ball in the street before he, with indecent skill, lobbed a 'no-look' pass into a wheelie bin.

Go and win me the title lads. But first, go on holiday. This was after the defeat at Arsenal and Leicester's players put the time off Ranieri granted them to various uses. Morgan stood on that windy field in Nottingham, coaching kids. King headed for the mountains, to Morzine in the French Alps, where his girlfriend Camilla's family have a place. 'I obviously didn't do any skiing but it was nice to get some fresh air, be a long way from anywhere. Nice restaurants and stuff,' he says.

'I think that break was big. That gave us the chance to reflect on the season. It was easy to get caught up in: "Oh, they are under pressure. They are top."

'We were Leicester City and top of the Premier League. None of us had been there before. It just gave us time to reflect, on life as much as football.'

So: Claudio Ranieri sent his players on holiday and like most things in a counterintuitive season, breaking convention worked. He allowed the squad a full week off following the Arsenal game on February 14, asking them to report back to Belvoir Drive on Monday February 22. Ranieri himself recharged in Italy. Although he still went to a match (his beloved Roma versus Real Madrid) and said, 'I was always thinking. I bring my laptop with me. If I have a spare hour I watch – then spend time to enjoy family – then another hour.'

The players were given fitness programmes to follow and GPS devices to wear while completing their allotted exercises. So it wasn't just tigers, fondue and country walks. When they come back, their exercise data was found to be good. 'They respected [the programmes] and worked well. I trust them,' Ranieri said.

But the proof would be in the pudding. Lose the next match, at home to Norwich on February 27, and 'Claudio's holiday' would start to be seen as one of the great foolhardy gambles; a bit like his substitutions in that infamous Chelsea–Monaco tie.

Trust is always a leap. But when repaid it brings the sweetest landing.

Ranieri had a selection problem. Simpson was suspended. De Laet was now out on loan. There was no available senior right back.

Using Wasilewski there had backfired against Arsenal. Albrighton played right wing-back in 2014–15 but offered much more in midfield. So Ranieri gambled again: he would trust a young Ghanaian who had never even been substitute for the first team.

Daniel Amartey was 21, a powerful but soft-spoken kid. He had signed from FC Copenhagen, having come to Scandinavia as a 16-year-old after a Swedish coach saw him star for a small team in Accra. The Danish season having closed down for the winter break in early December, it was nearly three months since Amartey's last competitive game.

But he did well when Steve Beaglehole's Under-21s beat Manchester City so Ranieri took the leap. Otherwise the line-up was unchanged.

It was a cold, clear, Saturday in Leicester and the King Power welcomed an old king, Martin O'Neill, who watched from the stands. With none of their rivals playing, Leicester could move five points clear – but fail to win and they would be knocked off the top if Arsenal won at Old Trafford the following afternoon.

Norwich were how Ranieri likes his own teams to be: desperate.

Early-season form had evaporated and the East Anglians were now locked in a grim survival struggle but they had lifelines: a two-week break (spent training), new signings and a good point grabbed in their previous match against West Ham.

And, for at least half an hour, Norwich were the better team. Playing a 5-3-2 that Leicester found awkward and threatening from set-pieces, Cameron Jerome should have given them a lead and one of their new recruits, Timm Klose, was making a difference at the back. Leicester worked and worked – as did Norwich – and the game became even. Mahrez got on the ball more. Vardy skimmed a shot close. Schlupp replaced Okazaki and added thrust – but with 12 minutes remaining things were still deadlocked.

Ranieri often talks about a semi-evolution of the Premier League. Evolution, because he finds matches more tactical, more European than when he first managed in England. But only 'semi' because, he says, in the last 20 minutes games still revert to the old end-to-end British style.

These are the minutes, he points out, in which both opportunities and dangers lie. And now he focused on the opportunities. Something had to give. So what if he matched Norwich's formation and trusted his players would be superior one v one?

Amartey, showing pace and good mentality, had let nobody down, but Ulloa came on for him. This enabled Ranieri to also go three at the back. King replaced Kanté: King would attack Norwich's box more.

Leicester heaped on pressure but Nathan Redmond, from nowhere, almost drove a long shot in for Norwich. Things were precarious.

One chance. One breach. One sniff. That is what Ranieri sought. And finally it came. Huth, probably climbing illegally, won a header against Redmond. King passed to Schlupp. Schlupp passed to Drinkwater. Drinkwater opened space by eliminating Alex Tettey with a skilful turn.

And he slid a pass straight down the pitch to Mahrez and now Mahrez was on the run. And Mahrez found Albrighton on his outside. And Albrighton crossed.

What a ball it was: low, fast and lasered right into that undefendable zone of the goalmouth where keepers cannot reach and defenders fear to intervene, since one touch could mean an own goal. Albrighton's ball travelled past Brady, past Klose, past Vardy too. And now past Norwich's Ryan Bennett. Ulloa jutted a leg.

And now it was 1–0.

And now Ranieri had his arms spread.

And now 'Fire' was playing.

And now kids on shoulders and tattooed men and grinning grannies bounced together in the King Power stands.

And Norwich were so tired.

And Leicester won.

• • •

Ulloa made the earth move. That very week, a group of first-year geology students from the University of Leicester set up seismometers in the basement of Hazel Community Primary School. The school is 500m from the King Power but the project had nothing to do with football. The students were merely seeking general data.

But, in the few days after the win against Norwich, they noticed an unusual 'spike' on their graphs. Saturday the 27th, just before 5pm, look at that!

The spike was when Ulloa scored.

A small earthquake, measuring 0.3, had been recorded thanks to supporters celebrating at the King Power. In May the university renamed its geology block, The Leonardo Ulloa Building. So, the footballer who as a boy crossed Argentina's place of geophysical wonder for a game is now associated with tectonic events. A fitting homage to Patagonia.

• • •

Keeping going, pushing into the 'red zone', wearing down opponents at the last: victory over Norwich was yet another one built on Leicester's great fitness and endurance. It was further tribute to the work of the conditioning department led by Matt Reeves. As 2015–16 progressed, more and more coverage was given to 'Leicester's fitness secrets'. But in reality nothing seismic was happening there.

It was more impressive than that. Reeves and his workers, abetted by Dave Rennie and his team, and overseen by Paul Balsom, were applying intelligence and values to their challenge. Simple as that. Nothing voodoo or space-age.

The 'Leicester's sports science' features inevitably focused on the gadgets and equipment used at Belvoir Drive, the colourful details about players' diet. *Cryotherapy and Beetroot Shots – Secrets of the Foxes' Success!* That sort of stuff. Yet if you really wanted to get Leicester's conditioning secret down to a tee, the 'T' involved was not 'Technology' but 'Trust'.

A golden thread of trust, something that should really exist at all clubs, but is actually a bit radical in football, ran through Belvoir Drive.

The manager trusted his sports science team, the sports scientists trusted the players and the players trusted each other, that nobody would let the whole group down. Giving the players a holiday then those players keeping up their GPS numbers by working out faithfully on the beach – that merely typified the different Leicester way.

First some stats:

> From August to the first week of February, adding together all first-team player lay-offs, Leicester lost a total of 184 days to injury. Arsenal and Chelsea lost 465 and 428 days respectively. Newcastle 1,042. At that point, eight Leicester players had played 80 per cent or more of possible minutes in Premier League matches.

And:

> Across the season, according to the conditioning professionals' website physioroom.com, Leicester suffered 16 significant player injuries, Arsenal 41, Tottenham 42, Chelsea 50, Liverpool 58, Manchester United 63 and Manchester City 74.

And:

> The team using fewest players in the Premier League in 2015–16 was Leicester (23). Player availability allowed Ranieri to make the fewest changes to his line-up of any title-winning manager since Sir Alex Ferguson in 1992–93.

So, let us drill into 'T for Trust'.

Guiding Leicester's conditioning 'is a very holistic approach', said Reeves in a February podcast. 'We need to involve the players in everything we do and get their buy-in to the interventions we put in place.'

He added it was equally 'vital' that he and his team were able to influence the manager. 'It's this three-pronged approach. The coaching department, sports science department and players themselves coming together to really understand what we're trying to achieve,' said Reeves. 'There's been a lot documented in the press about the spirit at Leicester, about the players really being together and fighting for each other but that's been created over a number of years, in some of the culture that's driven from the information we have and the way we treat them, empowering them to make decisions for themselves.'

Bear in mind what one of Uefa's lead doctors, Professor Jan Ekstrand, told the audience of the European medical conference Leicester organised in 2014. Ekstrand's keynote presentation was: 'Coaches are responsible for the injury pattern at elite clubs.' His theme was about players being over-trained. Also bear in mind that for his entire career Balsom has preached, 'load is by far and away the most important aspect' when it comes to keeping footballers prepared and fit.

Now to the training schedule at Belvoir Drive. Imagine Leicester have played on Saturday. What happens next?

On Sunday, players have the day off. Many clubs get their squads to come in for recovery work the day after a game but Leicester believe it is vital for theirs to take a mental break, stay at home, see their wives, play with their kids, meet friends – get out of that football 'bubble'. Of course, they still need to do recovery but that's where Trust comes in. 'They can be refuelling themselves. We place the emphasis on them,' said Reeves. 'Whether it's going to a local pool for a session, going out on a bike, taking the dog for a walk ... it's about empowering them to start that recovery process.'

Now Monday. Players arrive at Belvoir Drive and are split into groups. Those who were substitutes on Saturday work intensely: possession drills, small-sided games. But those who played just do more recovery. That could mean stretching the legs on the exercise bike, a few circuits to flush out the upper body; a cryotherapy session or ice massage.

Tuesday. A total switch. This is a day of intense work, of five-a-side tournaments and heavy lifting in the gym – really heavy lifting, with some players leg-pressing more than 500kg. There are sessions, too, with the 'NordBord' – a device for building eccentric hamstring strength that was introduced at the start of the season and is perceived to have brought major benefits.

And Wednesday? Another day off. Reeves acknowledges the unorthodoxy. 'You might look and say they don't seem to be training at all but our justification is we require them to work really hard on the Tuesday,' he said. 'And we want them to be really fresh for the Thursday session.'

Ah, Thursdays. This is where Leicester 'open up the areas'. To counter-attack with their rapidity and end-to-end scope, Ranieri's players needed to be used to shifting fast across big distances. The Thursday sessions were about getting running quickly over yardages and box-to-box and 11 v 11 games were employed. Then, after an hour and 20 minutes of this, 'The Runway'.

The drawback of training games with the ball is that only in special situations do players run at their maximum: a striker goes through and a defender has to sprint back, that kind of thing. But not enough of these situations exist and Reeves wants to be sure players are exposed to 'peak speeds' once a week. Peak speed training, he says, is crucial to avoiding hamstring injuries.

So there is The Runway, a drill involving a 10m acceleration, 20m of flat-out sprinting, and 10m deceleration. And there is no hiding place. The GPS data goes up in the dressing room – everyone knows if a player has been shirking under peak speed.

Friday is for Ranieri's *rifinitura*, the session where he rehearses his tactical plan for the forthcoming game with his players and practises set-pieces. There might be some (very competitive) five-a-sides. In all it is a short session (of less than 60 minutes) to avoid load.

And that is it. In a six-day gap between games Leicester players will do what is conventionally understood as 'proper training' only on two days. In training they mix long rests with short bursts – something Balsom preached and Sam Allardyce took on board to great success at Bolton.

Ranieri's instinct, upon arrival, was the Italian one of more training but he listened to Reeves and Rennie when they explained the longstanding schedule Leicester already had in place. Ranieri was open enough to trust it. And the players repaid him: they ran their yards, they pushed their weights, they withstood their ice – and were savvy on their days off.

They are a self-regulating group, you may recall. As King puts it, 'We know when it's time to work and when we can go out in Copenhagen dressed as turtles.'

• • •

Remember Toyota and *asa-ichi*? The Leicester thread of trust strengthened by feedback. Reeves believes it is absolutely essential to ask the players stuff.

They get morning questionnaires. On energy levels. On how muscles feel. To gauge the RPE (Rated Perceived Exertion) of an exercise the previous day – how hard it seemed.

On sleep: when did you drop off last night? How many wake-ups? Why did you wake up? For these, iPads with Google Forms are used: easier and less formal than staff with clipboards.

This 'subjective data' is put together with all the science-y 'objective' stats – like the printouts from the Catapult GPS vests and Polar Team heart watches players wear. Like the NordBord readings, the gym numbers. Maybe more than one player will say the same muscle seems tight, or the same drill was hard. Then you adjust the exercise.

For all technology's advances, 'you can't beat just asking a player how they're feeling,' Reeves believes.

The cryotherapy? Exposure to dry ice at -135°C does bring benefits. Cryotherapy is perceived to aid not just recovery but sleep, and Leicester installed a new £7m 'Whole Body Cryotherapy Unit' at Belvoir Drive in December 2015. Soon some players were asking for another chamber to be installed in the King Power home dressing room.

Beetroot shots? The players swigged those to boost endurance and under consultant nutritionist, Chris Rosimus, Leicester were right across the latest in refuelling. But you can buy beetroot shots in supermarkets and cryotherapy is nothing revolutionary nowadays. Cristiano Ronaldo even has a chamber in his house.

There was other science (like testing the density of the training pitch to see if it was too hard or soft on a given day) but the 'Trust' approach was where Leicester really differed. Vardy, for example, hardly trained for an entire month while waiting for a groin operation he underwent in

January and he was often taken out of shooting practice to conserve his precious hamstrings.

There is not one right way. Tottenham achieved incredible intensity levels via a quite different approach from Mauricio Pochettino: double-training, few days off and what defender Ben Davies described as 'crazy sessions' where the overall philosophy is basically 'don't be tired'. But Leicester's worked for them: contrast how they operated with the approach taken by Manchester City and Manchester United.

At City, when Guardiola took over, even though it was a new start under one of the world's best ever managers, stars came back overweight and Samir Nasri was banished from training until he shed some pounds. At United, van Gaal sailed close to mutiny with endless sessions that, at the start of his reign, could involve three, four full-size practice matches per week. When he emailed players video clips to watch, some of them would open them on their phones and leave the footage playing while doing something else, to fool the spyware he had his IT men attach to the messages. What trust there?

● ● ●

Going out of the FA cup, to Tottenham, after a replay, helped Ranieri's team. During Leicester's holiday, rivals exhausted themselves. Arsenal played Hull in the FA Cup then underwent a sapping defeat to Barcelona in the Champions League. Tottenham had three gruelling games, one involving a journey to Florence. Manchester City travelled all the way to Ukraine to play Dinamo Kiev.

The day after Leicester beat Norwich, Arsenal went down to Manchester United in a tired display and though Tottenham beat Swansea, their exertions would catch up with them against West Ham in the next game. From the beginning of March, City's energy and motivation ran low

On Tuesday 1 March, Leicester met West Brom at the King Power. For only the fourth time all season they had more possession than an opponent – then again they knew that Tony Pulis's *akat-ikit* (the opposite of *tiki-taka*) side would not want the ball.

The jolt was Salomón Rondón scoring for West Brom on a counter-attack, but fluently and collectively Leicester went forward and Drinkwater equalised when his shot went in off Jonas Olsson.

Vardy, sharp, headed against the bar. Then Drinkwater, playing so well, initiated a break, Albrighton found Mahrez who – with a flick so cheeky it was like he was back messing with those friends in his driveway – teed up King.

King, with finesse, swept the ball past Foster for 2–1 and yet any Pulis crew is always awkward. When Craig Gardner spun a free kick into Schmeichel's top corner West Brom levelled and hung on for 2–2.

Another chink for Tottenham and Arsenal, yet the following evening, Tottenham were outplayed at West Ham, losing 1–0, and Arsenal allowed Swansea to come from behind and beat them. Since their Valentine's Day selfies-fest, Arsenal had lost three in a row – their worst run since 2010.

Next, for Leicester, was something difficult: a 5.30pm Saturday kick-off, in the rain, at old Vicarage Road, Watford on March 5. Troy Deeney was big and dangerous and Vardy and Okazaki missed chances. Leicester would need something special to break such structured, disciplined foes. So up to the plate sauntered Mahrez again.

King was on by now and kept a move going, with Drinkwater, Kanté and Schlupp playing parts. Fuchs crossed deep; Watford cleared. Mahrez took pace off the ball with a soft-footed touch.

He faced a packed area. Most would have battered their shot in the hope of ricochets. But Mahrez, with subtler leanings, just shifted his angle and, showing lovely technique, bent a finish beyond Heurelho Gomes.

'We are top of the league,' sang Leicester's boisterous travelling support, 'we shall not be moved.' And they were not. Closing out for 1–0 and extending their lead thanks to Spurs and Arsenal drawing their North London derby, Ranieri's men ended the weekend in prime position.

The table:

1. Leicester— 60 points (+21 goal difference)
2. Tottenham — 55 points (+27)
3. Arsenal — 52 points (+16)
4. Manchester City—50 points (+21)

Albeit City had a game in hand.

● ● ●

The most influential person in the Premier League: that is what Sir Alex Ferguson called Steve Walsh. After a long and under-the-radar career, Walsh was suddenly attracting coverage. Hell, some people even now knew he was *not* the cult hero ex-Leicester centre-half of the very same name.

Rather, Walsh is a former non-league footballer who came into the professional game after working for many years as a PE head teacher – although, a little bizarrely, the *other* Steve Walsh was among his pupils at Bishop Rawstorne School, near Preston.

Our Steve Walsh, the recruitment one, was from a young age interested in putting together players and making teams. Mickey, his younger brother, played for Ireland, Blackpool and Everton, and Mickey remembers Steve, even aged 11 or 12, volunteering to be the manager of his junior team.

Steve took his coaching badges young and as a teacher spent ten years running the county side for Lancashire Schools. That role, travelling an area and assessing the best talent to form a squad, was a recruitment exercise in some ways and when Walsh joined Leyland Motors as a coach there was no money – so he had to again go scouring the area for players.

He next helped a friend, manager Martin Dobson, with opposition analysis at Bury – though in Walsh's Lancashire way he is deprecating about this stint: 'We call it analysis now but then it was "Tell us how they play and what you think and maybe we can do summat about it,"' he said.

After, Walsh did 'bits and pieces' for several clubs, including Notts County under Neil Warnock and then came a break: Gwyn Williams, a fellow teacher, was assembling a scouting team at Chelsea and hired Walsh, who quickly became the club's European specialist. He was still teaching and so would leave school on a Friday evening and go straight to the airport to go abroad, pack in a couple of games and return on Sunday evening. He kept this double life secret from most colleagues and his pupils. Secrecy, after all, is the scout's best friend.

Ranieri valued him at Chelsea and José Mourinho persuaded him to go full-time and when he left to become Newcastle's chief scout he struck a bond with one of their coaches, Nigel Pearson. Mickey Walsh became Pearson's agent.

Steve Walsh is a tall, spry-looking sixty-something, with the appearance of a retired police sergeant – but a kindly one – and has always worked hard, embraced technology, cultivated networks, developed knowledge of the game home and abroad. But none of that, nor any of his biography details, while quirky, really seems to explain why he became quite so good.

Drill down and, rather like Leicester's sports science, you find there is no magic formula. You find those simple but powerful things, collaboration and a people-centred approach.

'Walshy? Walshy's a good lad. Everyone knows Steve. He's built contacts. He's very meticulous, takes advice,' says a source, the right-hand man to the manager of several top English clubs. Like many involved in recruitment, the source prefers anonymity.

'You know that Steve does his diligence – because you see him at the right games,' the source continues. 'And he's not one of those scouts you see talking and not watching the game – you'd be surprised how many do that.'

But then we get to the nub.

'In recruitment, like a lot of things, you're only as good as the people willing to help you,' the source says. 'And Walshy? You want to help him. He's a nice guy. I've not heard anyone say a bad word about him.'

The source remembers putting two prospects Walsh's way on loan when Walsh was helping Pearson build a team at Hull, for no greater – or smaller – reason than that these were talented young players and Walsh was someone to trust. Both kids were great successes and one became Hull's captain.

Ferguson himself liked Walsh enough to let Hull and then Leicester get regular dibs on talents United were discarding. Drinkwater, James and De Laet came to Leicester that way. In a relationships business, being the guy people like helping, counts.

Leicester were in the Premier League's bottom six in spending on agents' fees and one agent remarks, a little cryptically, 'One of the things about Steve is he works *for* Leicester.' Was he suggesting others do deals that benefit themselves?

Another player representative, also anonymously, in an email conversation, described Leicester's recruitment system:

'When I get in touch,' he wrote, 'I know, crucially, that Steve has a) a clear understanding of what his club is looking for and b) the authority and influence to make things happen. That is not always the case at clubs. I have spoken to the chief scout at one Premier League club the same day my colleague spoke to the manager. The chief scout said they weren't interested in a player . . . and the manager said he wanted him.'

The agent noticed 'nine times out of ten' Walsh was aware of any European-based player, however obscure, suggested to him. 'It may or may not surprise you that a lot of clubs still don't seem to have comprehensive knowledge of the main European markets,' he noted.

He took Kanté and Mahrez as examples. 'I'm pretty sure if I'd offered him [Kanté] to all 20 Premier League clubs in summer 2015 a lot of chief scouts/directors of football would have made snap judgements – already 24 and only playing at Caen, a bit small, not for us. And Mahrez would have been looked at as "too cheap to be any good" by some clubs I know,' he noted.

'If you look at Leicester's title-winning squad, it's a healthy balance of local and national players, from the likes of Man United or Championship teams they played against, plus a sprinkling of quality from abroad – a squad that has evolved naturally and intelligently from their Championship days. And they don't stand still but recruit for the future – people will rave about them buying Demarai Gray at a good price in the next 12–18 months.

'It is worth looking at Steve's unique position within his football club too – I can't really think of many assistant managers who also head up the recruitment. He is seeing the squad on a daily basis, which is a huge benefit when it comes to his scouting duties.'

This agent's conclusion was that once you added in Jon Rudkin and Football Operations director Andrew Neville, who both joined Leicester in 1998, there was a level of stability and long-term collaboration in Leicester's recruitment that is very rare in English football. 'At other clubs you will find battling egos, inadequate skillsets, unclear roles, lack of authority in key positions etc. Leicester are joined-up in what they're doing.'

● ● ●

After Watford, Ranieri announced 'now there are only battles'. There were nine games left and the next was a Monday night match on March 14 against a Newcastle side who were fighting relegation and had a new manager, Rafa Benítez, to impress.

Such imperatives were sure to increase their edge. Ranieri showed his. On the Friday morning, King strained a hamstring in training and was immediately ruled out of the game. Yet, in his Friday lunchtime press conference, when Ranieri was asked about injuries, he just smiled and said 'none'.

Newcastle made the running and Benítez had clearly improved their tactics already. Their ploy was testing Leicester's defence with long, diagonal crosses – but Moussa Sissoko and Alex Mitrović could not quite convert.

Mahrez woke and, with a dribble-and-shot, won a corner. Huth headed it over. But then Mahrez won a free kick which he delivered deep. Albrighton collected, Steven Taylor repelled his chip, but Vardy headed the ball back across goal.

Eight yards out, Okazaki made a prodigious leap. With right boot head height he sent an overhead kick flashing past a stunned Newcastle keeper, Rob Elliot. The Japanese ran for the corner flag – backwards for some reason – with a grin as big as Tokyo.

It was Okazaki's first ever goal at the King Power and there can be few more spectacular examples of a player breaking a duck. Albrighton almost made it 2–0 but when Leicester reached their dressing room at half-time the reception from Ranieri seemed as warm as cryotherapy.

'The manager was so angry,' Okazaki reported. 'Yes, he is smiling most of the time, but he was mad. Maybe to see him angry like that is good for us. Luckily, he doesn't throw things.'

Ranieri was unhappy Leicester had not matched Newcastle's intensity and he thought his team lacked its usual positional discipline. The second half was more to his liking and as Leicester closed out another 1–0 Ranieri screamed at fans 'Come on!!' to elicit a late burst of clappers and noise.

Okazaki, tie askew but grin intact, came across as humble and relieved in an interview with the club channel. 'Today I am so very happy,' he said. 'I take into every game pressure. I am a striker and every match you don't score [at home] is negative.' Overhead kicks, in fact, are an Okazaki specialty – a similar effort for Stuttgart against Hannover in 2012 won him Bundesliga goal of the month.

With City dropping more points, against Norwich, and Arsenal in cup action, only Tottenham kept pace. The Newcastle win left Leicester five points ahead of Spurs, 11 of Arsenal and 12 of City – though Arsenal and City had a game in hand.

But Koeman, analysing Leicester versus Newcastle on Sky Sports, felt matters had been clarified. 'It is now a fight between two teams,' the Dutch coach said. 'Before this game it was a fight between four or five.'

Leicester versus Tottenham for the title, then.

No team had ever lost a race when in Leicester's position of five points ahead with eight games to play. But no team remotely like Leicester had ever won the Premier League.

Ranieri would have to relieve any tension the squad might feel – but he had already proved good at that. 'It literally felt like we had been relegated [at Arsenal],' Huth recalls. 'We had been on such a roll, then you lose and there's a two-week gap [before the next game]). You're thinking, "Oh, it's going to be ages before we perform again."

'We had eight days off training. I switched off and forgot about Arsenal. The manager said, "Go away. Go away with families. Or stay at home."

'I relaxed. And it really cheered me up. It really did.'

13
PLAYING AGAINST LEICESTER

'Normally the top teams dominate possession. The top four or five are also top four or five in the possession stats. Leicester are happy for you to have the ball. And that's their strength. They are the quickest team on the counterattack. So direct.

'They're happy for you to have the ball ... You're not set-up, you're out of shape because you've opened up to try and play ...

'... and within a couple of seconds Vardy has gone and Mahrez has gone ...

'... and the ball is over the top.

'We felt we were in an even game with them ... and yet we were 2–0 down by half-time and it ended worse.

'It's different to what you normally face.'

One of the more experienced and intelligent footballers in the Premier League, Leon Britton of Swansea, is trying to explain something traumatic. What it was like to play against Leicester in 2015–16?

Britton is driving home from a long day's study at a coaching course with the Welsh FA. The question is further stimulus for his active football brain. He wants to speak about the rareness of the Kanté–Drinkwater midfield partnership, the hidden roles that Okazaki and Vardy play, the collectiveness he saw up close from Leicester on the pitch.

It is fascinating.

Then again, Britton could have just said the same as Stoke's Marc Muniesa. 'All they do is run!'

● ● ●

Leicester, key place in the English Civil War, suddenly found itself frontline in the battle of football's Roundheads and Cavaliers.

To summarise (and probably marmalise) the history of the Civil War, fought from 1642-51, the parliamentarian Roundheads were for the people, extolling pared-down values. The royalist Cavaliers were for the elite and believed in style.

The old city of Leicester was a Roundhead stronghold. The Cavaliers, their name coming from *caballero*, were Spanish in influence.

When you consider where an underdog football club stood in the ideological divide gripping football more than 360 years later, perhaps the Civil War analogy is useful.

Muniesa's comment – overheard in the tunnel when Leicester went to

Stoke – was not intended as a compliment. He is a product of Barcelona's La Masia academy, that university of beautiful passing and grand temple for those on football's 'Cavalier' side. Stylish La Masia *tiki-taka* had been the game's dominant idea from 2006.

There were upstarts. Atletico Madrid, led by the piratical Diego Simeone, spearheaded the Roundhead challenge, finding ways, with humbler players and intense aggression, to win titles against Barcelona and knock them out of Champions Leagues. In Germany, playing self-described 'heavy metal football', Roundhead Jurgen Klopp dismantled the Bayern Munich reign of an old, possession-addict Cavalier prophet, Louis van Gaal.

By 2015-16 football seemed split down the middle between teams who sought the ball, and a style, when they stepped on the pitch, and others unbothered about possession – their focus was down-to-earth pragmatism.

Style and practicality have forever vied in the game since Scots came to Victorian England with an artful new idea: passing.

All they do is run. As Mahrez told *L'Équipe*, 'we're no Barcelona. We can't change who we are. We stay solid and counterattack.'

He described, affectionately, life under his manager. 'At training, Ranieri would hit us over the head with working on tactics. "Riyad! Keep the formation! Come back and defend!" He looks at your stats too. If you don't run, you don't play. I've clocked up 11km each match.'

Yet at the same time, this artist admitted that the 'place where I have really pushed on is [Leicester]' and Vardy said Ranieri had given him 'more freedom' than other managers.

So, think about all of that.

Leicester ran and ran. They did not even try to pass like Barcelona.

Ranieri hit them over the head with tactics and yet ... the team's star attacking players flourished and felt free. Some mix, isn't it?

Some act of coaching.

And, of course, Leicester won. By the end of the season 'doing a Leicester' had become a *thing*, a description applied to any clever, counterattacking, passionately hard-working small side, like Iceland at Euro 2016.

The glorious anomalies of Leicester-ball produced stats reproduced in every paper and on every football show. Like:

- *Average possession of Premier League champions from 2006 to 2015 = 58 per cent.*
- *Average possession of Leicester 2015–16 = 42 per cent.*
- *Pass accuracy of 2006–2015 champions = 83 per cent.*
- *Of Leicester = 70 per cent.*

One newspaper suggested Leicester had 'killed crossing'. More than one argued that, thanks to Ranieri, 'passing is dead'. And, in the *Spectator* magazine, a leading British journalist of his generation wrote about Leicester and of a 'con-trick in action', a 'triumph of brutality over the beautiful game'. A Cavalier, then.

Rather more admiringly, though, Rio Ferdinand observes, 'Everything in football is short and studied, Leicester do the opposite.' But what exactly was that? What was Leicester-ball?

• • •

Warning: terminology ahead. But stick with it. Leicester did more than run but nothing that was not beautifully simple. A young British coach, who has worked at the top of the Premier League and has both a playing and analysis background, offered to break down Leicester's play. It is better for him to be nameless, because Leicester are an opponent he must plot to beat, after all.

He started with three key concepts in modern football: compactness, spatial control, superiority.

Okay.

Compactness. Classic Italian school, he said. Look how Ranieri got his players to stay in a 'block' never more than 35–40m in length. They defended like this, sitting in a 'low block' (i.e., deep in their own defensive third). And look, he said, Leicester had 'horizontal compactness' too. Horizontal because if the opposition moved the ball from flank to flank, Ranieri's men moved with it in a tight shape.

Spatial control. Remember what Johan Cruyff told us, he said. *Defending is just about space*. And that José Mourinho is also 'classic Italian school'. And that Pep Guardiola famously said Barcelona were the best team at controlling the ball but Mourinho teams are best at controlling space. Well, Leicester controlled space brilliantly. Look how players had defined areas they operated in. Take Wes Morgan, said the coach, that big guy would never fancy a long sprint against a fast attacker. So, you know what, he was never left with one.

Superiority. Think 'quantitative' and 'qualitative' superiorities. Stick with it, don't worry about the terms. 'Quantitative' simply means having more men than the opposition in a given play situation. 'Qualitative' is just about your men being better than theirs. Leicester worked so brilliantly to produce situations of both types. For example, Fuchs supported Albrighton a lot so Leicester would have quantitative superiority on the left. But Mahrez is pure qualitative superiority: better than the opposition one-on-one, so on the right Simpson stayed back and it was about leaving Mahrez space and getting him the ball.

The coach noted another thing: Final Third Possession.

Not only does tactical research suggest counterattacks produce better-quality scoring chances than conventional attacks (you have more space on the break) but there is a study being done about Atlético Madrid that backs up a certain theory. Which is: *there is a big correlation between final third possession and winning; there is a much weaker correlation between overall possession and winning.*

'Final third' means the attacking third, by the way. Now look at the brilliance, the intelligence of Leicester in the final third, said our coach.

Leicester got the ball forward very directly. But once it arrived in the final third they often changed mode. A key to good counterattacking is realising when the counterattack is over and, at that point, slowing down the break, holding the ball and trying to work openings.

Leicester were masters. If they could not play Vardy clear, possession would go to Mahrez or Albrighton. Drinkwater and Kanté (or King) would support. Interplay would begin. 'What Leicester do is arrive quickly, but then recognise when it's time to keep possession and probe,' the coach said.

Now another anomaly made sense. Which was that while Leicester had the third-lowest total possession in the league, they had the second-highest percentage of passes in the opposition half.

• • •

Tactics are not really numbers, graphs and jargon – though these can help.

Really, they are about human beings. Little human decisions. What a manager suggests players do in a whole range of tiny situations. And how players are able to apply this – or use their own intuition and picture the play.

You could understand Guardiola's Bayern Munich on PhD level, with tracts and pictographs. Or you could just grasp that he thought Franck Ribéry and Arjen Robben could beat anyone, so he brought other players infield, even the full backs, and dreamt up passing strategies designed to leave his great wingers with one on ones.

Sir Alex Ferguson, with Aberdeen, once won a crucial European game by realising an opposition full back hated turning to his right.

Graeme Souness will tell you that long before the term 'false nine' was invented, Kenny Dalgish was one at Liverpool because of his genius at dropping back into space.

That's tactics.

So, Leicester. After our coach outlined the framework, he described how it boiled down to individuals applying skills.

Schmeichel? Well known among club analysts for having one of the biggest kicks in the game and a huge 'arm', just like his father, when throwing the ball out. The most important pass in any counterattack is the first one and Schmeichel often made the first one with a giant boot or hurl upfield that was incredibly accurate at locating Vardy. At this point it might be useful to know that Schmeichel started as a striker, so he knows how they think.

Vardy? Unbelievable at dropping into midfield when Leicester did not have possession, noted the coach. Two benefits. Helped the team defend. And gave Vardy valuable rests. In contrast, Harry Kane at Tottenham was always asked to press goalkeepers, necessitating tiring 'out-of-possession' sprints.

Drinkwater and Kanté? Normally using just two central midfielders, with a No.10/second striker in front of them, creates a flaw. Your midfield cannot naturally 'fan out' to stop opponents exploiting what Europeans call the 'half-space' down the sides. But Kanté and Drinkwater had such intelligence and energy they seemed able to block the passing lanes single-handed.

Mahrez and Albrighton? Incredible work rate when filling defensive gaps and so intelligent in 'final third' possession.

Britton backs up this sense of Leicester as having a classically Italian, very clear game plan enacted by individuals in outstanding ways.

'It's funny,' he says. 'They play a bit like a 4-4-2, but the two boys in midfield are so good at picking up second balls and on the transition, winning the ball back. At the King Power we [Swansea] tried a midfield diamond, to have four players in the middle to pick the ball up. But it didn't work because Kanté and Drinkwater are so good.

'Kanté is very fast around the ball. When you have it, he's instantly pressing you and you have to deal with the ball quick. He's not the biggest lad but strong, determined and wins it cleanly off you. They're not sliding tackles. It's an art form.'

And one of the biggest things Britton found, as a deep midfielder, was how good Vardy and Okazaki were at coming from behind to steal possession: 'They work so hard. You don't see them, I've got the ball, I'm looking forward, you don't get a shout ... and suddenly they come from behind you to take the ball.'

• • •

Cavaliers should be tied to chairs and made to watch the goal Leicester scored at Crystal Palace on March 19 on repeat. A win was crucial psychologically, allowing Ranieri's side to enjoy a March break with their lead intact. Selhurst Park, with its cheerleaders 'The Crystals' and trained eagle circling before the kick-off, rivals the King Power for offbeat ritual and is always testing. But Drinkwater was outstanding and Mahrez scored like this:

Simpson to Drinkwater.

Drinkwater to Kanté.

Kanté to Drinkwater.

Drinkwater to Huth.

Huth to Drinkwater.

Drinkwater hits long to Albrighton.

Direct. Yes, Drinkwater's pass travelled 40 yards, eliminating Palace's midfield. *Beautiful game?* Well, hadn't Leicester just done the Guardiola thing of detailed passing designed to spring a wing ace free?

And next:

Albrighton sees that Vardy and Okazaki are covered so he holds the ball until he can get it across to Mahrez. *Final third possession*.

And then:

Mahrez crosses, Damien Delaney defends. Drinkwater spies Vardy and sweeps a first-time pass to him. It is Vardy versus Dann and of course Vardy is too quick. *Qualitative superiority.*

Finally:

Vardy centres, Mahrez arrives and slots in. And rewind that tape, here is another thing you notice. Palace have actually defended well. Eight players back inside their own box. Alan Pardew could not ask more. But Leicester, from being in their own half just seconds ago, suddenly have seven men in or around Palace's area. Not quite *quantitative superiority* but still some effort.

Seeing the 1–0 victory through was not straightforward, with Delaney volleying against Schmeichel's bar, but at full-time exuberance flowed from Leicester's fans. The owners had gifted everyone a scarf reading 'Forever Fearless' and these were displayed while the supporters sang, 'We shall not be moved.' And they weren't, for after 15 minutes of this in an otherwise empty ground the stadium announcer had to beg politely for them to leave.

That was a moment the country as a whole realised the extent of Leicester belief. *Hold on, this lot really think they'll do it . . .* The Selhurst Park 'stay-behind' got great airplay on the evening's bulletins. 'We're waiting for Leicester: The Movie' said the BBC's Jonathan Overend. A Leicester fan explained on talkSPORT, 'It's not just what we're achieving, it's the commitment and effort of every one of our players. That's why we stayed behind as much as anything.'

• • •

Roy Hodgson had been at Selhurst Park and called Drinkwater into the England squad. Drinkwater was man of the match on debut against Holland on March 29. 'Singing the national anthem was huge – I always dreamt of it as a kid,' Drinkwater said. 'But maybe I could have moved [the ball] a bit faster.'

Typical, not to get carried away. It took the obligation of being MOTM to get Drinkwater before the cameras. Avoiding interviews was a habit and one Leicester had to explain to journalists. 'Quite a complicated character,' Pearson once told the press apologetically.

Drinkwater's rationale was his role model, Paul Scholes, who didn't talk to journalists and why should he? 'He was the sickest midfielder ever – so I thought I'll copy him,' Drinkwater said. He mentioned this when he gave his one sit-down of the season to the *Daily Mail*'s Martin Samuel. The interview was revealing. He who seldom speaks often has most to say.

It was Drinkwater, in this piece, who told the world about Ranieri and his 'dilly-dong' bells. From the Broadheath Estate in Altrincham, he had grown up sports-mad, doing rugby and athletics at school against Manchester United's wishes, and playing football at every chance. Sometimes just with 'popped balls' on the estate.

He was bright enough to gain nine GCSEs but admits his attitude at United's academy was 'not the best'. He resented others getting chances ahead of him. Always had talent, but didn't always apply it, Gary Neville recalled. At 21, after various loans, Drinkwater was sold to Leicester, days after dazzling at the King Power as a Barnsley loanee.

This changed him, he said. Knowing the 'safety net' of United was finally gone he 'knuckled down'. But it was a gradual blossoming. In 2014–15 he was still behind Esteban Cambiasso and his best friend Matty James in

Leicester's midfield pecking order. He played just two of Leicester's nine matches in their 'miracle escape'.

Ranieri liked him immediately, though, noting his skills but particualarly his spirit. 'When he makes mistakes he gets very angry,' Ranieri explained. 'I love him because he wants his best.'

After the Watford win, Drinkwater, King, Matty James and Ben Hamer went out in London to celebrate Drinkwater's birthday but an exclusive nightclub refused them entry and salt was rubbed in wounds by the fact the same club waved a group of Tottenham players straight in.

'It wasn't funny at the time, but looking back it was. Something to always hold over Drinky,' King laughs. 'I mean, Drinky plays for England, how's he not getting us in a nightclub?! I don't think he's quite come to terms with it.'

The affection in King's voice is obvious: 'Drinky' appears to be the lovable curmudgeon as far as teammates are concerned. And in Copenhagen the Mutant Ninja Turtle he chose to dress as was Raphael – the tough, deadpan but loyal one.

● ● ●

To understand the fine-tuning of Leicester's game, you have to listen to the players. '[Ranieri] comes into our team meetings where he's been up all night watching fifty or sixty clips of just one of the opposition's players and he will tell you exactly what he's done in forty-nine of them and what he did in the other eleven. It's mental how much detail he goes into,' said Vardy.

Leading up to matches, iPads were laid out at Belvoir Drive for players to watch – even while doing bike work in the gym. These were loaded with opposition clips and, earlier in the week, the same devices were used to debrief the previous performance.

'You click your name and basically watch the game through every clip you are involved in,' says King. 'You can watch our set-pieces, their set-pieces, our goals and their goals – to see if you had a hand in the goal or were at fault, for example.

'On the Thursday they put the iPads out again and they'll have the predicted line-up of the next opposition, the way each individual plays and the way their team plays as a whole. You scroll along the side and there'll be set-pieces, wide free kicks, where players run. Probably about eight pages of this.'

Training was videoed and discussed in team meetings – Ranieri sometimes played back footage of it. Players were encouraged to seek clips themselves. 'Which is good if you have nutmegged someone,' says King. "Right, let me see where I did that!"'

Huth was blown away by the preparation. 'All the clubs have got this stuff yet they don't make it available. Here they do. I mean, we have cameras at training. Who does that?!' he asks.

Albrighton tells of the detailed 'unit work' he did with the other attackers to ensure breakaways were coordinated right.

On match day Ranieri would have pinned up 'cribsheets' reminding everyone of tactical points and set-piece jobs. Then, Ranieri switched to motivation mode. 'He is quiet. He leaves us to do our own thing. He is maybe a little bit nervous himself,' says King. 'But his team talks are short and good.

'A lot of the time he says, "Make sure you play this like it is your last game." Or "Leave everything out on the pitch whatever happens . . ." And "Make the performance!" He often says that.

'You often go out of there thinking, "That's a good team talk." He is good with the whole emotional side of things.'

Troy Deeney spoke of how much talking he heard from Leicester players on the pitch, how much on-field organising they do. That self-regulating team again. In the dressing room Vardy and Huth were among the more vocal, while Morgan saved his leadership for the pitch. Schmeichel admits, laughing at himself, 'I talk a bit. Don't know if anybody is listening. I just talk rubbish, basically. A lot of it is pumping yourself up.'

And the opposition dressing room? At the King Power it is well-appointed but bare and you cannot escape who you are playing. The floor is Leicester-blue, the corridor is Leicester-blue, you emerge through double-doors, and the first thing you see is giant posters of Ranieri's team: like one of Vardy, in full-on battle cry.

Above the door to the pitch is, 'FOXES NEVER QUIT'. You hear the *Post Horn Gallop* playing and walk down a Leicester-blue tunnel where the last thing before the pitch is an overhead sign: #FEARLESS.

• • •

This was Southampton's 'welcome' on 2 April, a bright, spring Sunday. It was Khun Vichai's birthday and beer and donuts were distributed to fans. Ranieri's pre-match shtick was the usual 'step-by-step' one. He would not talk about the title, rather the next 'step' – the fact victory would put a Champions League place at hand.

Southampton started better. Their 3-4-1-2 shape took adjusting to. They were aggressive and their captain José Fonte smacked a shot from long range that, superbly, Schmeichel touched over. Sadio Mané beat Schmeichel after going through but Simpson stopped the seemingly certain goal after a prodigious bit of sprinting back.

Kanté versus Victor Wanyama looked like the smallest Russian doll in a set versus the biggest one, but he barged the giant Kenyan in the challenges. A Kanté tackle on Matt Targett . . . you could hear the *kerrunch* of it from the stand. And then Kanté bulldozed Mané. Fearless. Laws-of-Physics-less.

Much of this game was about Leicester's compactness. Urged by Morgan, they kept perfect distances, absorbing pressure, and Drinkwater began a counterattack where Fuchs found space on the left and crossed.

He could not have hit it better. Morgan, having rumbled up there for Albrighton's set-piece, was still in the area and left with only little Jordy Clasie trying to guard him. No contest. Morgan rose and put his head through the ball and powered it home.

Morgan's first goal of 2015–16. 'I was getting a lot of stick because I hadn't scored. Only Simmer and Fuchs were the same but I'm always in a position where I should be scoring more goals than I do. A vital goal as well,' Morgan says with a smile.

Southampton remained dangerous but the Leicester 'block' held and another 1–0 win was their reward. With Tottenham having drawn at Liverpool, Leicester now led by seven points, with six games left. 'There is only one chance in the life,' Ranieri said

And something odd but rather wonderful happened outside. Clutching beers as they stood outside the Holiday Inn opposite the King Power

Stadium, Leicester fans applauded Southampton's fans as their coaches pulled past. And were applauded back. Everyone, the opposition included, seemed to be enjoying Leicester's rise too much for tribalism.

But playing against Leicester: the King Power does its part against the opposition. 'The stadium is something different,' says Britton. 'We played them when they were trying to avoid relegation, the previous season, and I couldn't believe the atmosphere at the ground.

'It's not the biggest stadium but the noise they generate and support they give their team is incredible. The clappers are a bit different. It seems like the fans have a real good connection with their team, a togetherness. You can feel it. If you're trying to shout to one of your teammates you can't make your voice heard sometimes.'

• • •

The Premier League became a 'running league' a few years ago, says Joey Barton. Britton has seen the change. 'There's a lot of high intensity, really quick pressing. The new generation of manager is producing training sessions to reflect that game: they are pressing quicker, getting players to recover quicker. It's an 11-man game now,' he thinks.

Britton said Tottenham were the most intense team to play against in 2015–16 but Leicester were not far behind. He is always struck by their '11-man' style. 'Nathan Dyer mentions the team spirit, that the lads are very close and you see it on the pitch when you play them. Even brilliant players like Vardy and Mahrez put the team first,' he says.

Classic Italian? How about 1–0 results? The team who, back in September, were top scorers and the league's second-worst defenders, by April were on a run of winning five games out of six by that old *catenaccio* scoreline, 1–0.

Opponents, now conscious of Leicester's counterattacking power, were letting them have the ball, so Leicester were having to concentrate even harder, nick goals, then have the dogged mentality to hold out.

Morgan, Huth and Schmeichel loved it. 'We had five or six games where we proper grinded it out and that was great,' Schmeichel grins.

'Basically, it was crunch time,' agrees Morgan. 'There was more and more focus on: "Right, are they going to slip up? Is this the game where they slip up?" Even when we dropped points v West Brom, everyone was "Yep, that's them done." We didn't listen.' He was a centre-back in his element in such situations: '1–0s are the best. 1–0: it really sticks the fingers up to the opposition a little bit.'

Mentally, says Huth, the back four reached a point where 'it felt that once we were 1–0 up, a game was almost done.'

• • •

Vardy had not scored in six games and Ranieri was fielding questions about a goal drought. But teammates knew how important, even when not scoring, he was to Leicester's plan. When defending like they were having to do during the 1–0 phase, it was invaluable having such an outlet.

'Under pressure, or even in a normal game, you don't have to try thirty passes in midfield and still not get anywhere. You head it out and [Vardy's pace] gets us there without doing anything,' Huth says. 'And the other team has to run back; "Fuck's sake, we were only there five seconds ago."

'In terms of my clearances, I am trying to hit space where either Vards gets the ball or is fouled or we get a throw-in. I can head it to Drinky but sometimes I won't, I might aim for Vards. He [Drinky] hates me for it. But then we are up the field with relative ease.'

When Schmeichel got the ball, his first thought was to see if he could get it straight to Vardy or Mahrez. 'With Vards, it's about putting it a couple of yards in front of him to his right side, with the correct spin, so he can run onto it. With Riyad, it's more drilling it into his feet on the left, so he can control the ball and run with it. His touch is phenomenal. But even his heading game has come on hugely and if I drop it in the right place he can flick it into the big space where Vards can get.'

Nobody inside the team doubts Okazaki's importance. 'Maybe our most underrated [by outsiders] player,' says King. 'I know he has not maybe scored the goals he wants but it is he who allows us to play 4-4-2 because of his unselfish work off the ball.

'I read stats to show he is never too far away from Vards and never too far away from the midfield. That basically says he gets his position as a second striker right. He's almost perfect in terms of his distances.'

• • •

Sunday, April 10. Sunderland away. Sunderland under Sam Allardyce. Sunderland fighting relegation. Sunderland with Jermain Defoe in form. Chilly, far-off, Sunderland. This would be tough.

And it was.

For 45 minutes it was about the block and Morgan's leadership, Huth's physicality, Schmeichel's world-class standards. And Drinkwater and Kanté protecting, Fuchs and Simpson tucking in.

Even then, Younès Kaboul headed close – and a Fabio Borini shot cannoned off Morgan's chest, prevented from going in only by Schmeichel's instinctive leg. Okazaki skewered Leicester's best chance over the bar.

In cold sunshine, after half-time Leicester started opening out, and Drinkwater went through but DeAndre Yedlin was quick enough to bail Sunderland out. 0–0, Leicester seemed stuck and now only 25 minutes were left.

So, Huth won a header (how many Leicester counters started that way?) and Drinkwater received the ball, saw Lee Cattermole coming, and nutmegged Sunderland's captain.

Drinkwater did not need to even look. He knew Vardy would be off, chasing into wide, inviting spaces. He focused on making great contact and the swing of his boot was perfect, sending the ball spearing through the skies as if from a nine iron struck right at the pin.

He got the ball to drop to Vardy's right side, with the right spin and Vardy nudged it into the area and opened out his body. With such surety, he passed the ball round Vito Mannone and in.

In one header, one pass, one strike, all Sunderland's good work was gone.

There was an incredible reprieve, Jack Rodwell side-footing over Schmeichel's bar when Defoe's ricochet ran into his path. There was a miss, by Mahrez. Another, by Vardy. And another, by Amartey. And then quite a *coup de grâce*.

With Sunderland committed and Leicester on, yes, a counterattack, Demarai Gray embarrassed Yedlin and found Vardy, who knocked the ball past Patrick van Aanholt and then just steamrollered the young Dutchman when he tried a flimsy body check. On Vardy charged, round Mannone he veered, and then walked the ball gleefully into the beckoning net.

Vardy's return to deadliness took him past 20 league goals for the season. Not for 30 years, since Gary Lineker, had a Leicester player reached that mark. 'Legend of Jamie Vardy,' said a *Leicester Mercury* headline. The garlands were deserved for another so direct and punishing display.

• • •

All they do is run? Pat Nevin, whose eye is sharp, was a BBC pundit at the Stadium of Light that day. He would disagree. Uppermost in Pat's mind, on his drive home to the Scottish borders, was not Vardy but Ranieri.

'People say he's not "The Tinkerman" any more. Oh yes he is,' says Pat, 'but he tinkers subtly and beautifully these days. I remember that 2–0. Vardy was knackered. He'd been up against Sunderland's big centre-backs, Kaboul and Lamine Koné, and he was getting nothing, they were covering each other so well. And you were thinking "0–0."

'But then Ranieri has got Ulloa warming up. Where's Ulloa going to play? Behind Vardy? But Ulloa went on and stood right up on one of the centre-backs. And suddenly it was one against one.

'And the next time Leicester get the ball? Drinkwater plays it over the top to Vardy who only has one man to escape and he's scored. So simple, and the kind of move – one v one, ball over the top – that used to be a standard football ploy but isn't seen much these days.

'Everyone's going mad about Drinkwater and Vardy but I'm looking at the guy behind it. Ranieri. What a change. As Harry Potter said, "It's old magic."'

14

CRISIS

Claudio Ranieri was no Danny Simpson but had a ritual too. At his main press conference of the week, held in the ample media theatre at the King Power Stadium, he would come in and say an almost shy 'hello' – and then shake every journalist's hand.

Whether reporter, cameraman or work experience kid; whether a familiar face or foreign traveller, you got the same treatment. A quick, cordial handshake from a priestly, bespectacled Italian.

It seemed nothing at the start of the season. The Midlands 'beat' is intimate, involving a familiar and informed band of broadcasters, agency journalists and print reporters. Aston Villa, by tradition, is the most newsworthy club on the patch, not Leicester. At the start of the season a 'Friday presser' at the King Power would attract maybe eight or nine journalists, the local guys and maybe a Japanese or two who were following Okazaki.

So, initially, Ranieri was entering a large and largely empty room, and his greeting was just a way of spreading warmth amid cold, vacant seats.

For two months – well into October – this is how it stayed. Eight or nine reporters, hello from Ranieri, quick handshakes, begin. But, of course, things started growing. 'National' journalists started interloping. A foreign contingent grew. Not only Okazaki's Japanese but Italians tracking Ranieri began to appear. Then the big reporters from abroad – and, increasingly, America – started arriving in town on special assignment.

From March, there would be 20, 30, even 50 media people filling the theatre. You had to get there quick for the best sandwiches – though the crisps seldom ran out. And Ranieri maintained his ritual even though it took ever longer and was ever more challenging. He would push between chairs to get round all the hands. 'Okay? Everyone?' then finally go to the stage.

And, so, prior to Leicester's match with West Ham on 17 April he opened the door, saw the packed seats, the biggest audience yet, and thought 'not today'. He went straight to his seat behind the mics.

Well, Claudio Ranieri was no Danny Simpson – but he would never make that mistake of tempting fate again.

• • •

West Ham. If a team were ever going to test Leicester, the clever pundits felt it might be them. They were feisty, unafraid, and able to mix up their style under Slaven Bilić's impressive management. Their striker, Andy Carroll, was bruisingly 'unplayable' when fit and on his day. Their talisman, Dimitri Payet, was a Mahrez, a maverick from France, a late-bloomer, a game-changer. His delivery was incredible and West Ham especially liked putting crosses in.

This last point was relevant because there was a calculated gamble hidden inside Ranieri's game plan. Staying in a 'low block', and compact not just vertically but horizontally, inevitably invited the opposition down the flanks and meant Leicester had had to defend more crosses than anyone in the Premier League. With Morgan and Huth and Schmeichel so good in the air and Simpson and Fuchs adept at tucking in and helping out too, so far they had handled the ball flying into their box well.

Yet Payet's quality of delivery and Carroll's prowess in the skies were of a different order. And under Bilić's excellent coaching, West Ham's set-play routines could be more dangerous than anyone's.

The previous week, Arsenal had faced West Ham and played a beautiful game for 40 minutes, going 2–0 up and dominating their London cousins. So Bilić had tweaked things, made his team get the ball wider, cross it earlier. Carroll scored and then started bullying and inside eight minutes of play Arsenal were 3–2 down. West Ham's run of just two league defeats since November confirmed their menace.

Now, Ranieri knows Gérard Houllier. His four years at Chelsea coincided with Houllier's stint as manager of Liverpool and the pair have shared Uefa coaching forums as well as glasses of wine in the manager's room. Ranieri would know all about Houllier's diktat regarding facing the media – and, as someone who always puts strategy into his press conferences, might well agree.

Ranieri is no extrovert but he is a born communicator. He understands how to use his personality to impose a quirky authority in interviews.

Houllier famously said that 'the most important five minutes of a manager's week' are when facing the cameras and mics. Ranieri would probably choose his Friday *rifintura* as more vital while accepting what Houllier means.

Houllier's mantra was that what a manager says to camera is critical in setting the tone: players are watching, directors are watching, at home their wives and families and agents and friends are watching. How they think, how people in their circle think, will be shaped by what they see and hear in those moments. Did the manager seem in control? Was he positive? Worried? Did he like how I played?

And that is before you even get to your rivals and the supporters who are watching too. Ranieri is deliberate in his messages. '*Slowly slowly*', he would say throughout the season. '*Step by step*' and '*we must fight*' and '*our fans can keep dreaming*.' You could have compiled a Claudiology of tenets he reinforced week upon week. He is also big on tone.

He is Detective Columbo, going for the unthreatening and dotty persona to lull his rivals while knowing exactly what he is doing underneath. He knows the British press love a colourful line. 'We're the basement and the other teams are a villa with a swimming pool,' he would say. 'I'd like to say: "Yes we can!" But I am not Obama.' He found it very easy to keep that press onside.

So, pre-West Ham, no time for handshakes ('I would lose one hour!' he apologised), but all Ranieri's other ploys and charms were soon brought to bear as he sought to set the right mood for such a crucial game.

He wanted, first, for all to remember the difficulty of the match – 'Payet! Carroll! Noble! Valencia!' he said, reeling off the West Ham threats. Then he fired shots against complacency: no, he *still* would not talk about the title. Every week journalists tried to get him to admit it was a target but he always focused on a humbler goal. 'I understand your job,' he said. 'But for us it is important to clear everything. Don't read. Don't watch. And think only of the next match.'

The vibe was steely-but-smilingly-so and he maintained it with a gentle admonishment when someone asked if Leicester could learn from Liverpool blowing an almost similarly strong title advantage in 2013–14. 'Football is very strange,' said Ranieri. 'If you weren't here in Leicester, if you were with Chelsea or Manchester United and they were seven points ahead . . . you'd say it is finished. It's true, no?' Journalists took note and laughed.

'But in this moment you don't think this. Why? Because we are Leicester,' Ranieri continued. Then he suddenly grew strident. With almost a rasp in his voice he said, 'We have to fight. We have to be focused. We have to be strong.' Live on TV, that bit was for the fans.

There were no injuries except the long-term one to Matty James and so for the sixth successive game Ranieri picked his now standard XI: Schmeichel; Simpson, Morgan, Huth, Fuchs; Kanté, Drinkwater; Mahrez, Okazaki, Albrighton; Vardy.

Bilić sprang a surprise: no Carroll. The striker was on the bench as West Ham looked to pack midfield and match Leicester with a team of energetic hard-runners. The willing Emmanuel Emenike replaced Carroll and Victor Moses the more artistic Manuel Lanzini.

Match time. The *Post Horn Gallop* sounded magnificent. The clappers clapped. Kids waved flags. 'Hey Jude' played, *na na na naah*. Ranieri stood, blue suit, white shirt, club tie, in sunshine. 'The impossible team,' said television commentary maestro, Martin Tyler, 'chasing the impossible dream.'

The impossible soon happened.

Second minute. West Ham free kick. To be taken by Payet. With his brutal accuracy Payet pinpointed Cheikhou Kouyaté. He headed powerfully. It looked a definite goal. Yet, as the ball flashed right towards the corner, so did Schmeichel and, with mere fingernails, the keeper somehow got a touch. The ball spun off and struck the inside of the post, then spun the length of the goal line, hit the other post and bounced out. How did Schmeichel – how did Physics? – come up with that?

Leicester had started aggressively, Simpson rattling Payet in the very first seconds, but West Ham showed equal intent. After Drinkwater was unusually indecisive, and Huth put him in trouble, Mark Noble tore in and robbed Kanté. Another Noble tackle stopped Mahrez as he jinked towards a shooting position and Angelo Obgonna took out Okazaki, late and high. Ogbonna also headlocked Vardy at a set-piece. Leicester's best moment was a Huth header, but then:

18th minute. Payet free kick, headed up in the air by Michail Antonio. This time Schmeichel caught and strode through his box into space, just like a quarterback, before hurling the ball fully 40 yards to Mahrez, who was breaking. Mahrez collected, realised Moses was catching, and checked inside to assess his options.

Kanté was sprinting, small-quick-pistons, to his left and Mahrez fed a lovely pass into the support player's path. Winston Reid tried to get on terms but Kanté was clever enough to veer across the defender, who could not challenge for fear of a foul. The right pass from Kanté, and Vardy was clear.

One touch with the right boot teed up the shot, one with the left sent it low, hard, decisive, past Adrian. Vardy charged off and kung-fu-kicked a corner flag. Albrighton lifted him off his feet. Four, five, six teammates piled on. 1–0 Leicester and now you didn't fancy West Ham at all: it was eight and a half hours since Schmeichel had conceded a goal.

• • •

The Ranieri reappraisal had started in September, when Leicester were making comebacks every week and Vardy and Mahrez began flourishing. It was then that Ranieri's Chelsea reign was remembered a little more clearly by Englishmen.

Yes, Chelsea were a big-money project that resulted in failure for him, but only at the very end. Ranieri had predated Roman Abramovich and his billions and before the oligarch's arrival had built cleverly to create an attractive, improving team. And, always under Ranieri, it was now recalled, the dynamic and attack-minded players – like Frank Lampard, Joe Cole, Damien Duff – had flourished.

The treachery of CEO Peter Kenyon was retold. How he called Ranieri 'Dead Man Walking'. And it was also remembered – and felt significant – that Chelsea fans, former Chelsea players and even Abramovich himself, despite sacking him, still thought very well of Ranieri. Finally, people looked back and reflected that his conquerors had been Ferguson's United and Arsenal's 'Invincibles' – and those teams conquered everyone. So, the 'Clownio', the failure tag, was quickly thrown away.

A red letter day occurred on 4 October – not that the empathetic Italian would really have enjoyed it. But it was on that day that Liverpool fired Brendan Rodgers and Dick Advocaat stepped away at Sunderland. It meant the bookies were wrong: Ranieri was not first manager to go.

And those photos in his office kept having to come down as his rivals fell by the wayside. The 2015–16 season was England's worst ever for dismissals, with a record 56 suffered by managers across its top four divisions. The average tenure was 113 days. Eleven Premier League bosses went by the campaign's end. But not him.

Ranieri never forgot the bookmakers' slight. Even in the pre-West Ham press conference he brought it up: 'We have to fight, with a smile. Because our job [avoiding relegation] is done. You are laughing? It's true. That is the first miracle. No one remembers the first match. "Ranieri [will be] the first sacked." I remember it well!'

As Leicester's success built, his continental record was also better understood. 'How many managers actually win something? Unless you get the job at Barcelona or Real Madrid it's not a given,' Tor-Kristian Karlsen says down the line from Haifa. 'Ranieri has been successful in getting top three positions with many teams in a variety of countries. That is also an achievement.

'And some of his jobs, like Inter Milan and Juventus, were as the *traghettatore*, as Italians call it – the safe pair of hands, the interim man – and he was not allowed a project for the long term.'

People saw that now. Even Greece was reassessed: Ranieri only had four games, after all – 'Fifteen [training] days!' he told us – at a time when the entire country was in economic meltdown and Greek football was mired in scandal. 'Guardiola, Klopp or Joachim Löw wouldn't have done any better,' Karlsen argues and indeed Ranieri's replacement did worse.

By April, Ranieri's general popularity in England was transformed. Neutrals tuned in for a bit of him on Sky Sports News.

The RAF? . . . Kanté has a battery in his shorts? . . . Aw, isn't that nice what he said about his mother . . . go on, say 'dilly dong'.

Many lapped it up. And if the British laughed and no one asked about tactics – all the better, opponents would have to guess.

Steve Madeley, a Midlands beat guy, describes the season of Ranieri Friday 'pressers'. 'He gave the same answers every week. It became "How are we going to write this?" And yet everyone liked him. You came away thinking, "I haven't got a line . . . but what a nice bloke,"' Madeley says.

'No question made him lose his cool. But one thing he is master of is distraction. If you want a quirky tabloid line, he'll serve them up by the dozen. But get personal – "What would winning mean to *you*, Claudio, you've always been second . . ." then you'd see him get defensive.

'*Then* he went into a mode of polite self-justification. He'd explain at great length why it didn't work out at Chelsea or in Italy. It was then that you could tell, he's actually a very proud man.'

● ● ●

Another question the doubters liked posing about Leicester was – knowing nod – 'Ah, but how will they react if they go a goal down in one of these run-in games?'

Trouble was, Leicester never went a goal down these days. Vardy's strike was the sixth time in six that they had opened the scoring in a match. And now, in control of West Ham, in the sunshine, Leicester really did look like their title race was becoming a jog. A small thing happened that did not seem important at the time:

28th minute. West Ham passed the ball across their back line. Vardy, doing his usual pressing, ran at Kouyaté and, as Kouyaté received possession, dived in, flicking out a left foot. He caught Kouyaté's toes. Not the worst foul but Jon Moss, the referee, was over fast to issue the first booking.

Perhaps Moss's idea was to set an example, cool the players, but if so it did not work. This was a full-blooded game with a tinge of bad temper and so it remained. A Payet corner – defended. An Antonio shot – wildly over. Half-time came with Leicester still ahead.

• • •

The epithet for Ranieri, at Chelsea, was 'Tinkerman', on account of his use of a rotation policy, something new to English football at the time. But no manager made fewer line-up changes in the 2015–16 Premier League than he. So that slur was gone too. A little cheesily, Ranieri was campaigning for his nickname to now be '*Thinker*man'.

No one was quite going for that, but respect for him was now high enough that he was linked with the Italy job and, in April, named Italian coach of the year. *Corriere Dello Sport* made Leicester their lead front-page story one day: the first time in the newspaper's 92-year history a non-Italian team was afforded the honour.

The world was watching. A Finnish magazine carried a nine-page special. An Israeli newspaper had regular Leicester features. Members of a fans' group, the Foxes Trust, found themselves interviewed for German, Austrian, Swiss, Dutch, French and Norwegian publications in a matter of weeks.

Leicester were in *Newsweek*, *Washington Post*, the *New York Times*. Grant Wahl came over for *Sports Illustrated* and Wright Thompson for ESPN.com. Ranieri was invited to pen a column for *The Players' Tribune*, a magazine founded by baseball icon Derek Jeter, whose guest writers were normally NBA, NFL or MLB stars. Schmeichel was even getting Twitter messages from one of his heroes, serial Super Bowl champion quarterback, Tom Brady.

Leicester played big in Australia. 'There was plenty talkback about them on my radio show, with a huge surge of sentiment for them,' says Francis Leach, one of the country's major sports and music DJs. 'We're at heart a nation of ratbags who will always side with the outsider. And they came no better than that Leicester team.'

Attention was so unrelenting there was even an interview ban imposed on *Leicester Mercury* staff: talking to foreign television crews or reporters was taking up so much of their time. Decamping to the King Power from Connecticut, for the West Ham game, was the full production unit and presenting team of NBC Sports (including Leicester-raised anchor Arlo White). Two of the biggest six US audiences for English games had been Leicester matches and the channel reported a 'Leicester Spike' whenever Ranieri's men were on.

And then there was Wang Beilin. An online journalist for Chinese outlets SuperSport and CCTV5, she got hooked on Leicester after covering the 2014–15 relegation escape and, by now, Beilin was not only at the King Power reporting on every home game but had started travelling on the supporters' buses to away games – getting up at 5am sometimes –

just to follow Leicester as a fan. In the press room, queueing for soup at half-time in the West Ham game, she gave a giant smile and thumbs-up.

50th minute. Bilic had unleashed Carroll, who replaced Pedro Obiang at half-time, and Carroll started wreaking damage. At a set-piece, barging Morgan aside, he made a diving header which sailed close. Long throws, corners and free-kicks now peppered Leicester's box. A breakaway chance was spurned when Okazaki's centre evaded Vardy, and Huth headed Fuchs' throw wide.

• • •

TV audiences for Leicester games were up more than 23 per cent across metered markets worldwide, and 29 per cent in the UK, the growth such that global supplies of Leicester shirts ran out. Puma had only manufactured 25,000. Shirts were being sold, with certificates of authentication, like artefacts – for nearly £250 on eBay.

Narratives were everywhere. Endless publicity was being given to a vow by Gary Lineker, should his boyhood club become champions, to present *Match of the Day* in his underpants. This comedy take on Leicester's success became as repeated as dilly-dong.

And now a new actor tripped onto this stage. A middle-aged head teacher from West Yorkshire was about to make himself a worldwide bête-noire.

Jonathan Moss – Executive Head Jonathan Moss – co-runs a large school in a tough area of Halifax where nearly all the pupils are from ethnic minority backgrounds and its performance is 'Outstanding' say Ofsted. This admirable school leads initiatives like an anti-radicalisation effort aimed at Asian kids. Really, Mr Moss should be known and celebrated for that.

But that is not how it is for referees. Because match official Jon Moss left the King Power as The Bubble Burster, the whistle-toting killjoy who now endangered the dream. And this is how that infamy started:

56th minute. West Ham tried playing quickly forward, Reid sliding a long pass to Emenike. Huth went through the back of the Nigerian – foul, possibly – and Drinkwater seized the loose ball. He played his inevitable, and inevitably good, counterattack pass to Vardy, who moved into the box with a purposeful touch. Only Ogbonna was tracking him.

Momentum took Vardy away from goal and Ogbonna was quick so he appeared to make a calculation. Ogbonna's hand on his arm was Vardy's cue to thrust his leg across the Italian, creating contact, and go sprawling.

Vardy's take-off – two footed – looked unnatural and Moss was brilliantly positioned. He made a good call: no penalty but then he also decided Vardy had definitely dived. Definitely? That seemed brave. There was that hand on the arm, the contact after all.

Moss flourished a second yellow card and Vardy, for the first time since 2011, was sent off. And he did not leave the pitch well, berating Moss while jabbing a finger at the ref. West Ham's captain, Noble, had to help get him off the field.

● ● ●

Ranieri's rivals had been falling away. Wenger, without the league title in twelve years, saw another Arsenal season bitterly collapse. Wenger kept talking up his team's mentality but the reality was its displays of spirit came when there was less to lose.

Arsenal were great, for example, in the second legs of European ties following heavy defeat in the first. They would *almost* repair damage. After beating Leicester at the Emirates they contrived to win just one game in eight. The selfies were still online though.

Manchester City's focus dwindled after the announcement their manager was seeing out time. But, even before then, the team lacked an intensity and freshness of leg. City were good flat-track bullies but nearly always lost the big games.

Louis van Gaal was running his course at Manchester United. So many instructions, so little fun for players. United did not score enough and had too many ponderous days. Klopp's Liverpool were an early work-in-progress and Chelsea, while stabilised by Guus Hiddink, were in obvious need of a new direction.

The one still-potent foe was Tottenham. Mauricio Pochettino was close to his players and building a group ethic to rival Leicester's. His fierce training had produced a side of uncommon stamina and players like Harry Kane, Eric Dier and Dele Alli provided a core of young English talent to rally around.

This gave them a popularity beyond their own fanbase, just like Leicester enjoyed. And nor were they big spenders. 'Tottenham is a real story too,' Ranieri said.

After Leicester beat them at White Hart Lane, Spurs had reeled off six successive league victories, so they were clearly capable of putting together the kind of run that could overhaul Leicester should the Foxes falter. They thrashed United the previous weekend. This isn't over, Ranieri kept trying to say. Beware.

The King Power was getting deafening. *Chickah chickah chickah*. And mutinous.

Decisions Leicester's way were acclaimed sarcastically; decisions West Ham's were jeered. 'You're not fit to referee,' supporters raged at Moss. Morgan was required. Huth was required. Morgan required again. West Ham were applying ever more pressure.

Ranieri used up his substitutions: with 10 v 11 he sought power and energy. Schlupp was on for Albrighton, Ulloa for Okazaki and Amartey replaced Mahrez. But still the pressure came, and Morgan cleared valiantly for a West Ham corner.

84th minute. In fairness to Moss, both boxes were a nightmare. At each set-piece, players blocked and held and pulled and pushed. He let some go, he stopped the jostling at other times. West Ham had a corner and Huth and Reid wrestled again. Moss whistled, said to cut it out, and then signalled for Payet to take.

The first thing that happened after Moss's 'cut it out' warning was Ogbonna grabbing Huth. No action. The next thing was Huth pushing Reid away. No action. Then, Fuchs shoving Kouyaté, nothing.

Now Reid got a run on Morgan, who reached out with hands on either side of Reid's chest and Reid, almost as theatrically as Vardy, went to ground. This time Moss intervened. Penalty. What? Carroll buried calmly.

• • •

Some Sundays, more relaxed Sundays than this one, Ranieri visited the Cherry Tree pub in the south Leicestershire village of Little Bowden, for lunch with family. He dropped in to Gelato Village ice cream parlour – with his assistants Paolo Benetti and Andrea Azzalin – in Leicester's St Martins Square. He went to the city's indoor market to buy shellfish and octopus.

In Stoneygate, if you were very lucky, maybe you would see him taking his dog for a walk.

He was always approachable. Open to locals, and part of local life. He felt very close to supporters; at Sunderland he was moist-eyed when he saw some old ladies celebrating among Leicester's following. 'The people say to me, "Good luck, Claudio,"' he told his press conference. 'And I say, "We need it. A lot."'

So, right now, he probably knew how supporters felt.

86th minute. Leicester just could not get that ball clear. 1–1 now, 11 versus 10, West Ham smelt flesh and pinned them in their box. Bilić's full backs became full-time wingers. Carroll lurked in the middle. Payet waited for openings. Michail Antonio gathered on the right, shook off Ulloa and beat Fuchs, then crossed. A half-clearance skimmed off Simpson's head, and now Aaron Cresswell chested the ball.

The left back was on an angle, and the edge of the area, but this ball sat up perfectly and Cresswell has good technique. His beautiful volley flashed over Schmeichel's head. Just as at Arsenal they had gone from 1–0 up to 2–1 down after a red card.

• • •

The issue Ranieri could not escape, the one question that was beyond being dispelled with Columbo charm, was this. Could he win?

You reappraised his career and saw the good work. But could he win?

You tutted at his treatment at Chelsea ... but could he win?

You applauded the work at Leicester, loved the jokes, liked the man ... Could he win?

You agreed Moss had been inconsistent and Leicester's position in this game was unfair ... But could he win?

Could Ranieri win?

His 'nearly man' history was this. His Roma side were top of Serie A with four games left in 2009–10 but finished second. His Juventus team were joint top in January but finished second. His Chelsea finished second.

Nine times he had finished in the top four of a league, but never finished first. In his last 21 seasons, on only six occasions had his team's performance not tailed off during the second half of the campaign. And there was that botched Champions League semi with Chelsea versus Monaco. '*Zero tituli*' was the acidic Mourinho jibe.

So, Claudio Ranieri.

Could he win?

• • •

Nine more minutes were played, including five of stoppage time. It was a moment of management truth. Were Leicester prepared right, both physically and mentally, for a comeback? Were the right three substitutes on the pitch? Ranieri was making small but urgent instructions from the side: were these the right ones?

90th minute. Defending Fuchs' long throw Ogbonna hooked his arm round Huth's neck and pulled him down. No penalty. What? The King Power sang, 'You're not fit to referee.'

95th minute. Schlupp stopped, nursing his leg after taking a kick, and West Ham fatally disregarded him. Kanté took possession, Schlupp was okay now, and Kanté slid a pass to him. Schlupp went for the box and reached it as Carroll came across. Clumsily, Carroll checked him, leading with forearm rather than the permitted shoulder. Moss was again perfectly positioned. And again brave in his interpretation.

He signalled to the spot and it all came down to Ulloa. Third in the Leicester penalty pecking order, the big Argentine took a breath. He ran up fast. He hit it true. Adrián was nowhere. 2–2. Leicester rescued the point.

● ● ●

April 17, 2016 should have been an auspicious date for Leicester for it was the very last day of the 2015–16 season when it was possible to look back and say 'a year ago, Leicester were bottom of the Premier League.' On 18 April 2015, that win at Burnley lifted them off 20th during 'the great escape'. But today, this 2–2 did not feel auspicious.

At least something had been salvaged and Ranieri's decisions had proved good. He defended Vardy ('he never dives') and tried to project positivity in his press conference. But his reaction to Ulloa's equaliser had been telling. As the whole stadium celebrated – or, in West Ham colours, raged – he just looked on impassively, the only one out of 32,000 people, with a stiff upper lip. What turmoil lay concealed?

Vardy's reaction to the red card drew criticism and the penalty box shenanigans inspired articles about 'Dirty Leicester', even if statistics far from supported this characterisation. In 2015–16, in fact, Leicester had fewer bookings than any side except Arsenal and Everton.

Vardy faced an automatic one-game ban and the threat of further games out because of his dissent. There would be an FA hearing. Leicester's four games did not seem easy: Swansea (home), Manchester United (away), Everton (home), Chelsea (away).

If Tottenham could win at Stoke the following day, Leicester would have to win three out of these four to be certain of becoming champions. And play at least one, but probably two or three, of these games without Vardy. All this at a time Mahrez was a bit off the boil.

And in the press room Beilin was crying.

• • •

Tottenham went to Stoke. They were brilliant. They were 'perfect', said Pochettino. Kane, sublimely, curled in to set them on their way. Alli scored, Kane scored, Alli scored again. At one of England's most difficult grounds, the Britannia Stadium, they strolled it, 4–0.

Statisticians noted both their defence and attack had the best numbers in the Premier League – their goal difference was +39 to Leicester's +26. Spurs supporters at the Britannia sang, 'Leicester City – we're coming for you.'

Kane had shown great front, the day before, when he took to Instagram after watching Leicester drop points. He posted an arresting photo: four lions, with bloodlust in their eyes, padding through snow.

Leicester City . . . coming for you.

15

KINGS

You are Andy King and in a GCSE class at Furze Platt comprehensive in Maidenhead. Your mother texts – yet again – and you cringe because, to a 15-year-old, a habit she has seems so uncool.

King can still visualise that tiny moment when it all began. The schoolroom, his phone ('Nokia 3310, silver one') and his mum's way of writing. 'She would text all in capitals,' King sighs, 'and that annoyed me.'

Everyone thought he was going to be a footballer. He was bright enough to do plenty else but just daft about the game. The aim was getting out of Furze Platt to a full-time club scholarship as soon as he could.

He had played at Wembley and he was too good for the other kids. Teachers forbade him scoring in PE class – so he just dribbled through the rest and kicked a ball against one to put it in.

Definitely going to be a footballer. Yet Chelsea released him. Around the same time they were dumping Ranieri they were axing youth players. King, their academy prospect since the age of eight, was told, 'Yeah, we like you, we've always liked you, but Chelsea are changing.'

We want to be the best in Europe so we are scouting youngsters from all across the world now; sorry, no scholarship, they said.

End of a dream. He went back to school. But Chelsea had at least been good enough to email other clubs with his details and the offers of trials were coming in. Reading, Wycombe, Sheffield United . . . each time his mum would text. Always in those stupid capitals. And each time King thought 'fine', put his phone away, and got back to concentrating on class.

But this message felt different as soon as he read it. LEICESTER WANT TO LOOK AT YOU. 'I remember showing my mate and proper buzzing off it. I thought . . . *Decent* . . . Leicester were in the Prem, on the way to be relegated but still in the Prem, and I thought, "from Chelsea to Leicester – that's doable."'

● ● ●

The papers purred about Tottenham. 'Harry Potter' raved the headlines about magic Kane. Leicester . . . he's coming for you.

They carried news, too, of the Football Association charging Vardy for his dissent against Jon Moss. There would be a commission, video evidence and on top of the mandatory one game ban for the red card Vardy faced the likelihood of being banned for at least one additional match. He requested a personal hearing, anxious not to miss more than the Swansea and Manchester United games. If the commission decided to be draconian he could even get a three-match penalty and miss the entire remainder of the run-in.

'I want to stay calm and speak about football. I don't want to tell you my feelings,' Ranieri told journalists after West Ham. Players kept their counsel too, though many were still irritated – and remained so even after the season was done.

'The 2–2 game? That was, er, *interesting*. Put it that way. [Moss] was "keeping it interesting". Quote, unquote,' recalls Schmeichel. '11 v 11, we would have won that game. No question. At 10 against 11 we managed to come back against some odds that were out of our control.'

Says Albrighton, 'It was an annoyance that [the outcome of the game] was not in our hands. The worst thing is [before Vardy's red] we were comfortable. Even two days later I was still seething.'

Schmeichel interjects, 'I think we still are. We still are.'

Morgan is the first to apologise to teammates if he feels he has made an error, but the penalty? 'If you make a mistake then you always hold your hands up,' says the captain. 'But the referee, for me, in that game, just found it hard to keep control.

'I was doing my job. I am getting pulled and head-locked when trying to score goals at the other end. And, there, when I literally put my arm against a player and he goes down – falls in the wrong direction to where I "pulled" him! – the referee gives a penalty.

'[Moss] is basically calling decisions for one and not for the other. But it happens. Probably the less said, the better.'

Graham Poll, the former referee, criticised Leicester's 'dark arts' in the aftermath. He said, 'They've been getting away with it all season.' Others, like Martin Keown, defended Huth and Morgan.

Losing Vardy: what would Leicester do without someone involved in more goals than any other in the Premier League? Since promotion, Leicester had played twelve Premier League games without Vardy starting, and won just three. Then Pochettino waded in. 'It's a big impact for Leicester because Vardy is one of the best players in the Premier League,' said Tottenham's manager, applying pressure. 'Sure, it's a big impact for them.'

● ● ●

For once Steve Walsh cannot take credit for a player. Jon Rudkin and 'Beags' – Steve Beaglehole – were responsible for getting King to Belvoir Drive in the autumn of 2004. A few weeks prior to Leicester's trial invite, King had scored twice for Chelsea against Beaglehole's Under-18 team. Once he was available, Leicester's youth chiefs were not slow to act.

Angie and John, his mum and dad, brought King up from the Thames Valley, a two-hour drive. He remembers the trial match: Sheffield United, back pitch, 6–1, he scored a header. The next week the Kings drove up again. Andy scored again, against MK Dons. How about training with us for a week, asked Rudkin, Leicester's academy manager then.

This meant King staying in 'digs' with older players, some aged 18, 19, and his mind raced: 'Are they going to do all this stuff to me?' But the lads were great. And so was his week. He loved the training under 'Beags'. And when his parents came, King remembers the scene in the bottom car park of Belvoir Drive: Rudkin chatting to his dad and then walking round to him and saying, 'Well, Andy, how would you like it if Leicester offered you a scholarship?'

His parents knew that was that and spent the journey home exchanging proud glances but he was too innocent to realise no academy manager would pose that question without following up with an offer. So, two days later, when his dad came off the phone and said, well, that was Rudkin, there is a contract – he was 'buzzing' all over again.

And King is still wide-eyed, and 'buzzing' as he recounts every small detail of how he and Leicester became an item. Twelve years on he remembers it all like yesterday. This is love. 'If I was ever to move, which fingers crossed doesn't happen,' he says at one point, 'I would be so nervous going into another changing room.'

You doubt he would, actually. King is friendly, perky, quick-witted, good to be around. He is like your favourite younger cousin in demeanour. Culture, before eating strategy for breakfast, has to start the day somehow. Leicester's rises each time a bright-eyed King flings back the covers: *How are we today? Decent.*

He is its guardian on the playing side – just as the long servers like Rudkin and Rennie are on the staff side. And he remembers the lot. Five permanent managers and three caretaker regimes in his first three years; the debut at 18 under Gary Megson, the first goal – a glorious 35-yarder – just after his 19th birthday.

He remembers relegation to League One; away days at clubs so sunken that, like Hereford United, they no longer exist; the toils of the Championship. Memory banks like these are what keep organisations going – but of course King offers even more than that. Leicester keep him on and on and on – because he is a very good player.

Some facts about King:

He is one of the very few in football history to play in a game where a club dropped to its lowest ever position (defeat to Brighton, 2008, sinking Leicester to sixth in the third tier) and then in a match where they ascended to their highest (3–0 v Newcastle 2015, when Leicester first topped the Premier League).

He was one of only two players, aged 27 or older, in the 2015–16 Premier League, who had never – not even on loan – played for another club.

He is Leicester's top-scoring midfielder of all time – and they have had some good ones.

And, as everyone kept reminding him by now, a unique achievement was in his grasp:

Andy King could become the first player, with one club, to win League One, the Championship and then the Premier League.

The biggest problem in King's life is dimming that Leicester-blue light that tends to shade his every thought. 'If something happens at the club, I kind of feel it more than other people,' he says. 'Even if it's got nothing to do with me. I am not great at switching off.'

• • •

Turning Leicester blue for a day was the kind of campaign local newspapers love. The *Leicester Mercury* launched it a day after the win at Sunderland. Then title fever raged unchecked. A sensible city was suddenly giddy. 'This is going to happen, isn't it?' was a headline in the *Leicester Mercury*.

The campaign – 'Backing the Blues' – was an idea to celebrate the club's heroics by asking residents to wear blue, decorate their homes blue and get up to stuff like a 'Ranieri Ride' for cyclists. The city council pledged landmarks like Town Hall, Clock Tower and New Walk Museum would be illuminated blue. The date set was Friday 29 April: two days before the team played at Old Trafford.

Ranieri, in a rare moment of dropping his guard, allowed himself to be quoted inviting Prince William to any title celebrations.

'Backing the Blues' filled a desperate need for new angles on Leicester. Every journalist was out of them. There had even been an in-depth feature on Vardy's plaster cast. What next? An interview with Wasilewski's beard? More and more fans gathered daily outside Belvoir Drive to mob the cars. But dropped points, Vardy's ban and Spurs' spike in form noticeably cooled things down.

Suddenly the daily 'Backing the Blues' update was on the *Mercury*'s inside pages and not the front. Come on guys. Lilu Fine Indian Dining offering blue cheese naan bread on the 29th? That could have stopped the presses just a few days before.

Even the significant news that Leicester were now assured automatic Champions League qualification (after Manchester City's draw at Newcastle) got downplayed. Summing up the mood was a letter to the *Mercury* from an elderly fan from Ashby-de-la-Zouch. 'We seem to have one way of playing – get the ball to Vardy and let him do the rest. I don't think we have time to bring another dimension to the way we play . . . The way

I feel at the moment is I wish we were just halfway up the league in a safe position as part of a four-year plan,' he wrote.

Ranieri, having spent all season playing down expectations, all of a sudden needed to pump everybody back up. He did not worry about the players – that dressing room would self-manage – but he did need the King Power, for Swansea on Sunday, at its raucous best.

Enough of playing these crunch games 10 versus 11. Leicester wanted to be 12 v 11 with their 'twelfth man' to be fully involved.

So . . . Ranieri gave the press conference of his life. Before it he had sat down with the club's media manager Anthony Herlihy and talked through how it should be approached. The tone and message were carefully planned. Of course his first decision was, unlike pre-West Ham, he would shake every single damn journalist's hand.

Once this ritual, at great length, was completed, Claudio began.

Rob Dorsett, the trusted Sky Sports reporter who gets to kick off all Leicester conferences, began with a line of questions about Vardy. Ranieri kept shutting them down. Even questions, like a gentle one about Roy Hodgson voicing support for his player, that any manager would normally take on.

Dorsett changed tack. How about three Leicester players, Mahrez, Vardy and Kanté, all being nominated for PFA Player of the Year? And here was the chance. 'Amazing . . .' Ranieri started. And then his faced changed, and he leant forward to grip his microphone.

'And . . . also . . . hey, man! We are in the Champions League. WE ARE IN THE CHAMPIONS LEAGUE, MAN! Dilly-ding, dilly-dong! Huh?'

The room changed too.

'You forget!' continued Ranieri, now leaning back and waving his hands.

'You speak about *blah blah blah*! But we are in Champions League! Fantastic. Terrific. Well done to everybody ... the owners, the players, the staff, everybody. Even Anthony.'

Herlihy willed away blushes as Ranieri gripped his shoulder. 'It is fantastic!' the manager said.

But now his voice dropped like a storyteller, getting to the good part.

'Now we go ... straight away ... to try and win the title. Yes! Only this. Only this remain.

'I know Pochettino. Mauricio ... keep calm!

'Now is the right moment to push. I believe!

'Five points ahead. I think they [Spurs] will win [their remaining games]. And we [will] win ... and then ...'

It was Oscar-winning stuff. Every reporter left the room with renewed confidence about Leicester's position, and Ranieri's performance dominated headlines and bulletins, just like the star actor hoped. A city reflated. The players, the staff too.

● ● ●

King was born in Barnstaple. He has been there just the once – on the day he arrived into the world, quite by surprise. Mum and Dad were on holiday in North Devon and on the eve of their departure for home, Andy made his move. Angie suddenly went into labour – two weeks ahead of due date. Going back to Maidenhead would have to wait. She was rushed to the local hospital, where she had her son.

Now this may be the only recorded instance of Andy King being in the wrong place at the wrong time. For his career is built on beautifully judged arrivals. Like runs into the box that lead to classic 'goalscoring midfielder' goals. By April 2016, he had 58 in nine seasons for Leicester, and inside the club, from dressing room to laundry room, people felt there would be at least one more 'Kingy moment' before the campaign was out. A goal and a goal of meaning, perhaps – because his strikes have a habit of being important.

King was among Ranieri's options as he looked to rejig the team. Ulloa would stand in for Vardy, that was obvious, but might there be a further tweak? Bringing in Schlupp, another fast player, was a thought. King had the most Leicester goals in the squad (including Vardy) but the thing about him, though always desperate to start, is he will always accept what is best for the side.

'Obviously I'd like to play more but when the team's winning you can't take yourself out of a 25-man squad and ask, "Why am I not playing?"' says King. 'It's not hard for me to play that [back-up] role if it's what the manager wants.'

At this point there was a further way he was looking after the greater good: as Mahrez's chauffeur. With the Algerian on a six-month speeding ban it was King who often drove him back to Stoneygate in his black club 4x4.

• • •

Other Kings were in supporters' thoughts as Swansea came round. Old monarchs of the cold. The 'Ice Kings', Leicester's greatest previous side. In

1962–63 this team were top of the First Division (the former top tier) with five games to go but blew their lead to the extent they finished fourth. Their similarities to the current Leicester team were striking.

The 'Ice Kings' players were misfits too. Signed cheaply, too. And likewise came from humble places like the factory floor.

Leicester had an imported manager (Matt Gillies, a Scot) and were known for a powerful dressing room spirit. They had a great goalkeeper (Gordon Banks), a Mahrez-like maverick (David Gibson), a quick scorer (Mike Stringfellow) and a centre-half (Frank McLintock) to rival Morgan.

There was even a King (Ian King) in the squad.

Their team hardly changed from week to week. It defended solidly and was devastating on the break. And, just as 53 seasons later, Leicester's groundsman was celebrated: the 'Ice Kings' name was because during England's worst winter in 200 years, Leicester's use of a chemically treated top soil allowed them to keep playing at Filbert Street while rivals kept having matches postponed.

But with five games to go the 'Ice Kings' had imploded. The old guys, many who continue living locally, still do not really know exactly why. But they do agree something damaging happened before their final run of games – they lost star players (like Gibson and Banks, through injury) and their winning formula was suddenly gone.

Four games left. No Vardy.

The 'Ice Kings', eh?

Ranieri chose Ulloa and did make a further twist to his selection for the visit to Swansea on Sunday April 24. Schlupp replaced Albrighton. King remained on the bench. Schlupp is easygoing and Ranieri wanted him pumped. 'Jeff, I need you, you are so powerful . . .' he told the player.

It was unseasonably cold but a gospel choir, now regulars outside the King Power, were warm in smile and voice. Leicester were 4-2-3-1 again: Schmeichel; Simpson, Morgan, Huth, Fuchs; Kanté, Drinkwater; Mahrez, Okazaki, Schlupp; Ulloa.

The King Power, oh the King Power that day . . . 'We Are Fearless', said one giant flag. Across two great banners spread 'History Makes Us Who We Are'.

The first song sung after the *Post Horn Gallop* was 'We Shall Not Be Moved'.

'We are Going For It!' was the stadium announcer's cry.

The clappers clapped slower, firmer, louder than you had ever heard before: rhythmic, aurally hypnotic. 'Hey Jude' boomed, *na na na naah*. Ranieri stood ramrod straight in his overcoat, right out by the pitch. *This* was what Ranieri wanted. This stadium in the palm of his hand.

Swansea started well enough but the scurrying of Kanté and the closing down of Drinkwater were soon scratching at their calm. The noise would not be stopping. Pressure: Ashley Williams, usually tough of mind, blew a mental fuse. His attempt to clear was casual and straight to Mahrez.

Mahrez moved into the box, slowing time the way he does, liquidly checked left, then stroked a shot past Łukasz Fabiański. 1–0.

Now Morgan, fighting for territory, won a free kick. Drinkwater delivered and Ulloa, rising, and almost already smiling as it struck the net, powered a header in. 2–0.

Schmeichel stopped what he had to. Morgan held the defensive line. Drinkwater and Kanté were two men against the four in Swansea's packed central midfield but it was almost, it felt to Swansea players, like Leicester had the extra man in there.

Mahrez floated where he pleased. Okazaki worked until he was drenched, and then worked some more. And Ranieri's picks? Schlupp's power and speed ensured a new outlet for breakaways, meaning Leicester could keep playing their favourite game and Ulloa, once Argentina's unknown striker, was stamping his name all over the game.

Ulloa outmanning a defender (Federico Fernández) who'd played in a World Cup finals for their country was, like little Kanté muscling big Leroy Fer around, a further image of against-odds Leicester.

The noise, the clappers, keep going. Second half: Fernández lost a 50–50 to Schlupp, who made the box and, after Williams blocked, got the ball to Ulloa for him to score at the far post. 3–0.

And then King was on, Demarai Gray too. Gray sped down the right, his youthful audacity dazzling. King headed back to him, Fabiański parried his shot and a third substitute, Albrighton, slammed it in for 4–0.

Under their biggest pressure, Leicester had recorded their biggest win of 2015–16. 'We're going to win the league,' sang fans, no longer shy. And another song ... *Mauricio* . . . *keep calm* . . . was, 'Tottenham Hotspur, we're coming for you.'

Vardy, in grey gilet, clapped from a private box and Fabio Capello, there for Italian TV, effused about Ranieri. Capello had spoken to the BBC, pre-match, about how tension might 'block the legs', but Leicester had seldom looked to be running so free.

'Four-nil to the one-man team' came the new song, then, 'Barcelona, we're coming for you.' Through the final moments nearly the whole stadium was on its feet, clappers going, everyone singing, and at the final whistle Ranieri was on the pitch – bumping chests with Huth and Morgan in ironical sports jock celebration.

The manager had got his motivating just right, but so had that self-managing dressing room. Social media was back to play a part. Harry Kane's Instagram pic of the lions? Just like the Arsenal selfies it had merely served to hype up Morgan and co.

'That is when I thought, "Right, we are going to win this,"' says Schmeichel. 'You saw them [Spurs] thinking, "We have got them now," and I think they got a little overconfident.

'That [Kane's post] probably wasn't the cleverest thing. That is not the type of stuff we do. And it fuelled us, I think. It was defiance now: "We are not going to let this happen."

'You can see it in our performance [against Swansea]. You could see that we were just ready for it – and you could feel it in the dressing room before the game. There was no way we were going to go out and get anything less than a win. Definitely not.'

The 'one-man team' thing? There is not a Leicester player who does not appreciate Vardy's uniqueness. But had people learned nothing? Leicester, from laundry room to dressing room, to the tan leather cabin of the owners' helicopter, were a collective. No Vardy? *Doable*, as Andy King might say.

'I suppose the media have to create some type of story: "There is no Vards – are they going to win?" We proved that we are a full team,' says

Morgan. 'That we are good. Everyone is a good player. Everyone can do their part.'

● ● ●

Spurs hosted West Brom the following evening. They started on fire, hit posts, skimmed bars, and forced a first-half goal when Craig Dawson put the ball into West Brom's net. Yet there was a flattening of the atmosphere at White Hart Lane as a second Spurs goal refused to arrive and West Brom dug in, and with 17 minutes remaining, Dawson equalised. And now a Spurs player, Dele Alli, faced FA trouble for a punch.

The situation had flipped again. Worst-case scenario with four games left had been that Leicester would have to win three to secure the title but now, with three games to go, just one victory was the very most they would need. *Hey, man!*

● ● ●

Andy King thought about Matty James. And he thought about his own brother and sister, Dave and Sally.

James was his friend, his fellow Copenhagen turtle – and, for three previous seasons, his midfield rival. But exactly a year ago James ruptured a cruciate ligament and his 2015–16 had been in such contrast to the rest of the squad. He suffered, he waited, he rehabbed, he pushed. He got back on the field. But in January, on a terrible pitch at Blackburn, he tore his meniscus playing for the Under-21s.

James strove again, but for the last month had known he would not be making it back into the first team before the end. He put on his bravest face (apart from to Drinkwater, his closest pal), always saying 'yeah, good' when the lads asked how recovery was progressing. Privately, though, he had some low, low times. King thought about Matty and Matty's mum and dad: while everyone else was so happy, how was all this for them?

Always, Dave and Sally are in mind. 'My mum and dad drove me to Chelsea three times a week from the age of eight. Tuesday night, Thursday night, Saturday or Sunday. The support they've given is absolutely brilliant,' King says, 'but I'm especially lucky about my brother and sister.

'They could easily have thought, "Oh, he's the favourite child, why are our parents always with him?" But they never once moaned about, "Oh, Mum, I want to go to the cinema on Tuesday, why are you taking Andy to football?" Or, "Dad, why are you never here on a Sunday? I want to do my homework, but you are always watching him play."'

In *The Winner Within: A Life Plan for Team Players*, by Pat Riley, the great NBA coach, a key chapter is 'The Innocent Climb'. In it he describes the phenomenon of a sports side comprising unselfish members, without a history of title-winning, beginning an 'innocent climb' to greatness. Such a side achieves greatness when team members dedicate themselves to one another, trust their bonds, and fearlessly follow instinct.

'Innocence' is not naivety, Riley asserts. Naivety is not understanding what it takes; Innocence is knowing, but casting away personal feelings. Andy King is innocent in the Riley sense. On he climbs ... *League One, Championship, Premier League* ... but his thoughts are about the group. And others were similar. King was not called 'Mr Leicester' for nothing.

'The crisis of yesterday is the joke of tomorrow,' said H. G. Wells – one of the many aphorisms quoted by Riley. One-man team? The lions of Tottenham coming for you through snow? Now the laughter was from the boys of Belvoir Drive.

Ken Way, Leicester's sports psychologist, is someone who has worked with world champions, on television and in big business. What was his trick that helped the squad dispel pressure during the run-in? Not long before the Swansea game, Way gave Oliver Kay of *The Times* a self-effacing interview.

Vardy used him, he said – but then Vardy always had. Having had doubts about the step-up when he first joined Leicester in 2012, the striker started consulting Way then and had not stopped. But it was small stuff. Keeping the mind clear for scoring goals.

As for the others: Way was very underemployed. So much so, that during the run-in he had been able to go on holiday.

'I was concerned, earlier in the season, about how [the pressure] might start to affect the players but it honestly hasn't. It's not a stressful situation. It's only stressful if you allow it to be,' Way said.

Nothing had suddenly 'clicked' in Leicester's mentality, he added – the squad had always been like that.

It is what Peter Schmeichel swears. A regular visitor to Belvoir Drive, to see Kasper, he 'can guarantee' the mood there was 'exactly the same' when Leicester stood on the cusp of the title as when they were battling relegation. Leicester innocently climbed.

Fighting relegation? Now *that* was pressure, players like King, Morgan,

Schmeichel, Huth, kept telling journalists. Leicester could win the title in their next game, at grand Old Trafford, a dream circumstance – but when Schlupp met reporters 48 hours before the match, what he really wanted to talk about was not glory but the chef, the laundry ladies, the kit man, and all the other unsung staff. The ones who had been to the brink and back with the team itself.

Schlupp had been at Leicester since he was 12, almost went to Manchester United once, but like King was a happy one-club man. King knows where Schlupp was coming from. 'Rach[el] who works in the office ... Macca the kit man ... the two laundry ladies ... Dave the physio ... Like Jeff said, seeing those people made you realise you were in a privileged position at the top of the league.

'Delie and Sheila [in laundry] had their money cut and almost lost their jobs when we got relegated a few years ago. [Former captain] Matt Elliott had to do a whip-round just to keep them in a job. To see people like that, who have been through the whole thing – from League One all the way up – keeps it all kind of grounded,' King says.

The steps of Leicester's climb worked for them in the closing weeks, King believes. In 2009 the team won League One. In 2014, the Championship. In 2015, seven victories from nine to avoid relegation, there was another experience of going down the stretch, having to win, and pulling it off.

'As the run-in came to an end and it was us versus Tottenham. You were thinking, "Hold on, I know it's a different league, but seven or eight of us in this squad have won the Championship. Some had won leagues in foreign countries. Hold on. We are used to being in this situation."

'You looked at Tottenham and they didn't really have that. Most of their players had played in the Premier League a long time but never been in [a title] situation. One thing I have said for a long time now is that when the pressure is on, you cannot say Leicester crumble.

'[The 2013 play-off loss to] Watford was as bad as you can imagine,' says King. 'Whatever happened could not hurt as much as that game. From Watford we got promoted, then the Great Escape. So, when people said this year, "They are going to crumble," I am thinking, "We are not."

'This is a strong, mentally strong group of players. We don't crumble.'

● ● ●

After the Swansea game, once the players had showered and changed, the gleaming, blue Agusta A109S whirred skyward from the grass at the King Power Stadium and Khun Vichai's helicopter took Mahrez, Kanté and Vardy to London for that evening's PFA awards. Mahrez won. 'Backing the Blues' day was a great success, with blue sausages and 'Vardyccino' coffee among the attractions, as city-folk allowed themselves a little giddiness again. Someone put a scarf round the statue of Richard III.

Steve Madeley reckons it took Ranieri '20 minutes' to do all the handshakes in the most packed media room yet before his pre-Manchester United press conference. But this time the message was straightforward. No dramatics, no dilly-dongs. *Focus*, said Claudio. *Work*.

'Everything is in our hands and if our strength is to be concentrated, solid – we have to continue,' he said. Reminded that after 28 years in management, all those nearly seasons, he was one game from winning his first major title, he smiled thinly.

'A good opportunity,' he said. 'Let me be calm.'

Good news was Vardy's personal hearing went well: he would only be banned for this one further game.

That Sunday, on May 1, Leicester city centre again turned Leicester blue, as thousands packed the pubs in club colours. The scarf stayed on old Richard. Blue candles were lit in Leicester cathedral. Away tickets were offered for £1,850 online. Those Leicester fans who made it into Old Trafford mocked the doubters one more time, raising a banner saying 'We Are Staying Up.'

But Manchester United were not rolling over to become somebody else's footnote. Ranieri retained the starting XI from the Swansea thrashing, yet United were a different proposition and immediately Leicester were pinned, penned and forced back. United, in one of their best 30 minutes of the season, attacked in waves and Anthony Martial knocked home after an unanswerable United move.

For the first time all season Leicester had conceded in the opening ten minutes and Jesse Lingard looked certain to make it 2–0 but, somehow, Schmeichel saved. 'Come on, boys,' shouted big Wes.

And, from Leicester's first significant attack, with a burly header, he scored. He ran to the support, arms out, grin so wide.

It was an even game from there. Maybe King, on as substitute, should have won it. Maybe – no definitely – Huth was naughty to pull Marouane Fellaini's hair: he too now faced a ban. Drinkwater was sent off, late on, for a second booking. 1–1 full-time.

Leicester would have to wait for the title but a point, after such a difficult start, with such high stakes, felt not far from a win. Because Tottenham had to win at Chelsea now. 'We'll be watching tomorrow night,' Morgan told TV with that big Viv Richards smile.

In the Sky Sports studio Graeme Souness, not Leicester's chief admirer throughout the season, held up his hands. 'Manchester United were fabulous for half an hour but it's as if . . .' he said, '. . . the small team comes to the big team, the big team gets the great start and a goal. You think the small team's going to start feeling sorry for themselves . . . but to a man, none of them threw the towel in. You could just see them grinding themselves back into the game. In the second half they were the better team.

'That 90 minutes typifies what the season has all been about: "When adversity comes we deal with it." It's really, really hard to be anything other than utterly in awe of this team.'

Would Ranieri be watching Spurs play Chelsea? He did not plan to. Monday was his mother's birthday and they had a date: he would be treating Renata, 96 years old, to lunch in Rome. Rosanna was going too.

Claudio went. They all ate wonderfully. He had steak and chicory, followed by strawberries with lemon and sugar. They spent two hours talking. He was relaxed, Renata said, and he spoke about what things were like at his football club.

'Claudio told me he had found a great group of players who have trained like true professionals and finally everything has fallen into place and my son has found himself,' Renata revealed.

He calls her every night. But now he had to go. He had decided, after all, to watch Tottenham play at Stamford Bridge and a car waited to take him to Ciampino Airport. With Khun Vichai's £43m Gulfstream 650 laid on, Claudio and Rosanna flew back to East Midlands and then went on home.

If the fans sing 'Jamie Vardy's having a party,' why not live up to it? Most of the squad headed for Melton Mowbray and the striker's house. Together, fittingly together, they would watch Chelsea versus Tottenham there. And in the centre of Leicester the bars filled up again. And in houses, perhaps from behind sofas, residents of all ages watched their televisions too.

● ● ●

An Eden Hazard goal concluded the 2014–15 title race on 3 May. And on 2 May 2015–16? Hazard . . . well . . .

Spurs began at Stamford Bridge ablaze with intent. Son Heung-min missed early but Kane rounded Asmir Begović and finished a sublime, one-touch move, by rolling the ball in. Son went through for 2–0 just before half-time.

But Chelsea players, with bitter history between the clubs, had promised to stop Tottenham winning the title, and affection for their former manager had Chelsea supporters holding 'Let's Do It For Ranieri' placards.

Roared on, Chelsea pushed back and Gary Cahill converted at a corner. Diego Costa nearly tapped in an equaliser and Spurs were suddenly losing impetus, making fouls, losing discipline.

Then Hazard, Hazard of all players, Hazard whose pitiful season was a symbol of the Premier League elite's decline; then Hazard, who started off the whole weirdness of 2015–16 when he fatefully called for treatment at Swansea on opening day; then Hazard . . . well . . .

Hazard took the ball just inside Tottenham's half. He burst forward, suddenly so dynamic. He threw off markers. He passed to Costa, who drew defenders in, and then returned him the ball. He received it a yard inside Tottenham's box.

And he did not need space, and he did not need time. He shaped his body, swept his right foot, and this was geometry.

Hugo Lloris was set but Hazard's right foot spun the ball. Lloris dived, but this was past him. And Hazard scored.

And . . .

Chickah chickah chickah.

Fearless.

Chase now over.

Leicester City. Bloody Leicester City! Champions.

16

FEARLESS

And so they came. From their quiet houses, down their mellow streets, from every corner of a modest city they came – except nothing was quiet or mellow or modest any more. Not now.

Not tonight.

Lads danced with arms round each other, bouncing in the light rain. A woman and girl, in pyjamas, walked arm in arm. They laughed as they followed those thronging towards the stadium.

People running. People carrying bottles. People swigging from cans.

A grey-haired fella in a jubba, grinning wide. Boisterous teens in 'Jamie Vardy Party' T-shirts. Men in wigs. Men in shorts – though it was chilly. Men carrying kids: on one's shoulders, a tiny girl, her face painted blue. It was 10.45pm by now, but bedtime rules had gone.

Drivers beeped their horns in football-chant rhythms. You heard the first honks on the roads within a minute of full-time at Stamford Bridge. Motorbikes revved. Attached to a car roof was a giant football. Windows wound down and camera phones were thrust out, recording the noise and nonsense of moments for which there was no pack drill, no plan.

When Real Madrid win something their public know it is tradition to head to Madrid's Cibeles Square. In Munich you pull your lederhosen on, grab your flags and head to Marienplatz and Munich Town Hall.

But this was Leicester. *What did we do when we saw off Tranmere to win that Worthington Cup, Dad?* No, nothing prepared anyone for this.

The King Power seemed the logical place to go. So, turning Raw Dykes Road and Aylestone Road into the world's happiest traffic jam, the cars headed there and the people jogged on pavements towards the stadium concourse.

A people carrier was parked right in the middle of the growing, dancing crowd and an elderly couple were inside it. As you got closer you noticed something about the old man: his hair was spiked in a Leicester blue Mohican.

Nobody really found the right chant. 'Championes', 'Ran-ieri', 'Les-tah' (to 'Hey Jude') all had turns, but none became the song of the night, nothing did.

Nothing quite was the defining image. Lads climbed on a Portakabin and danced under a giant #FEARLESS sign. But, 'Is that it?' carped fans of other clubs when those images spread on social media.

Yet that was the point. This was Leicester, this was no city of extroverts, of triumphalism, of preparedness for success. One thing you noticed about the King Power party was the (relative) sobriety: plenty there were Asians and not drinking. Merely joyful.

And you know what? It was different, nice.

Aleem, Adil, Mahira, Riz – they came. 'This has put us on the map!' said Riz. 'Haven't eaten all day,' 19-year-old Aleem added.

Andy Miller, with his sons Luca and Ethan, and friends Roy and Matt – they came. Andy thought about the journey, his 30-odd years of supporting his local club. 'Losing Martin O'Neill ... having David Pleat in charge ... playing in front of just 7,000 at Filbert Street ...' he said, reeling off the low points. 'Oh, Grimsby away, 0–0 ...

'And when we got smashed 4–1 at Ipswich. New Year, 1995. God. The lights on my Vauxhall Nova had gone and I crawled home in drizzle, everyone flashing us the whole way.'

Luca, eight – 'he's got school, but it doesn't matter' – looked at his dad like he was speaking Swahili. 'Everyone who was a fan pre the Premier League remembers it being like this,' said Andy. Roy and Matt agreed between swigs from a champagne bottle. 'Back then everyone had a chance,' Andy continued. 'Nobody decided in advance who the top in England would be.'

He praised Pearson, for starting to bring the right type of player to the club. He laughed about reading Khun Vichai's 'Top Five in three years' pledge in the paper.

Ranieri had made a difference, he said. So had nobody really getting injured. And, of course, 'team spirit – we've got team spirit.' But it still did not make sense. Andy said, 'Tell you what I remember: that first game versus Everton, back in the Premier League [a 2–2 draw, August 2014]. I'm thinking fucking hell! They're just playing the ball about, just playing with us. I thought, "we're going to struggle to touch the ball in this division, let alone win a game."'

There was more noise and nonsense in town, on Horsefair Street and Gallowtree Gate and Town Hall Square. A younger, boozier, crowd had spilled out of the bars and towards the Clock Tower. Some tried to climb it. Some had a football that they were hoofing about. To one side was a Buddhist guy banging bells against a drum as some lairy lads danced beside him.

You went past the Sporting Success Statue on Gallowtree Gate, a bronze commemorating the 'heady' years from 1996–8 when Leicestershire were cricket champions, the Tigers won the Pilkington Cup and Leicester City were ... COCA-COLA CUP WINNERS!! You thought, just maybe, there will be a new sculpture on the way.

• • •

Defining imagery did emerge, in the end, but not from Leicester itself. It zapped its way from Melton Mowbray to phones, websites and televisions around the world. Vardy (of course) was having a party. With the squad round at his to watch the Spurs game, Herlihy, with a club camera guy, was there.

The media team had realised that if Leicester won the title that night the world would want a window on their celebrations. The players took some persuading. Morgan, as always, was the dressing room conduit. This was a private get-together.

But, as usual at this club, one group listened to another and yielded to expertise. And a collaborative outcome was reached. The PR lads could come – so long as they were unobtrusive and the players approved what they put out.

Tipped off by an agent, television stations, chiefly Sky Sports, wanted to gatecrash, but the club stood firm and kept the cameras out. Because there was a risk: if Leicester did not win this Premier League then the whole evening at Vardy's might come to look like a terrible episode of counting chickens.

But anyway, what the hell, everyone said, and Vardy passed round the Jupiler beers.

● ● ●

So. You are Andy King and you are round at a teammate's place, supposedly to celebrate winning the league with all the lads. But Tottenham are 2–0 up and rampant after 45 minutes. Beer bottle down. 'We sat there and thought, "Well, this is awkward." Like, "I need a water because we have training tomorrow."

'Everyone had arrived buzzing and started drinking but now it was "Hold on . . . we have a game. There is a game we need to win on Saturday!"' King says. 'If there weren't people outside I honestly reckon most players would have left at half-time.'

Ah yes, the people outside. Steve Madeley was covering the story for *The Times*. He arrived at Vardy's an hour before Spurs kicked off and there were 'about 25–30' fans outside it. Most were not there in the hope of revelry but autograph hunters who wanted to catch the players arriving in their cars. Madeley went back to his vehicle to view the game online and a Sky Sports truck parked in front of him.

He was focused on the match. At full-time he re-emerged and walked round the truck, which had been blocking the view to the street. Suddenly there '400–500' fans outside Vardy's; 45 minutes later there were approaching 3,000.

Police closed roads. Security guards, summoned earlier, were stopping punters getting through Vardy's gates or climbing on the low wall of his garden.

Vardy's is a new-build detached house – footballerish but not lavish – in a residential street of similar homes. But now this place heaved like Mardi Gras. Or, as a reveller with hidden tabloid-headline talent put it, like *Vardy Gras*. So there was no way out. The players stayed for the second period. 'When Cahill scored, we were buzzing. When Hazard did what he did we were like ... the place went absolutely as wild as you would imagine,' grins King. 'We broke Vardy's TV.'

How?

'As everyone crowded into the wall [after Hazard scored] it was hit. There was another further round so it was fine. But it was unbelievable. When the final whistle went ... and it wasn't even a nervous last five or ten minutes because if anything Chelsea were going to score again.'

Tottenham rather lost it in those last minutes, with four bookings (taking their match total to nine) in quick succession, with players in melees, spats and gouging eyes. 'If Chelsea went forward, somebody would smash one of their players but that was fine: there is nobody better at surrounding the ref than Chelsea players. They could waste five minutes, going in, pushing, blah blah blah,' says King.

'Then [Spurs] had a free kick. Everyone was like, "Ohhhh." Then it was blasted wide and everyone cheered. The final whistle went and for fifteen or twenty minutes everyone went mad.'

The defining imagery was captured then. The club grabbed such great pictures: group shots of the lads, arms round shoulders, almost tumbling as they hugged, grinned and roared simultaneously. Pure team bliss. Fuchs filmed a bit of the scene and his footage, together with the club stuff, scorched around cyberspace.

In the UK alone, Twitter activity spiked 86 per cent that night.

Wasilewski stole the spotlight. Clad in an off-beat T-shirt plainly either the expensive work of a cutting-edge designer, or just a white garment he had let his children scrawl on, he thrust his giant, bearded, grinning self into the centre of almost every shot.

And, the next day, some priceless extra footage emerged of 'Was', like one of those 'World's Strongest Man' contestants hauling a vehicle, dragging a giggling Morgan along the floor of Vardy's kitchen.

But then, after the initial joy, something changed for a while. Says King, 'It went flat for twenty minutes. People tried to digest it. "*What now?* We have won the Premier League." It was almost like something had died a little bit because you had reached the goal you had dreamed about. *Now what?*

'Lads were calling or trying to FaceTime their families, stuff like that. We sat around for twenty minutes going, "What has just happened there?"'

A bit like the moment caught on film of Danny Willett, in the club house at Augusta, having won golf's Masters, not sure what to do and ending up in an awkward phone conversation with his wife?

'Yeah,' King agrees. 'I have read other stuff where people find they have reached their thing and then a bit of them goes.

'Do you watch *Only Fools and Horses*? It's like when Del Boy and Rodney had got that money from the watch. Someone calls asking, "Are you going to be interested in these fires?" Del is like, "Yeah." Rodney is like, "Del, we don't trade any more." It kills Del inside.

'It was obviously not to that level for us, because there is different stuff for this team to now go and achieve. But we had so much pressure. "Are they going to do it? Are they going to do it? Are they going to do it? This is their chance."

'So when it was done, the relief for everyone was like, *ahhhh*. We all took a twenty-minute deep breath. And then we started enjoying ourselves again.'

• • •

Middlesex Road, where you enter the Belvoir Drive training ground, made for another mad street scene the following morning. Police stopped photographers standing on residents' bins to get vantage points. Forty or fifty fans kept a vigil in the rain. There was a man with a beautiful Lambretta scooter parked there, bearing the legend 'Fearless'. There were American, Italian, Japanese camera crews. The postman and a linen van were applauded in.

The Agusta helicopter touched down, bearing Top and Khun Vichai. On the door to the physio room Dave Rennie hung a sign: 'Closed due to unforeseen circumstances'. Underneath was a picture of the Premier League trophy and 'CHAMPIONS'.

Ranieri held court to a dozen or so journalists. They applauded him in and applauded him back out again. His last words were to thank everyone for their 'respect' throughout the season – though he added, 'I know next year you will have to criticise me again . . .' And of course he shook hands.

He was candid and disclosed some things he had been keeping to himself, some of his thinking as the title run evolved. He told how important it had been, after arriving, to just observe how the group worked; how he ignored the negative press about his appointment. A crucial moment, he said, was changing from the back three to 4-2-3-1.

Another step, he said, was realising Mahrez was more dangerous on the right flank cutting onto his left foot, and Albrighton the opposite: on the left cutting onto his right. He twigged, at a very early stage, that counterattacking was Leicester's weapon.

The 3–1 at Manchester City was the moment he knew the team really could be champions but it had been vital not to overthink, to stay 'step by step' and thus retain fearlessness. 'We were like climbers, if you look down: "Oh God." No, come on, look up,' he said.

Then Ranieri, the players, the staff – and a Vardy impersonator – boarded a silver coach: the owners were taking them to San Carlo restaurant, in Granby Street, for celebrations. Simpson's tweet was heartfelt: 'I swear to god I fucking love this team. You don't understand. No one does. Fucking unreal. I don't know what to do.'

In the middle of all this now was Schmeichel – but twelve hours previously he had not been with the lads. Instead he was in a car racing down dark roads from Cheshire, long after midnight, to Melton Mowbray. To join them late. And here is why.

In very Schmeichel-ish, none-of-that-nonsense, fashion, he had shunned the party. 'I, personally, had not watched any of Tottenham's games until then. And I had no intention of watching that game either,' he explains. So he stayed in Alderley Edge, with Stine and the kids. His brother-in-law was visiting and they went for dinner.

They got back home and he switched his phone off and started putting little Isabella to bed. 'My wife came in to say goodnight to our daughter and I looked at her [Stine], she sort of looked back, and I could see in her face that something had happened. "There is something wrong. Tell me now!"

'So she told me that Tottenham were 2–0 up. I thought, "Well, I might as well watch it. There's nothing to lose."'

Son Max, six, joined him in front of the television. About five minutes before Hazard scored, Max fell asleep, sprawled across Kasper's lap. There he stayed. So, when Hazard's goal went in and subsequently full-time arrived, one dad in Cheshire was screaming history's biggest silent 'Yesssssssssss!' Punching the air, taking care not to budge a snoozing six-year-old.

'I tried to celebrate but I couldn't really. I was just sat there,' Kasper grins. He knows nothing could have been more fitting.

His goalkeeping, a family business. His life, family focused. Yup, the moment fitted; for the memory bank that moment will do.

Kasper got Max off to bed then jumped in the car and when he got to Melton Mowbray the Vardy Gras was still going on. 'I mean, there is one thing watching it with the lads,' says Kasper, 'but the family are there . . . have always been there . . . are the ones you spend time away from. Your kids make sacrifices that they didn't ask to make.

'People only really see the 90 minutes a week. They don't see the work that goes in. All the way through your youth. All the time you spend away from your family. So, it was nice to share that moment with family. You know, you share moments with your teammates every day.'

• • •

The little, low-key notes of Leicester's symphony of dreams. Maybe it was those that were most important now.

The world media celebration was extraordinary. In Italy, *La Gazetta dello Sport* had 'King Claudio' above an image of Ranieri as Julius Caesar. But none of the big stuff quite had the meaning of a small video made by a Turkish broadcaster a week before.

It was simple. The Turkish crew just took a camera around Leicester inviting ordinary folk to thank Ranieri. Vicky from Leicester market, young kids, old ladies, Asian lads, a young group of black friends and, memorably, 'from everyone at Leicester station!' – these were simple messages of appreciation.

The last speaker was a woman who patted her heart. 'Follow your home town and believe ... Leicester is true testament,' she said. When Ranieri saw it he welled up. 'All my sacrifice,' he said, 'is this.'

The types of people in that video. The local. The loyal. The ordinary lives enriched by a team's success – a payout far greater than the thousands of pounds being received by punters who gambled at 5000-1. Those Leicester betting stories were fun – but a bit like 'Dilly-ding, dilly-dong', they were the froth, the spume, atop deep waters of happiness and meaning.

The day after the title was won you thought of the folk in the video – how is their day today?

You thought of people like Chandu Dave. How were the odds-and-sods in the Lost Bar doing? How was Andy Miller's hangover?

What of Jasbir Rupra's family? He, a 67-year-old, loved Leicester but had never attended a game. His son, Perminder, a season ticket holder, took him to the Newcastle match on 14 March. He had, Perminder said, 'the most amazing night'. Leaving the King Power he had a heart attack. Leicester fans staged a minute's applause to honour him at the Southampton game. Perminder said this made him love his club even more. What did today mean to him?

And not just in Leicester: around the world followers of forgotten teams, locals from modest cities – they could also smile.

Why not? Solidarity lived. The last home game was Everton and an Everton fan donated two match tickets so a Leicester dad could take his boy: on the black market such tickets were being offered at £15,000 a pair.

• • •

Andrea Bocelli is a Grand Officer of the Order of Merit of the Italian Republic. He has a star on the Hollywood Walk of Fame. He has released 40 best-selling albums and sells out concerts in every corner where he sings.

He could probably gargle and it would move people. But what was Bocelli doing around 5pm on 7 May 2016? He was seen in a corridor of the King Power, pacing in deep focus, rehearsing as if the next performance was his first. His humble professionalism struck chords at a football club.

Bocelli had come to visit them, Leicester City, little Leicester, having followed their story and then called Ranieri to ask if he could sing at their celebrations. Ranieri has had worse offers. And so Bocelli was getting ready to take to the pitch. The *Post Horn Gallop* was incidental music – just this once.

The stage that was assembled for the blind tenor – who lost his sight in a football accident – was very Leicester. Bocelli's agent had called: what will Andrea be singing on? No one had really thought. He needs a stage! Flowers! the agent said. So a can-do young club employee grabbed some paper and sketched something out. Bocelli's rep approved.

The stage looked wonderful: Leicester blue and with seven giant square pots of blue-and-white flowers swaying in the breeze. And so Bocelli came out, led by Ranieri. Ranieri thanked the fans then with a very Caesar-like arm (but kindly smile) signalled for quiet. They did not obey quickly – quietness did not come easily today – but when they started hushing, Bocelli began.

And his song started, *None shall sleep!*

and went on, *watch the stars that tremble with love and with hope.*

and ended, *I win! I win! I win!*

That's the translation, anyway, from the Italian that he sang in. The song was 'Nessun Dorma', since the Italia 90 World Cup, English football's favourite aria.

● ● ●

With any other club, any other players, the game itself would have been mere exhibition; just filler before a trophy presentation. But, like Bocelli in the corridor, pushing yourself was something ingrained in Leicester.

Players still had memories of winning the Championship in 2014 but then being thumped by Brighton as they took it easy in their next home game and even now, even as Premier League champions, that still gnawed at them. This would not be another squib. Way they saw it, they still owed the fans.

Everton were dire, the only eleven men in the stadium who wanted to be elsewhere. But Leicester were electric. Huth, for his Fellaini hair-tug, and Drinkwater, for his Old Tafford red card, were banned, so King and big Wasilewski started.

After five minutes, from a lovely King chip, Vardy scored on the half-volley. He added a second-half penalty and late on, to his annoyance, missed from the spot. Kevin Mirallas's fine solo effort was Everton's consolation. 3–1. 33 goal attempts: one of Leicester's very best performances of the season.

Their other and best goal came from King. Told you he would strike again. Okazaki led a break and played to Mahrez and Marhez dribbled, throwing jinks and stepovers at Leighton Baines. Baines was not quite fooled and managed to knock the ball away but King was arriving and King was unerring. His crisp, first-time finish was so natural and Joel Robles had no chance to save.

'A lot of people had said to me, "I think you're going to score." With this whole journey I've been on fans were willing me. Riyad puts a great chance on my head and I head it straight at the goalie . . . but when Riyad got it again I thought, "This is me . . . I am not missing this."

'The emotion when that went in . . .' he says. 'I have a really nice photo in front of the fans. It just happened I was stood in front of it. A sign that said, "Made In Leicester".'

Full-time. Presentation time. And lions again. When the title was secured Vardy had posted a very *chat shit get banged* tweet: a picture of a cartoon lion slithering down a cliff towards oblivion, his riposte to Kane's 'coming for you' lions tweet.

The lions at hand now were gold and on the handles of the great silver Premier League trophy. And Morgan accepted it with Ranieri, lifting eyes to the heavens. Then they both smiled. Then thrust it up. Players piled forward and the fireworks and ticker tape launched. *Watch the stars . . . I win! I win! I win!*

● ● ●

It was the time for families now. Khun Vichai and Top, father and son, took the trophy. The players had turns holding it and beckoned their nearest and dearest to join them on the pitch.

The photographs taken that day may end up meaning more to them than their medals. A lovely one: Kasper, with Stine, Max and Isabella at the front – and Peter in the back row among other close family.

Huth was there with his wife and boys. The Outlier: and Huth was not as misty as the rest.

'As a person, I am not emotionally less ... but I am very even. The moment is flat line for me,' he admits. 'Even when we lifted the trophy it was amazing but I wasn't overwhelmed. Maybe because we had a week's celebration beforehand. When Hazard scored the goal, the 2–2, that was probably the bigger emotion.

'But it wasn't the best day of my life.'

What was? 'Kids. My kids being born. Every day since then. The kids.'

King? 'That Saturday was the best day of my life. I'm just going to put it out there. That two hours at the end on the pitch with all the family and friends, seeing your teammates and their families and friends, seeing how happy everyone was, how happy the supporters were . . . it is not going to get any better than that for me,' he says.

With King were his mum, dad and girlfriend Camilla and her family. His brother and sister and their partners and children, too. And friends from school. 'I had about twenty people there,' he grins and pulls out his phone to show the pictures. 'These are the people who have dealt with me during the highs and lows of my career and these are the people who had to be there.'

Maybe the very most meaningful pictures belong to Albrighton. 'Let me reel them off: Chloe, Matilda-Beau, Dolly-Boo, Lisa, James, Madeline, Terry, Carol, Darren, Connor, Rosie, Jack, Jack, Steven . . .' he smiles, going along the many faces. 'I managed to get a photo of us all with the trophy. Every single one of the people who are most special to me were all on the pitch. It's so much more than a picture. It's a massive thank you.'

Chloe and the girls. Mum and dad. Sister and brother. His three very best mates. And other family. And Marc is wearing a T-shirt. It bears a picture of Sue Davey, Chloe's late mum. Connor said there was no way she should miss the celebrations.

Albrighton was so determined to have everyone there to share this moment that he had bought a box for the last game, at Chelsea, believing the trophy would be presented then. Cue a panic when he realised the presentation would be at the King Power. He only had eight tickets for the Everton game. 'I was devastated, because I needed everyone to be there. They were the ones there when things were going bad.' In the end Leicester found him tickets (and Chelsea refunded his box).

'We just had an unbelievable occasion,' Albrighton says. 'I keep going back to the pictures.'

• • •

Champagne flowed. Not always where Ranieri wanted. During his press conference an excitable Austrian burst in to empty a magnum over the manager. Ranieri stayed dignified but his expression said it all. Christian: not the time and place for there to be No Fuchs Given.

Ranieri was not the only Italian drenched. Outside the King Power, long past 10.30pm, soaked by the rain, were ragged but exuberant travellers. These were from the 1,100 young fans from Italy who had made their pilgrimage to the Leicester miracle, joined by Edoardo Magro, the 'Jesus of Leicester' with 'Drinkbeer' on his back.

None had tickets. Just being outside the King Power was good enough and now they wanted to hail Ranieri. Their tale was an example of how Leicester had captured far-off imaginations.

In Italy, of foreign games shown on TV in 2015–16, only *El Clásico* drew bigger ratings than Leicester matches. The country's biggest morning radio DJ had a running joke that 'today I won't talk about Leicester again' – then always did.

A group formed via Facebook, using the hashtag #Macchinataignorante – meaning 'ignorant car tripper'. The idea of being in Leicester was hatched and forty cars and seven coaches were filled by all the fans. Most were teenagers, or around 20, kids whose entire upbringing had been in the age of football being about cynical money. There, in a distant land, Leicester represented something different.

'The last five years, only the big, big football teams who spend a lot won,' Magro explains. 'And with a little budget Leicester managed with unknown players, from nothing, to win one of the most difficult leagues.' That Ranieri, an Italian, was central to the wonder, further appealed, Edoardo adds.

● ● ●

Five days on, one space in the King Power car park was still taken up. Filling it were seven giant square pots with blue and white flowers, now bedraggled. What to do with Bocelli's decorations? Nobody appeared to have figured that out.

Had anybody figured out anything? What had Leicester just done? Football did not know. And did not want to, perhaps: that thought occurred. Very quickly mainstream and social media filled up with – transfers, sackings, star players, big clubs, super-managers – the old guff all over again. The Leicester story, over the summer, would be increasingly relegated.

But how had they done it?

'A unique season' was always Ranieri's starting point. He was ever at pains to modestly say it was rare for *all* the big clubs to fail *all* at the same time. Happens once every fifty years, he reckoned. So let's start with those big clubs.

Manchester United: still in the aftershock of Sir Alex Ferguson retiring. Struggling for identity. A club with fully seventy sponsors and unprecedented commercial imperatives. Whose manager worked to an inflexible, grand philosophy.

Manchester City: buried in money, with an overarching ambition to be at the hub of a global 'City Football Group'. Who were always building stuff, unveiling projects, moving to the next phases of the masterplan. A club, racing ahead of itself, announcing its next manager in the middle of the season, a club racing ahead of the here and now.

Chelsea: personality cults. Abramovich. Mourinho. Certain big star players. Wars of interests: club doctor versus manager, manager versus recruitment, fans versus owner. Fall-out everywhere as Mourinho's reign unravelled.

Arsenal: a softer but still unmistakable personality cult, where Wenger does it his way without input or challenge. Patterns – including those of underperformance – that recur.

Liverpool: transition. And transition again.

Leicester were no one-man cult. Lacked grandiose designs. Had no factions, no commercial distractions. No thought except the football to be played. They had a new manager yet next-to-no transition – because the underlying structures were so strong.

People worked together at this club. Golden threads of trust ran through it. There was a circle from owners to manager to staff to players to fans. And, something basic: football was about winning, to them. Not top fours. Not philosophies. Winning. Fighting and winning when you had to: from promotion campaigns to the 'great escape', this is what a strong dressing room had learned to do.

But still . . . *Leicester!*

Why them and not, say, Tottenham, Southampton, West Ham – other admirable antidotes to the big powers?

Maybe there is something in what the old football heads have always said: 'It's about the players.'

King would go along with this. 'When asked what's won Leicester the league I see people say, "team spirit and togetherness". This is the Premier League!' he says. 'You don't just win it like that. I could get eleven of my mates and we would have great "team spirit and togetherness". You have to have outstanding players.'

There *were* outstanding players at Leicester. Even if it had not been obvious at first. A brilliantly put together and balanced team, with quality, experience and mentality, in all the positions and – well, look back over the tapes – three real world-class performers.

Mahrez, Kanté and Schmeichel – truly outstanding at what they do. And Vardy, used right, would worry any opponent of any class.

The manager was world class too. Look at Ranieri's list of clubs. Okay, he had not won, but how many coaches had done so many big jobs well? How Leicester's big rivals performed was actually irrelevant in some ways. Leicester's points total – 81 – would have won them the league in other years.

But ... what was Leicester's *secret*? The very question suggests an attitude that where there is success, there is something singular behind it. Something that you can pull out. Copy perhaps. Or buy. Now that attitude is *very* Premier League.

If there was *one* thing about Leicester it is that nothing there was singular. These were people, departments, workers, coming together and showing teamwork every single time. Maybe Drinkwater said all that ever needed to be said: it was just about a bunch of lads that got along. And, top to bottom, a whole club that got along.

It does not feel as if that happens much in top football these days. And there is another thing: is every success not something unique? Does the story of every team not rest in many ways on the individuals?

Perhaps the Leicester miracle started not only at Watford in 2013 but with a Bangkok duty free shop. With an Italian, who had unfinished business, talking football over steak.

On a hillside pitch in Yorkshire. A skinny kid practising in a *banlieue* gym.

With a silent little boy of giant talent. With a big kid lapping a pitch to sweat off pounds. In a Berlin suburb, a Birmingham family. With a text to Year 11 Andy King.

We have no trouble, in other fields, in accepting that the right individuals, combining in the right way, can sometimes achieve the extraordinary. Maybe it just happened in football for once. In the Premier League, from 8 August 2015 to 15 May 2016.

● ● ●

Stamford Bridge. Sunday, 15 May. Last day of the season. The end of a week of parties. There was one at the King Power after the Everton game, one for Leicester's club awards, and a London dinner where Vardy was made the Football Writers' Player of the Year.

There was a mooted lunch with David Cameron that never materialised but the players did get together at a restaurant. It was for their annual meal paid for by dressing room fines. 'Cheers Riyad' was the toast. Mahrez was easily the most regular offender on security cam breaking the 9.30am rule. His fines would have been more but he was so good the team cut deals: 'Riyad, score on Saturday and we'll forget about the hundred quid.'

Any other club, any other players, and it would have been a flat farewell at Stamford Bridge. Nothing at all rode on this. Indeed there were things – a victory parade through Leicester another goodwill trip to Thailand – the players could have done with saving energy for.

But Cesc Fàbregas scored a penalty for Chelsea. And Leicester could not help themselves. They pushed, they fought and with eight minutes left Drinkwater rattled a shot past Thibaut Courtois from 30 yards. Not beaten. A draw. Another good game. Edoardo was in a pub – he had a ticket and wanted to be in the stadium as 'Drinkbeer Jesus' again but stewards would not let him enter in costume.

The victory parade: now they also came – the sections of Leicester who had not quite been or felt included in the club's success yet. But the event in Victoria Park was free for all, and so communal it appealed to everyone. Women in blue hijabs came with their kids. People of the St Matthew's estate – little Hamza from the shop next to the mosque (despite being a Chelsea fan) – they were there too.

In a city with a 330,000 population, an estimated 240,000 turned out for this party – and there were only five arrests. Kasabian played. Banners of every player were hung on lampposts along the parade route. A bus carrying the squad started off in Jubilee Square.

On that warm May evening, the bus crawled up London Road, past the Turkish bakers, the Islamic lawyers, the English pubs, the Pakistani flag reworked in Leicester colours. Past the three old Caribbean gents watching the world go by. Past a nice homemade supporter's sign: The Bubble Will Burst.

Kids smiled, adults wept and who could be begrudging? Finally the bus made it to Victoria Park and a sea of blue-shirted love. But Claudio had to go. The owners' helicopter sped him to a Battersea helipad and from there he raced to his London home and changed his suit. He and Rosanna then rushed to the League Managers Association dinner at Old Billingsgate.

He was manager of the year. To the warmest applause, wearing a slightly bemused smile, he took the stage and accepted his award. He thanked Rosanna. Then joked 'I don't know what has happened. I don't know if I'm here . . . or on the other side [the afterlife].' And then he told everyone how it was done.

'I say to my players, "I want to see you play English football and I put my little tactics,"' Ranieri began. '"Italian tactics, English heart. We can do something special."

'And they followed me,' he said. And that was that.

17

EPILOGUE

Stop the clock, freeze the picture, frame and cherish the moment. Sunday, 17 April, 2016, at King Power Stadium, approaching 2.40pm: when the Leicester 'title-winning XI' broke up forever.

No one knew it at the time but after Claudio Ranieri substituted Marc Albrighton in the 54th minute of Leicester's turbulent game against West Ham that April day, his 'classic' 2015–16 line up would never appear on the pitch as an XI again.

So cherish them: Schmeichel; Simpson, Morgan, Huth, Fuchs; Kante, Drinkwater; Mahrez, Okazaki, Albrighton; Vardy. The Magnificent Eleven ended as a playing unit then and there.

In that West Ham match Jamie Vardy was sent off two minutes after Albrighton left the field. By the time Vardy played again, Robert Huth and Danny Drinkwater were serving bans, Huth's keeping him out for the remainder of 2015–16. Then, in July, after returning from an impressive Euro 2016, N'Golo Kante quit Leicester for Chelsea. They do say it is always the quiet ones.

The Srivhaddhanprabhas offered Kante a huge new contract to remain but still he left. He suggested Chelsea represented his chance to play for 'a big club'. After all Leicester had done they were still on the wrong side of that old divide between football's supposed elite and also-rans. 'I thought everybody wanted to stay with Leicester and continue to fight. But I made a mistake. One did want to go – Kante is finished with us and he has gone,' were Ranieri's sharp words.

He said this on August 19, four weeks after Kante's departure. Initially his take on it had been more generous but by then Ranieri had realised Leicester were in a new struggle – life after a miracle, how do you live it?

Leicester had lost to Hull in their first game of the new Premier League campaign, to Manchester United in the Community Shield, and disappointed in a glitzy, globe-trotting International Champions Cup pre-season tournament. The giant gap extraordinary little Kante would leave on the pitch was already clear.

Steve Walsh also left, joining Everton as director of football. The doubters could doubt again: '*told you* Leicester wouldn't last,' they said. But Riyad Mahrez surprised them by signing a new four-year contract to dash the hopes of big suitors. Jamie Vardy turned down Arsenal and renewed his deal. Kasper Schmeichel, Wes Morgan, Andy King, Danny Drinkwater and Ranieri himself also extended their contracts.

Vardy got married over the summer. So too Robert Huth. Marc and Chloe Albrighton were wed in a great family bash at Peckforton Castle in

Cheshire. The interior of Belvoir Drive had a revamp. Gary Lineker indeed presented *Match of the Day* – well, a section of it – in his underwear. And life started to go on.

The narrative revolved around the 'big clubs' once more. Pep Guardiola's impact at Manchester City and José Mourinho's at Manchester United, dominated coverage. A glut of mega-transfers in to the Manchester clubs – like Paul Pogba's £89m move to United from Juventus – made it seem football was all about bags of money again.

The bookies? Though the *Financial Times* estimated betting companies lost £50m in payouts when Leicester won the title, Leicester were still shorter odds to be relegated than to be champions a second time when the 2016-17 campaign began.

For Leicester's trophy parade in May, banners of each player in the title-winning squad were hung from lampposts around the city and stayed there throughout the summer and so it felt symbolic when they were finally taken down, on the weekend the King Power hosted its first match of 2016-17. Arsenal, appropriately Arsenal, were the visitors. There was a new razzmatazz in the stadium, including cheerleaders, that felt unnecessary, but the clappers were there. And the *Post Horn Gallop* sounded. And the sun shone.

And when new signing Nampalys Mendy went off injured and Andy King came on, Leicester had an XI featuring 10 of the 'classic' line-up plus 'Kingy' – who was as important as any of the 10 anyway. And a 'click' seemed to happen. Leicester had a familiar speed and purposeful simplicity and collectiveness in their game. The electricity was back. The fearlessness.

They should have won – but the referee, Mark Clattenburg, wrongly rebuffed a late Leicester penalty claim. 'Our spirit. I watched our spirit. Very happy,' Ranieri said.

The challenge, for him then, and for successors forevermore, would be not emulating 2015–16's success level: impossible. Rather it would be preserving what lay behind it.

Life goes on, football goes on, but you felt that electricity against Arsenal and you saw Ranieri's twinkle and you knew that not all was lost.

PICTURE CREDITS

Action Images via Reuters/Livepic: p. 1 top (Dylan Martinez); p. 1 bottom (Darren Staples); p. 5 top (Paul Childs); p. 5 bottom (Carl Recine); p. 7 bottom (Eddie Keogh); p. 10 bottom (Carl Recine); p. 11 top (Carl Recine); p. 12 top (Darren Staples); p. 16 top (Alex Morton)

Plumb Images/Leicester City FC via Getty Images: p. 3 bottom; p. 4 bottom; p. 6 top; p. 8 bottom; p. 9 top; p. 10 top; p. 12 bottom; p. 13 top & bottom;

Press Association Images: p. 2 top (Nigel French/PA Wire); p. 2 bottom (Mike Egerton/EMPICS Sport); p. 3 top (Simon Bellis/Sportimage); p. 4 top (Tim Goode/EMPICS Sport); p. 6 bottom (Barrington Coombs/PA Archive); p. 7 top (David Klein/Sportimage); p. 8 top (Matt Dunham/AP); p. 9 bottom (AP); p. 11 bottom (Mike Egerton/PA Archive); p. 14 top (Simon Bellis/Sportimage); p. 14 bottom (Nick Potts/PA Wire); p. 15 top (Mark Baker/AP); p. 15 bottom (Mike Egerton/EMPICS Sport); p. 16 bottom (Nigel French/EMPICS Sport)

Jonathan Northcroft is the soccer correspondent for the *Sunday Times*. He is a frequent contributor to BBC Radio 5 Live's football programs, and a regular guest on Sky Sports' Sunday Supplement show. Inaugural winner of the Jim Rodger Memorial Award for young sports writers in Scotland, he was shortlisted for Feature Writer of the Year at the Sports Journalists Association awards in 2006 and Football Writer of the Year in 2016.

NATION BOOKS

The Nation Institute

Founded in 2000, **Nation Books** has become a leading voice in American independent publishing. The imprint's mission is to tell stories that inform and empower just as they inspire or entertain readers. We publish award-winning and bestselling journalists, thought leaders, whistleblowers, and truthtellers, and we are also committed to seeking out a new generation of emerging writers, particularly voices from underrepresented communities and writers from diverse backgrounds. As a publisher with a focused list, we work closely with all our authors to ensure that their books have broad and lasting impact. With each of our books we aim to constructively affect and amplify cultural and political discourse and to engender positive social change.

Nation Books is a project of The Nation Institute, a nonprofit media center established to extend the reach of democratic ideals and strengthen the independent press. The Nation Institute is home to a dynamic range of programs: the award-winning Investigative Fund, which supports groundbreaking investigative journalism; the widely read and syndicated website TomDispatch; journalism fellowships that support and cultivate over twenty-five emerging and high-profile reporters each year; and the Victor S. Navasky Internship Program.

For more information on Nation Books and The Nation Institute, please visit:

www.nationbooks.org
www.nationinstitute.org
www.facebook.com/nationbooks.ny
Twitter: @nationbooks